Campaigning
for Congress

Campaigning for Congress

Edie N. Goldenberg
Michael W. Traugott

University of Michigan

a division of Congressional Quarterly Inc.
1414 22nd Street N.W., Washington, D.C. 20037

Printed in the United States of America

Second Printing

Library of Congress Cataloging in Publication Data

Goldenberg, Edie N.
    Campaigning for Congress.

    Bibliography: p.
    Includes index.
    1. Electioneering — United States. 2. United States. Congress
— Elections. I. Traugott, Michael W. II. Title.
JK1976.G64   1984   324.7'0973   84-1840
ISBN 0-87187-283-8

To

Katie and Joe
on their 50th

and

Santa, Elisabeth, and Chris
for patience and understanding

Contents

Tables and Figures

Preface

Congressional campaigns play a vital role in the U. S. system of government. Under ideal circumstances, campaigns provide the information that voters use in choosing people best suited to represent their interests. But what really happens during primary and general election campaigns? What are the actual conditions surrounding the selection of our U. S. representatives?

Much of the accepted wisdom about congressional campaigns ignores the substantial variety in districts and resources that opposing candidates bring to the contests and construes electoral outcomes too narrowly. Our research, based on a representative national sample of 86 contested House races in 1978, shows that these variations make a significant difference in the vitality of the campaigns and that the results have an importance beyond that of simply winning or losing. In this book we take a close look at why campaigns develop the way they do.

Chapter 1 presents a picture of contemporary congressional campaigns, including the role of the mass media, and challenges traditional views of the influence campaigns have on eventual vote choice. Chapter 2 describes the various sources of data used in our analysis and introduces the principal actors in the campaigns—the candidates and their managers. Chapters 3 and 4 focus on the development of campaign strategies and tactics in different types of district contests.

Because most strategic decisions require money for their implementation, tracing how that money is collected and how and when it is spent is crucial to understanding the nature of congressional campaigning. This process is discussed in detail in chapters 5, 6, and 7. The energy and resources of campaigns are mostly devoted to increasing the candidates' recognition with the electorate. To accomplish this, candidates can make personal appearances in their districts, but, using the most current technology, they rely more on computerized direct mail messages, television, and other types of media. Chapter 8 discusses news coverage of the campaign and how the fit between congressional districts and media markets affects the choices managers make to promote their candidates.

There is more at stake in an election campaign than who wins and who loses; the results can be analyzed from a broader point of view. Chapter 9 concentrates on how the voters responded to the campaigns and whether candidate recognition was increased. Chapter 10 analyzes the effects of the campaign on election outcomes and discusses the long-term consequences for political careers. Running a poor campaign rarely causes a House incumbent to lose, but the campaign can affect how well he or she performs relative to expectations. In Chapter 11 the various pieces of the process are reassembled in four case studies describing typical congressional contests. The conclusion presents a summary of the findings and relates them to other types of elections.

The research on which this book is based has benefited from the intellectual support and stimulation of a number of colleagues. From the beginning, Warren Miller was a source of encouragement. He assisted us in the integration of our work with the 1978 American National Election Study. He was a careful and thorough reader of our earlier manuscripts and of a draft of this volume. Other Michigan colleagues who provided guidance and editorial support include Phil Converse, Don Kinder, and John Kingdon. Gary Jacobson consistently and graciously exchanged data and ideas with us, for which we are grateful. At critical stages in our research, Tom Mann, Bob Teeter, and Mary Lukens also contributed important data elements. It would have been impossible to work our way through the Federal Election Commission reports without the assistance of Kent Cooper and his staff at the Public Records Division.

The research could not have proceeded without the cooperation of the 167 campaign managers who consented to interviews and gave so freely of their time and knowledge. The data collection effort was supported by the National Science Foundation under Grant Number SOC-78-18710. At the University of Michigan, the Center for Political Studies, the Institute for Social Research, the Department of Political Science, and the Institute of Public Policy Studies provided invaluable aid during the data analysis, including support for computer time, research assistance, and released time for sabbaticals. We completed the first draft of the manuscript while both of us were on sabbatical, and Edie Goldenberg was graciously supported for some of her writing by the Woodrow Wilson International Center for Scholars and Florida Atlantic University.

The efforts of a number of research assistants made possible the extensive original data collection reported here. At various points, four people were of critical importance to data collection, management, and analysis efforts. They are Frank Baumgartner, Susan Evans, Charles Franklin, and Giovanna Morchio. Other students who made substantial contributions to the project include Antonia Bloenbergen, Julio Borquez, Sean Casey, Julia Dabbs, Harley Frazis, George Golubovskis, John Hoffman, Carolyn Huston, H. W. Perry, Mark Peterson, John Schuster, Kathrin Sears, Rob Simmons, Rick Sloan, Joel Smith, Janet Topolsky, and Lisa Vogler.

Manuscript preparation often was complicated along the way by the occasional separation of the authors and by the use of different word processing systems. It is a tribute to the perseverance and skills of Kathy Dorando that the entire manuscript was assembled for delivery to the publisher. For assistance along the way, we also thank Nancy Brennan, Donna Gotts, Joyce Meyer, and Karen Roper.

We are grateful to Jean Woy, formerly of Congressional Quarterly, for her initial support of our project and to Joanne Daniels, director of CQ Press, for the encouragement that ensured completion of the manuscript. The reviews by Alan Abramowitz, Robert Agranoff, and Robert Peabody provided many helpful suggestions for revisions. The quality of the current text is due to the sustained effort of our editor Carolyn Goldinger. Any errors of omission or commission remain our sole responsibility.

Edie N. Goldenberg
Michael W. Traugott

Chapter 1   Studying Campaigns

Campaigning for Congress always has been an ordeal for challengers and a necessary evil for incumbents. Members of the U. S. House of Representatives who seek reelection usually win, but winning or losing a particular race is not the only measure of campaign success. Elections and the campaigns to win them play a central role in traditional democratic theory, which describes the ideal functioning of a political system like ours. The offices at stake involve the selection of representatives who pass laws and appropriate money for governmental operations. The people affected by these decisions, the constituents, have very little regular contact with their elected representatives. The campaign provides a setting in which citizens and those who seek to represent them have an opportunity to communicate with each other directly and through the mass media. The campaign period is especially important in this regard because members of the electorate are not continuously interested in politics. The stimulus of campaigns—their organized activities and events and the attendant media coverage— heightens public interest in politics, even if only for a brief time.

Ideally the debate between candidates in competitive races should inform the electorate through public discussion of important issues. The incumbent presents and defends a record of service while the opponent usually challenges it and promises better. Serious attention to issues occurs generally only where contests are held between candidates with equal personal, organizational, and financial resources. Too often, however, contemporary campaigns are not waged by such equally matched opponents.

The incumbents enjoy considerable advantages over their challengers. Their work affords contact with some of their constituents, solving problems that arise in dealing with the federal government. Much of this work is performed through offices maintained in the district with allotments of federal funds for space rental and staff. Senior citizens needing information about Social Security benefits, veterans interested in pension rights, or high school students interested in attending one of the military service academies and their families all contact their U. S. representative for assistance. Franking privileges provide members with free postage for their newsletters, in which they communicate with constituents about legislative matters in Washington. As elected public officials, incumbents generate coverage in the local media by announcing new federal projects or grants in their districts or by holding press conferences when they return home. It is difficult for challengers to establish and maintain equivalent contacts with potential voters.

Campaigns are also one of the most important mechanisms for recruiting and sustaining political leadership. Because the outcome of any one election has implications for the next, campaigns should be viewed as part of a dynamic selection process. Unsuccessful challengers can do better than expected and emerge as popular choices for the next election. Victorious incumbents can do worse than expected and appear vulnerable in future races, or they can annihilate their challengers and become candidates for higher office. The study of campaigns is, therefore, an exercise in understanding not only the short-term but also the long-term winners and losers.

This book is about the contemporary campaign process in contests for the U. S. House of Representatives. While the research reported here draws primarily on information collected during and after the 1978 midterm elections, it serves as more than an investigation of only one set of 435 congressional contests. It emphasizes the development of campaign strategies and tactics, the allocation of a candidate's resources, the information about the campaign that becomes available to potential voters, and the consequences of campaigns for electoral outcomes. These consequences are real and significant for candidates who have sufficient resources to implement their best strategies.

Campaigns are also important for constituents. The quantity and quality of the political debate they witness is a function of the vitality of the campaigns that candidates wage. But understanding campaigns also requires knowing the factors that may limit their importance. Depending on how the boundaries of a congressional district were drawn, people who identify with one party or the other may exercise consistent control at the ballot box. If so, the minority party will have difficulty recruiting strong candidates, and general election campaigns will be quiet and ineffective. Even active campaigns, however, do not always result in effective communication with potential voters. If the fit is poor between a district's boundaries and the area served by local media outlets, then the news coverage of congressional races will be limited. Campaign advertising in the media also will be limited. As a consequence of media market characteristics, voters in different districts receive different amounts of information about their candidates.

Since 1960 there have been significant changes in the style and technology of political campaigns for all levels of office, and the costs have been rising steadily. Presidential campaigns, the most expensive, are now publicly funded, once candidates raise a certain amount. Senatorial and gubernatorial campaigns also cost a great deal; candidates for these offices must raise their own money, and they spend a great deal of it on mass media appeals that are based on information generated through sophisticated surveys of the electorate. Some campaigns for House seats also have become quite expensive, costing as much as half a million dollars or more spent primarily on media advertising. Recent House campaigns also have become more dependent on professional managers and consultants and the specialized techniques of their trade.

A substantial difference exists between the minimal significance that academic studies have attributed to campaigns and the influence attributed to them by candidates, political consultants, and members of the media. According to most previous research, the outcomes of congressional elections are clear in advance and virtually unchangeable. Incumbents usually win unless they have been placed in jeopardy by scandal or gerrymandering. Consequently, the most important factors are thought to be those largely beyond the campaign's influence, such as the voters' party identification, rather than the strategic behavior of candidates during the campaign.

On the other hand, the practical "how to" literature concentrates upon manipulable factors such as the visibility of the challenger to potential voters and the campaign themes presented through the media. From this point of view, a candidate's performance in an election can be influenced substantially by the campaign that is waged. Winning or losing is not always the most important result; how well the candidates do relative to expectations of performance can be of equal significance. Campaign professionals and politicians, interested in advancing their careers, have long understood the importance of the campaign for producing a "good showing" as a step toward running for higher elective office or a leadership position in the House.

This bifurcation in the perspectives of academics and activists developed in part because of the unique nature of the period during which early academic studies were conducted. In their first systematic efforts in the 1940s, scholars found no significant campaign effects on individual voter preferences. In subsequent research, they adopted methodological approaches that made continued attention to campaign effects difficult. As a result, the "minimal effects" perspective lingered for several decades.

Minimal Campaign Effects:
An Accident of History

The first systematic studies of the effects of campaigns on voting behavior
were conducted in the 1940s with the advent and general application of the
survey method.[1] In an elaborate study involving seven waves of interviews in
Erie County, Ohio, Paul Lazarsfeld and his colleagues at Columbia University questioned potential voters about their reactions to the presidential
candidates in 1940. Using a panel design in which the same people were interviewed repeatedly, the Columbia researchers measured voter attitudes
frequently, observing changes in them over time and relating those changes
to developments in the campaign. Because the studies were concentrated in
a particular locale, it was possible to assemble contextual information, such
as local media content, and link it with the survey measures. This approach
represented a significant advance over earlier studies, and its findings
molded the research perspectives of most other scholars in the field.

Yet, in many regards, presidential politics during the 1940s were unlike
those of any period since. The distribution of partisanship in the nation had
undergone a realignment in the 1930s, mostly because of the trauma of the
Depression, and the country switched effectively from Republican to
Democratic allegiance. Among newly mobilized voters, party affiliation
undoubtedly was strong. Lazarsfeld later acknowledged that by 1940 most
voter perceptions about Franklin D. Roosevelt had become rather stereo-
typed as a consequence of his two previous campaigns.[2] Most attitudes
toward Roosevelt were crystallized in advance of the 1940 campaign, and
there was little new in the arguments to challenge voter attitudes. Moreover,
there were few issues of any sort on which the major parties were split.[3]
These special features made this election period unproductive for observing
strong campaign effects on voting behavior.

To measure the effects of changing campaign events, Lazarsfeld,
Berelson, and Gaudet interviewed the same respondents once a month for
seven months. To their surprise, they found that half of the respondents
already had decided upon their candidate by the time of the first interview in
May. Furthermore, another quarter had made up their minds by the time of
the conventions in late June and mid-July. As a result, only about one in four
was left to formulate a preference during the three months we normally think
of as the general election campaign period.

Media Influence in the Campaign

Based upon this work, the Columbia University researchers concluded that
the campaign—and especially the mass media's influence in it—served
primarily to activate and reinforce a voter's partisan predispositions, but
only rarely did it influence a voter to defect and vote for the candidate of the

other party. Because most people selected newspapers or radio broadcasts in agreement with their political preferences, there was little opportunity for conversion. Media effects on vote choice appeared to be minimal. Only 8 percent of those interviewed in 1940 actually switched their votes from one party to the other during the study. Instead, by reading newspapers or listening to radio broadcasts that bolstered their initial partisan preferences, voters were motivated to go to the polls and were reinforced in their candidate preference.

Had this first important election study been conducted at a time when voters were more susceptible to influences beyond partisanship, when issue conflicts between the two parties were sharp and substantial, and when more people were exposed to media content at odds with their partisan leanings, then perhaps media effects would have been identified and the course of subsequent election research altered. For those few potential voters in 1940 who were exposed to media information at variance with their own political predispositions, the effects of media exposure on conversion were striking. Among Republicans, those who were exposed to predominantly Democratic media were three times as likely as readers of Republican media to defect and support the Democrats (47 percent compared with 15 percent); Democrats who were exposed to predominantly Republican media were twice as likely to defect (49 percent to 25 percent) as those who were exposed to Democratic media.[4] The authors attached little significance to these media effects because so few people in Erie County were converted. The possibility of selecting information according to partisan preference no longer exists in most communities, which today have have only one dominant daily newspaper. Moreover, voters' attitudes toward candidates for other offices, including the U. S. Congress, probably are less resistant to challenge than were attitudes toward Roosevelt in 1940. The findings of limited media effects certainly warranted further study before they became generally accepted wisdom.

Nevertheless, the second systematic inquiry by the Columbia group began with an assumption of minimal media effects on voting behavior. As a consequence, the study design did not incorporate variation in the partisan nature of media coverage. There was virtually no variation in campaign content across the news outlets in Elmira, New York, in 1948. The choice of that site precluded any assessment of media effects on vote choice. What could be done was an analysis of how the amount of *exposure* to media content affected the knowledge that individuals had about candidates and issues. Lazarsfeld and his colleagues found that the more people read about and heard about the campaign in the mass media, the more they knew about election issues and the more accurately they perceived the candidates' stands on the issues.[5] Individual voters often lacked detailed information about the campaign, but usually they had the crucial general information needed to make a choice.

Studies of the National Electorate

Beginning in the 1950s and extending for more than a quarter of a century, voting studies adopted a national perspective. A series of biennial studies, conducted by Campbell, Converse, Miller, and Stokes at the University of Michigan (1960, 1966), extended the Lazarsfeld work with a particular emphasis on the role of party identification for the individual's vote choice. These studies focused on variations in the electorate's response to national campaigns, but they did not investigate local variations in the campaign and in popular responses to them. Collecting relevant media content data in national studies is no simple task. It is difficult to identify in advance the media that respondents will read, hear, or watch in a national sample that spans many different geographical locales, and it is obviously more costly to collect and analyze media content from a large number of outlets.

Media coverage of the campaign is only one element in the political context, or environment, within which voters decide which candidate to support. Although the Michigan researchers did not study the impact of media context on vote choice, they were interested in other contextual factors, such as the voters' places of residence, particularly whether they lived in urban or rural areas; their family situations; and their places of work, including industry and occupation. They looked at neither the presidential campaign activity in each locale nor at the media markets in which potential voters lived. The neglect of this kind of contextual data was not bothersome to most scholars because they assumed that media and campaign effects were unimportant. Prior research seemed to indicate that survey-based measures of exposure captured these effects in an adequate fashion.

That assumption, especially for congressional campaigns, was reinforced by research findings from a 1958 study that showed the public to be largely unaware of their congressional candidates (Stokes and Miller, 1962) and by a consistent preoccupation among researchers with winning and losing as a central measure of electoral outcomes. A view of the public as essentially uneducable within the campaign context, and the prospect of studying a set of incumbents who nearly always won, discouraged further interest in research on campaigns. Attention turned instead to a variety of factors largely beyond the control of either candidate for congressional office—incumbency, the state of the economy, and public assessments of presidential performance (Cover, 1977; Cover and Mayhew, 1981; Erikson, 1971; Ferejohn, 1977; Fiorina, 1977; Jacobson, 1981; Johannes and McAdams, 1981; Mayhew, 1974; Tufte, 1975).

Another assumption that guided academic work was that many basic conclusions about voting behavior that were drawn from studies of presidential elections were applicable to congressional elections as well. This assumption was not made entirely by choice, but rather as the result of the predominantly presidential focus of virtually all large studies of national elections until 1978. In that year the American National Election Study conducted by the University of Michigan used congressional districts instead of counties as primary sampling units and included in the interviews of potential voters a number of questions specifically related to congressional elections. Published works based on the 1978 study pointed out the dangers of extrapolating findings from the presidential case to other types of elections and identified a number of substantial gaps in our understanding of congressional elections (Hinckley, 1981; Maisel and Cooper, 1981). All of these studies, for example, emphasized the importance of incumbency advantages in House elections, especially the high levels of recognition that incumbents enjoy among potential voters and the overall popularity of incumbents in their districts.

With few exceptions, these studies did little to explore how incumbency advantages vary across districts or whether some challengers could overcome them during the campaign. A few studies compared House and Senate races, noting that challengers to Senate incumbents are more likely to win than are challengers to House incumbents (Abramowitz, 1980; Hinckley, 1980). One suggested explanation is that while media coverage of House races is skimpy, coverage of Senate races is sufficiently ample to permit challengers to become known (Ragsdale, 1981; Westlye, 1983). Media coverage also varies a great deal across House races, but systematic studies of this variation have been rare.

Nevertheless, past research has provided impetus for the 1978 study of congressional campaigns and their effects. Five intriguing observations stimulate renewed attention to congressional campaigns. First, the range of outcomes in congressional elections varies substantially from district to district, although national averages of party voting change very little from year to year. Some incumbents win big; others barely survive or lose. Second, the amount of money spent during the campaign, especially by challengers, does matter. Third, the effects of mass media content often are far from minimal. Fourth, there are variations in the extent to which challengers are visible throughout the campaign. While a few become quite well known to residents in their districts, many are unknown even on election day. And last, campaigns are more than individual events with immediate winners or losers. They are part of a dynamic process of career building with implications beyond the particular election at hand. Each of these observations merits elaboration.

Recent Research on Campaign Effects

Before Thomas E. Mann's analysis of the 1974 and 1976 races, studies of congressional elections tended to ignore the amount of variation in congressional district outcomes. As Mann demonstrated, this variation is substantial. From 1972 to 1974, for example, the national popular vote shifted an average of six percentage points from the Republicans to the Democrats. The shift within individual districts, however, varied from 28 percentage points in favor of the Republican to 36 percentage points in favor of the Democrat. The range in the partisan shift across districts for the 1974 to 1976 elections was even greater. Mann showed that this variation across districts was not due to a few atypical cases, but rather that it represented widespread district variability. Furthermore, this variation was not due simply to the partisan makeup of the districts or to incumbency advantage. In fact, Mann convincingly argued that incumbency advantage also varies substantially: some incumbents are much more successful than others in capitalizing on their "advantage." [6]

Moreover, Mann's analysis undercuts traditional assumptions about public ignorance of congressional campaigns. Some voters who cannot recall the name of congressional candidates in their district (the traditional information test) are able to recognize the candidates' names when presented with them and to evaluate candidates positively or negatively. Because most voters are provided the names of their congressional candidates on the ballot on election day, Mann argued that the traditional test of name recall is unreasonably severe. With a revised measurement approach, the public's knowledge of congressional candidates appears more substantial and its behavior becomes more explicable. Mann's work also shows that national trends cannot account for the varying electoral results across congressional districts. Studies of congressional elections should include district-level variables in general and campaign-related variables in particular in an effort to account for the electoral results of congressional races.

This is also the message of scholarly work on campaign spending (Dawson and Zinser, 1976; Glantz, Abramowitz, and Burkhart, 1976; Jacobson, 1975, 1978, 1980; Palda, 1973; Welch, 1977, 1980). Controlling for national factors and the partisan division in the district, Gary Jacobson reported that a challenger's proportion of the two-party vote is primarily a function of how much the challenger spends in campaigning and that the challenger spends as much as can be raised. In contrast, the incumbent spends in reaction to the spending levels of the challenger, but without much demonstrated effect on the outcome of the election. More recent evidence suggests that incumbents spend both to preempt serious challenges and to react to them (Goldenberg, Traugott, and Baumgartner, 1983). In any event, these studies underscore the importance of the candidates' campaign activities, especially for challengers and contestants for open seats, although they do little to explain just what candidates buy with their money that matters so much.

The major roadblock facing most congressional challengers is becoming known to people in the district. The mass media afford one of the most effective means of achieving visibility, providing they devote sufficient coverage to the candidates and the race. How much attention candidates receive, why attention varies across districts, and what consequences flow from different types of media content are important questions yet to be answered.

Recent studies have identified media effects on election outcomes, individual voting decisions, political knowledge and beliefs, political trust, and issue salience (summarized in Becker, McCombs, and McLeod, 1975; Kinder and Sears, 1984; McCombs and Shaw, 1972). This revisionist literature reconsiders the minimal-effects tradition of media research initiated with the Lazarsfeld work and begins to specify the conditions under which certain types of media content *do* make a difference. Content varies from newspaper to newspaper (Miller, Goldenberg, and Erbring, 1979), and that content can be linked with the electoral choices of individuals and resulting election outcomes (Coombs, 1981; Graber, 1980; and Robinson, 1974). With the resurgence of interest in the effects of the media on public opinion has come renewed interest in the importance of the media in the campaign.

One other significant change in perspective on the role of congressional elections is due to reconceptualizing campaigns as dynamic elements of congressional careers (Bullock, 1972; Cover, 1977; Erikson, 1971). While incumbents are odds-on favorites to win any particular reelection effort, over the course of their careers, their chances of losing become more substantial. Winning a seat in the U. S. Congress is a formidable task, and incumbents are most vulnerable to defeat during their first or second reelection attempts. Then a long period of relative security sets in. At the end of their careers, the risks of electoral defeat rise again, but this time from intraparty challengers in primaries.

Although challengers have difficulty defeating incumbents, it also seems increasingly clear that popular perceptions of an incumbent's vulnerability can be heightened by a succession of strong challenges. Contests in a district are appropriately viewed as a series of events between individuals in certain candidate roles that shift over time. Although rare, incidents of personal scandal and misfortune do arise. They can be particularly fatal if they crop up during the campaign. Candidates previously given no chance at all can become serious contenders overnight through no particular effort or fault of their own (Peters and Welch, 1980).

There are also major tides of public sentiment that may sweep unlikely challengers into office. Sometimes the winners ride on presidential coattails, as when Lyndon Johnson's landslide victory over Barry Goldwater in 1964 resulted in the heavily Democratic 89th Congress. Sometimes the public expresses extreme dissatisfaction with presidential performance or behavior, as in the off-year election of 1974, when the residue of the Watergate episode swept unusually large numbers of Republican representatives out of office.

The wide variety of settings in which congressional elections take place, their frequency, and the large number of seats at stake are all reasons why they represent ideal subjects for the study of political campaigns and their effects. House races provide a rich assortment of political contexts in which the strategic behavior of "political elites"—candidates and their campaign managers—can be observed and the popular response to it can be assessed.

The importance of campaigns for electoral outcomes and the role of mass media in them warrant reevaluation. Not only are the candidates' patterns of resource allocation of interest, but so are the resulting levels of information in the electorate. Questions about the effects of media, the development of campaign strategies, and the consequences of campaigns for the outcomes of congressional elections guided the study of House races upon which this book is based.

Notes

1. These studies are described in detail in Paul F. Lazarsfeld, Bernard Berelson, and Hazel Gaudet, *The People's Choice* (New York: Columbia University Press, 1948) and Bernard R. Berelson, Paul F. Lazarsfeld, and William N. McPhee, *Voting* (Chicago: University of Chicago Press, 1954).
2. See Lazarsfeld, Berelson, and Gaudet, xxv.
3. Ibid., 28-39.
4. Ibid., 96.
5. See Berelson, Lazarsfeld, and McPhee, 248-251.
6. See Thomas E. Mann, *Unsafe at Any Margin* (Washington, D. C.: American Enterprise Institute for Public Policy Research, 1978), 16-18.

Candidates, Managers, and Districts

Chapter 2

The same features that make House elections a particularly rich setting for analyzing the consequences of campaigns also create problems for researchers. All 435 congressional districts hold elections every two years. This provides a sufficient number of races to study, but it makes assembling information about them quite difficult. In accordance with the U. S. Constitution, each district is expected to be of approximately equal population at the time of redistricting, currently about 500,000 residents, but districts vary widely in nearly every other respect.

For example, Figure 2-1 shows the congressional districts in Michigan as of the 1978 elections. At that time, there were 19 districts, and their land area ranged from 34 square miles in the Thirteenth District, located in the city of Detroit, to approximately 23,000 square miles in the Eleventh District, which comprised some or all of 27 different counties.[1] The southeastern region of Michigan is highly urbanized. There are seven districts alone within Wayne County and its major city, Detroit. In contrast, in central Michigan— the Tenth Congressional District—only one-third of the residents live in urban areas. The ethnic and racial composition of the districts is related to these patterns of residence. In Michigan, 11.2 percent of the population is black. Across all 19 districts, the proportion of blacks ranges from 0.3 percent to 70.0 percent.

The media markets are as diverse as the congressional districts. In southeastern Michigan, the Detroit television stations have signals that cover nine counties and encompass eleven districts, not counting territory covered in neighboring Ohio and Canada. On the other hand, the Eleventh District falls into two television markets, one centered in Marquette and the other in Traverse City. The patterns of newspaper circulation and the charges for

Figure 2-1 Michigan's Congressional Districts Established May 15, 1972

television advertising in this district are quite different from the Detroit market.

To conduct an analysis that takes full account of the rich variety of environments in which congressional elections take place, several data resources are necessary. In this study, those resources include personal interviews with political elites (the candidates' managers) and their constituents, administrative records, content analysis of newspapers in the districts, and information about each district's makeup, history, and recent electoral results. Each of these is described in some detail below along with characteristics of the managers, candidates, and congressional districts studied.

Data Resources

The core of the study is a representative national sample of congressional districts in the continental United States in 1978. The seats being contested were in the U. S. House of Representatives for the 96th Congress, with the winners serving from 1979 to 1980.[2] Several major data collection efforts formed the basis for the research reported here.

The Managers' Survey

The most substantial data collection resulted from personal interviews conducted across the United States with the campaign managers for both of the major party candidates in 86 contested races. An attempt was made to interview each manager both before and after the election.[3]

The first interview was conducted in early September at the start of the general election period, after both candidates had been selected and each could develop a strategy with a known opponent in mind. The emphasis in this preelection interview was on the development of campaign strategy and planned resource allocations. In particular, managers were asked about the strengths and weaknesses of their own candidates and organizations as well as the equivalent characteristics of their opponents. They also discussed the central issues in the campaign, important voter groups in the district, and anticipated effects of national political figures and forces on the contest in their district. Under a guarantee of confidentiality, they spoke freely and in some detail about the basic elements of their tactics, their fund-raising plans, and anticipated expenditures. Attention was given to expected relations with and treatment by the press, as well as the campaign's advertising strategies in the media. Managers also were asked which candidate would win, whether the outcome would be close, and whether each candidate would be able to raise enough money to run a successful campaign. These questions were used to develop measures of the managers' overall assessments of their chances of winning.

In the postelection interviews, the emphasis was on how campaign strategies had changed over the course of the campaign and why, how resources were allocated, and how the election's outcome had been affected by the campaign. Information also was sought about how events during the campaign forced the managers to alter their original strategies, if at all. Many of the questions in preelection interviews were repeated to assess whether expectations were in fact fulfilled—particularly with regard to the candidates' ability to raise money and decisions about how to allocate it.

American National Election Study

A second substantial data collection, which plays an integral part in the following analysis, is the 1978 American National Election Study (ANES), conducted by the Center for Political Studies.[4] This survey was the fifteenth in a series of election studies dating back to 1952. A total of 2,304 adults were interviewed in the 108 districts that formed the basic sample; 1,843 of them lived in the 86 contested districts where elite interviews with the managers were conducted. The primary objective of the election study was a detailed analysis of the public's attitudes and behavior in the setting of congressional elections; people were selected for interviewing in small samples from each congressional district.

The 1978 election study provided basic measures of voters' familiarity with and assessments of the candidates, including levels of recognition and recall as well as evaluations of the candidates' personal characteristics and knowledge of their issue positions. Furthermore, information was available about the contact of citizens with their candidates, participation in campaign activities and events, and exposure to campaign news coverage and advertisements. These data permitted an analysis of how individuals responded to different types of campaigns.[5]

Other Data Sources

At a number of points, independent ancillary data collections were undertaken to verify the general quality of the managers' survey responses. Most significantly, substantial effort was devoted to automating detailed expenditure reports that the candidates were required to file with the Federal Election Commission.[6] These data show how much money was spent in congressional races and for what purposes.

The political information environment in each congressional district was captured through collections of two additional sources of data—newspapers and campaign literature. The first involved a content analysis of the major circulation daily newspapers in each district.[7] The material obtained from this effort included straight news articles, editorials, opinion columns, letters, and paid advertisements placed by the candidates. As part of the independent and simultaneous American National Election Study project, interviewers made two trips to each candidate's headquarters in order to collect samples of literature, position papers, and campaign paraphernalia. This second type of political information was coded for general thematic content by the ANES staff, and portions of these data were incorporated into the analysis presented here.

Measuring the 'Normal Vote'

In addition to these major data collection efforts, the generation of one additional measure—the "normal vote"— warrants discussion. Arthur Miller (1979) provides the most current technique for estimating the normal vote of·a constituency from information about the partisan identifications of a representative sample of its potential voters. Such information was available from the Democratic and Republican congressional campaign committees for 37 of the 86 contested districts in this study.[8] Estimates were needed for all 86 races, and they were derived statistically, based upon observations in the initial 37 cases of relationships between partisan identification and a variety of demographic measures available from the U. S. Census for all districts. These procedures are described in detail in the Appendix. The resulting estimates of the Democrat's expected share of the vote were subtracted from the actual 1978 election result for the Democratic candidate in each district to yield a set of deviations. The differences between actual and expected votes formed the basis for analyzing the effects of the campaign in the district. They reflect the net result of various campaign influences on voting decisions.

Who Runs for Congress?

To provide a setting for the 1978 congressional races, it is useful to describe the congressional districts that were sampled, the candidates whose managers were interviewed, and the managers themselves. It is also useful to compare the sample districts with the full set of congressional districts in 1978 and to compare the sample candidates with the full set of candidates in races for the 96th Congress, as well as with members in earlier Congresses. These comparisons establish the suitability of the data in terms of how representative they are of races, candidates, and campaign staffs in general. They also provide a perspective on how the 1978 election compares with other midterm elections and how the 96th Congress compares with other legislative classes.

The Sample of Districts

The basic ANES sample consisted of a one-in-four selection from the 432 congressional districts in the continental United States. The design of the sample ensured that it was representative of the voting age population in terms of geographic region, urbanization, past voting behavior, proportion of black population, and proportion of families with incomes of $15,000 or more.[9]

Of the original 108 districts, only 86 had contested races in which two major party candidates were running for the House. In many respects, these 86 races reflected accurately all 435 contests in 1978. There were as many Democratic candidates in the sample of contested races (63.0 percent) as in the entire set of 435 districts (63.4 percent). The historical vote division favored the Democrats in 49.1 percent of the sample districts compared with 50.2 percent of the entire set. The proportion of uncontested races out of the original 108 districts (20.4 percent) was only slightly higher than in the full national set of races for the 96th Congress (14.0 percent). A seat in the U. S. House of Representatives is one of the most secure elective offices available: one in seven incumbents is safe because there is no general election competition at all. A record number of 58 open seats were contested in 1978 (13.3 percent of the total), which compared closely with 11 in the sample (10.2 percent).[10]

Despite the careful sampling procedures, it is still important to ask whether a sample of districts designed to represent potential voters serves to represent candidates as well. Jacobson (1981) has raised questions about the adequacy of the 1978 sample of districts in these terms, in particular relating to the vitality of the challenges. During the general election itself, 19 incumbents lost. Fourteen were Democrats, two elected in 1976 and seven in 1974. In the sample, however, only one incumbent eventually lost. This is an important point. The 1978 sample of congressional districts resulted in a set of candidates who seem to represent all candidates running that year in most important respects except that strong challengers appear to be underrepresented. The findings presented in this book are based upon analyses that take the strength of the challengers into account. As a result, the underrepresentation of vital challenges in the sample means only that we have smaller numbers of vital contests to analyze. It does not distort the analysis presented here in ways that would alter the conclusions.[11] What it does mean is that the findings about the effects of vital campaigns on electoral outcomes may have even wider significance than is apparent based upon the sample data available.

The Sample of Candidates

Out of a possible 172 major party candidates running in the 86 districts in the sample, detailed information on the campaigns of 167 was assembled through the managers' interviews. These were the campaigns of 85 Democrats and 82 Republicans, representing 22 contestants in 11 open races, 71 incumbents, and 74 challengers. To compare the characteristics of these candidates with data from other studies, it is most convenient to consider the winners in 1978 separately from the losers.

Winners become members of the House. Appropriate comparisons for their characteristics are with all 435 members of the U. S. House of Representatives in 1978 and in earlier Congresses. Based upon the available demographic data, the sample of winners appears to reflect quite well the characteristics of their population in 1978. For example, at the start of the 96th Congress, the average length of service in the sample of incumbents who won in 1978 was 9.0 years, compared with 8.4 years in the House as a whole, all of whom were, of course, incumbents. The sample of winners in 1978 also appears to fit smoothly into trends in House membership since World War II. This point is of special interest because the ability to generalize from findings based on an analysis of the 1978 sample depends both on whether the sample is adequately representative of all races in 1978 and on whether the 1978 races, as a whole, were typical of other off-year contests.

An assessment of how typical the 1978 races were in these terms is difficult to make because there are few demographic measures consistently available for comparative analysis over time. Therefore, characteristics of the House are hard to track except in the most rudimentary terms. But one way in which Congresses have been described is in terms of the collective seniority of House members—the number of "careerists," or members who have served 10 or more terms, and the number of junior members (Bullock, 1972; Dodd and Oppenheimer, 1981). The proportion of careerists increased from World War II until 1972, when one-fifth of the members had served that long, and has been declining since. By 1978 only one-eighth of the members were careerists, fitting smoothly into a trend begun years before. Concurrently, of course, the proportion of less senior members has been on the increase since 1972.[12]

The number of very senior and very junior members in Congress has significance for the vitality of campaigns that are fought and the probability of incumbent defeats. Junior members often face strong challenges in their first or second reelection bids. Senior members become increasingly vulnerable to intraparty challenges in primaries. As Figure 2-2 shows, the prospect of a House member leaving office through defeat at any given election remains low (usually only in the range of 3 to 8 percent). Nevertheless, a substantial portion of members eventually will be defeated at the polls (Erikson, 1978). During the 1960s, when major redistricting efforts took their toll, general election defeats reached their postwar peak. They have since declined, but successful primary challenges then increased, particularly against members with unusual longevity. Over time, the freshmen become more secure, but the senior careerists face repeated serious challenges until they retire or lose. Counting retirements and defeats, there were 77 freshman representatives (41 Democrats and 36 Republicans) who began their service in the 96th Congress, and nearly one-half of the en-

Figure 2-2   The Retention Rate of Congressional Incumbents Seeking Reelection, 1960-1982

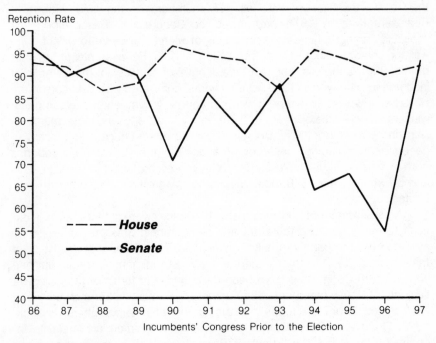

Incumbents' Congress Prior to the Election

Source: Abramson, Aldrich, and Rohde (1983), 192.

tire membership had been elected for the first time in 1974 or 1976. Six of the eight most senior members in the 95th Congress had retired before the election; for the first time there was no member serving who was born in the nineteenth century.

The average age of members is an indicator of turnover in the House, and it has been declining in recent Congresses. Incumbents in the sample of 86 competitive races were 49.9 years old as compared with 50.4 years in all 108 sampled districts, and 50.1 years for all members. While the average age has been declining, the average level of education has risen through the years. Whereas barely two-thirds of the members who served 20 years ago had college educations, now more than 96 percent of the members have a college education. This compares with 98 percent of the incumbents in the 1978 sample.

Systematic data on the demographic characteristics of challengers in congressional races are much more difficult to come by. Most of them lose, and data collections have tended to concentrate on officeholders or winners. While there have been several excellent studies of winners and losers in races in a single state (Hershey, 1974; Kingdon, 1968), there have been only two national studies that looked at the characteristics of unsuccessful candidates and their campaign organizations. Robert Huckshorn and Robert Spencer (1971) studied the losers in the 1962 races through the use of a postelection mail questionnaire.[13] Jeff Fishel (1973) applied similar techniques in his study of the races held in 1964.

The challengers in both Fishel's and Huckshorn and Spencer's studies tended to be younger than the incumbents and to have less political experience than those who had served. The average age of Fishel's nonincumbents was 44 years compared with 53 for the incumbents. Huckshorn and Spencer further distinguished between challengers in marginal races and those that were less competitive, and they observed that "contests in which chances are favorable attract younger candidates." [14] In the 1978 sample, the average age of all the challengers was 44.9 years, about 5 years less than their incumbent opponents. The candidates in open races who felt they had a chance to win were the youngest, 37.5 years old on average. Only 18 percent of the challengers had held prior elective office, and the challengers were less likely to have college educations (85 percent) than the incumbents. These data on demography and seniority show that the 1978 sample of candidates compares quite well to the population of candidates in 1978; the data also are consistent with data on candidates of equivalent status in earlier years.

Management of Congressional Campaigns

Although the candidates are the principal actors in political campaigns, the teams of advisers and managers they assemble play critical roles in orchestrating their activity. In conjunction with the financial resources the candidates accumulate, these staffers are the foundation for a successful campaign effort. The variations in the characteristics and qualifications of the managers are much greater than for the candidates and more sharply a function of other campaign resources. Candidate status plays an important part in explaining the quality of these management teams.

The data presented in Table 2-1 show the distribution of the staffing patterns for six key positions in congressional campaigns. In addition to the manager, these are lawyer or counsel, accountant, press aide, treasurer, and advertising or media specialist. Virtually every campaign had a designated campaign manager and a treasurer. The managers were most likely to be salaried employees, although almost as many were volunteers. Their characteristics are discussed in greater detail below.

The Federal Election Campaign Act and its financial reporting requirements have made their mark on the character of congressional campaign staffs. Virtually every campaign (96 percent) had a treasurer, although

Table 2-1   Campaign Staffing in Congressional Races, 1978

	All Cam-paigns	By Party		By Candidate Status		
		Demo-crats	Repub-licans	Incum-bents	Chal-lengers	Open Races
Campaign Manager						
Salaried employee	43%	36%	50%	50%	32%	52%
Paid consultant	9	7	10	4	15	5
Volunteer	33	43	22	29	35	38
Other arrangements	5	4	5	4	6	0
Didn't use services	11	10	12	12	12	5
	(157)	(81)	(76)	(68)	(68)	(21)
Treasurer						
Salaried employee	5%	5%	5%	10%	1%	0%
Paid consultant	5	7	3	8	3	5
Volunteer	84	84	84	81	84	95
Other arrangements	2	0	4	0	4	0
Didn't use services	4	4	4	2	7	0
	(157)	(82)	(75)	(67)	(69)	(21)
Advertising/Media Specialist						
Salaried employee	16%	11%	22%	15%	15%	24%
Paid consultant	39	43	35	47	26	57
Volunteer	23	26	19	23	27	9
Other arrangements	3	5	1	1	3	9
Didn't use services	18	15	22	14	29	0
	(153)	(81)	(72)	(66)	(66)	(21)
Press Aide						
Salaried employee	35%	28%	42%	34%	31%	50%
Paid consultant	8	6	10	5	9	15
Volunteer	31	32	30	25	35	35
Other arrangements	3	4	3	5	3	0
Didn't use services	23	30	16	31	22	0
	(155)	(81)	(74)	(67)	(68)	(20)
Accountant						
Salaried employee	10%	9%	11%	21%	0%	5%
Paid consultant	14	18	11	23	6	15
Volunteer	53	50	56	36	63	75
Other arrangements	2	1	3	0	3	5
Didn't use services	21	22	19	20	28	0
	(153)	(80)	(73)	(66)	(67)	(20)
Lawyer						
Salaried employee	1%	1%	0%	0%	0%	5%
Paid consultant	5	6	4	9	3	0
Volunteer	50	43	57	39	57	62
Other arrangements	5	7	3	3	6	9
Didn't use services	39	42	37	49	34	24
	(155)	(81)	(74)	(67)	(67)	(21)

almost all of the individuals who filled this role (84 percent) were volunteers. Most campaigns had an accountant on their staff. While one-half (53 percent) were volunteers, one in four (24 percent) was a salaried employee or paid consultant. The vast majority of the campaigns also had advertising/media specialists and press aides who were either salaried employees or paid consultants. Most of the campaigns also had a lawyer, usually a volunteer, although this was the least likely slot to be filled.

The staffing of campaigns reflects a recurring difference between the resources of incumbents and their challengers. In general, the incumbents' staffs were more likely to be composed of paid professionals than those of their opponents. The managers of incumbents, for example, were most likely to be salaried employees, while challengers more frequently used volunteers or paid consultants who contributed part-time effort to the campaign. Although the proportions of managers who were classified as "volunteers" appear to be similar for incumbents and challengers, there are two different types of individuals who filled this role. For incumbents, many volunteer managers were congressional staffers temporarily off the Washington payroll and assigned to the district office. Despite their volunteer status, they often had substantial experience from previous campaign work. The volunteers who assisted the challengers, on the other hand, tended to be friends and family members or local party activists who worked without pay. Many were amateurs with no prior campaign experience.

The financial experts on the incumbents' teams also were more likely to be paid. While the difference is slight for treasurers, 44 percent of the incumbents employed paid accountants while only 6 percent of the challengers did. Almost two out of three incumbents' campaigns employed a salaried staffer or paid consultant for media and advertising, while fewer than one-half (41 percent) of the challengers' campaigns did. In open races, where the expenditures usually are much greater, the vast majority of the campaigns compensated their advertising and media specialists (81 percent) and press aides (65 percent).

The manager is the team leader for the campaign, responsible for the strategic decisions about scheduling the candidate's time and effort, the design and implementation of the game plan, and the allocation of resources. The average age of all the managers was in the late thirties. Incumbents tended to have older managers, usually a reflection of the length of their associations with the candidate and greater experience in past campaigns.

The data presented in Table 2-2 show the professionalization of the managers in campaigns of candidates with different status. In about one in seven campaigns, the candidate was also the manager. Challengers were more likely than incumbents to run their own campaigns. Huckshorn and Spencer found in 1962 that only 4 percent of the challengers employed salaried managers, although the proportion rose to 22 percent among the

Table 2-2 Professionalization Among Managers of Congressional Campaigns, 1978

	All Campaigns	By Party		By Candidate Status		
		Democrats	Republicans	Incumbents	Challengers	Open Races
Manager Is						
The candidate	15%	11%	20%	3%	30%	5%
A congressional staffer	22	27	17	52	0	0
Someone else	63	62	63	45	70	95
	(167)	(85)	(82)	(76)	(74)	(22)
Number of Previous Campaigns						
None	16%	12%	20%	11%	19%	20%
1 – 2	18	13	22	18	19	10
3 – 6	27	36	18	24	25	40
7 or more	40	40	40	47	36	30
	(158)	(78)	(82)	(66)	(72)	(20)
Professionalization of Manager						
Professional	66%	68%	64%	84%	54%	56%
Amateur	34	32	36	16	46	44
	(146)	(76)	(70)	(61)	(67)	(22)

candidates in "marginal" districts. By 1978 professional campaign management had become more common for challengers, but incumbents still were more likely than their opponents to benefit from professional staff support. In the 1978 sample, one-half of the campaign managers for incumbents (52 percent) were members of their congressional staff who were assigned back to the district or ran the local office in conjunction with the campaign. Their familiarity with the member's record, office operations, and the district were obvious advantages in organizing their candidates' campaigns.

Previous experience in running political campaigns is another advantage that incumbents' managers have over their counterparts. Across all of the campaigns, one-sixth of the managers indicated that they had no previous campaign experience, but the proportion of inexperienced managers was somewhat greater for challengers (19 percent) than for incumbents (11 percent). Of equal significance, more managers for incumbents (47 percent) were very experienced (running seven or more campaigns) than those for the challengers (36 percent).

The information relating to the person who occupies the position of manager, the compensation arrangement, and past experience can be combined to form a measure of the professionalization of the position.[15] Overall, two-thirds of the campaigns were managed by professionals, but incumbents enjoyed a substantial advantage over challengers or candidates in open races. Almost all incumbents' campaigns (84 percent) were run by professionals, compared with bare majorities for challengers and candidates in open races.

Human resources, then, represent one of the major advantages that incumbents enjoy in their quest for reelection. Their campaigns tend to be managed by people who are experienced and earn their living by doing this kind of work. Overall, their campaign staffs are relatively large, heterogeneous teams possessing a wide variety of skills necessary to cope with a campaign environment that is becoming more complex, broader in scope, and increasingly reliant upon technology.

Attitudes also play an important role in the development of strategy and the conduct of campaigns. Not all managers begin each campaign with the same assessment of their chances to win. They feel more or less confident based on the strengths and weaknesses of their candidate and the opponent; the resources they have at their disposal; the characteristics of the constituents, which they usually have to take as a given; and their own experience and abilities. These uncertainties are not felt equally by the managers. No managers for incumbents began the campaign expecting to lose, for example, although some expected that considerable effort would be required to secure reelection. At the same time, no managers for challengers were certain that they could win, although many were confident that they had a reasonable chance.

The significance of these assessments is that they set the tone for a campaign and regulate its activity, and this fact is true for both incumbents and challengers. These attitudes are grounded in their expertise, the resources they have to work with, and the equivalent qualities of the opposition. In the next chapter, the basic strategic planning of the campaign is discussed in terms of the relationship between the properties of the district the managers begin with and how they develop campaign strategies to deal with them.

Notes

1. As a result of the redistricting of states that takes place after each decennial census, Michigan now has 18 congressional districts. The map in Figure 2-1 and the associated statistics were taken from the *U. S. Bureau of the Census' Congressional District Data Book,* 93d Congress (Washington, D.C.: U. S. Government Printing Office, 1973), 241-261.

2. The sample was based upon a one-in-four selection from the 432 congressional districts in the continental United States, excluding the one district in Alaska and the two in Hawaii. The sample was designed by the staff of the American National Election Study in conjunction with the Sampling Section of the Survey Research Center at the University of Michigan.

3. The actual interviewing was performed by the Field Section of the Survey Research Center only in those districts where both the Democratic and Republican parties fielded general election candidates. The interviews lasted approximately one and one-half hours. The designated respondent was the campaign manager, operationally defined as the individual who, regardless of title, was responsible for planning strategy and empowered to allocate campaign funds. In 25 of the campaigns, this individual turned out to be the candidate, but most typically the manager was a regular campaign staff member, paid or otherwise. The preelection interviews were conducted in September 1978, while the postelection interviews were conducted in January 1979. A total of 167 candidates out of a possible 172 were interviewed for a 97 percent coverage rate, although some managers were interviewed only once. In the preelection phase of the study, 153 candidates were interviewed for a response rate of 89 percent. In the postelection phase, 144 candidates were contacted again, and 14 more consented to be interviewed for the first time for a response rate of 92 percent.

4. The data for the 1978 American National Election Study were collected with the support of the National Science Foundation under Grant No. SOC77-08885. The principal investigators were Warren Miller and the National Election Studies/Center for Political Studies. The data were made available by the Inter-university Consortium for Political and Social Research. Neither the original collectors of the data nor the ICPSR bear any responsibility for the analysis or interpretations presented here.

5. Although there were too few people interviewed in each district to provide adequate representation of its constituency, analysis could proceed by considering all of the respondents in certain types of districts together.

6. Line-by-line information reported on Schedule B Itemized Expenditures for the period of July 1, 1978, through the end of the year provided a check on reported levels of financial activity as well as an indication of how the money was spent. We are grateful to Kent Cooper, director, and the staff of the Public Records Office of the Federal Election Commission for their assistance in securing microfilm and computer printout copies of various financial reports and for assistance in interpreting them.

7. The American National Election Study employed a clipping service to collect campaign stories, editorials, advertisements, letters to the editors, and the like from selected newspapers in the sample of congressional districts. This decision was based on cost considerations: the clipping service was much less expensive than subscribing to the newspapers and employing people in Ann Arbor to clip them. An independent assessment by the authors of the accuracy of the clipping service showed that the number of clippings delivered was substantially, but not uniformly, below the actual number of campaign stories and ads in the papers. Consequently, the results reported here on content coverage of the campaigns are based upon a subsample of the selected newspapers for which microfilm could be obtained through the University of Michigan Library and then content analyzed. A more complete discussion of the analysis of the clipping service data can be found in "Accuracy of Newspaper Clippings," by Edie N. Goldenberg, unpublished memorandum, Ann Arbor, Mich., June 30, 1981.

8. The assistance and contributions of Market Opinion Research Corporation, especially Robert Teeter and Mary C. Lukens, and of Thomas E. Mann and the Democratic Study Group are gratefully acknowledged. Marginal distributions of party identification in districts falling in our sample were received from these two sources in two forms. For 12 congressional districts, data were received for a seven-point party identification scale; for an additional 25 districts data were received that aggregated party identification to summary Democrat-Independent-Republican distributions. All of the data were reported to be obtained from telephone surveys, with some prescreening of respondents for registration status and likelihood of voting. The data were collected for 9 districts in 1980, for 21 in 1978, for 6 in 1976, and for 1 in 1974. Sample sizes were generally between 300 and 400 respondents, except for two districts with 500-person samples and two districts with samples of only 154 and 54 respondents.

9. These criteria represent relevant data that were available in computer-readable form at the congressional district level. For a more detailed description of the sampling procedures, see *Codebook for the 1978 American National Election Study*, vol. 1. (Ann Arbor, Mich.: Inter-university Consortium for Political and Social Research, 1980), vii-x. Also see Irene Hess, "Comments on the Sample of Congressional Districts" (Memorandum, Ann Arbor, Mich., February 1980).

10. This summary of the results of the 1978 elections is taken from "House: Modest Gains for the Minority," *Congressional Quarterly Weekly Report*, November 11, 1978, 3250-3253.

11. The underrepresentation of strong challengers in the 1978 sample in terms of their expenditures would be problematic if (a) those sampled were unrepresentative of all such challengers in general or if (b) conclusions were based upon statements about House candidates without considering vital and nonvital races separately. Although the evidence available about the population of House challengers is limited, there is nothing in it or in the characteristics of the incumbents they face to suggest that the vital challengers in the sample present a distorted picture of all vital challengers in 1978. So far as generalizations to all candidates or to candidates by party or status drawn from the sample data are concerned, the analysis presented in this book examines relationships for different types of candidates and races according to the vitality of the contest as measured by perceptions of the managers about likely outcomes.

12. Changes of this magnitude in average characteristics of members of the House reflect substantial differences between freshman classes and the incumbents who return for additional terms. A relatively low turnover rate in a legislative body with many members means that many kinds of demographic and compositional changes will be slow to take place. In looking at the composition of successive Congresses, a substantial portion of the information represents the persistent characteristics of members with seniority who are serving one more term than last time. For a description of these changes across the first 170 years of the U. S. House, see Bogue, Clubb, McKibbin, and Traugott (1976).

13. Huckshorn and Spencer actually used three different questionnaire forms in their postelec-

tion mail survey: a 13-page survey of defeated candidates, a 10-page survey of nonincumbent winners, and a 7-page survey of incumbent winners. The associated response rates were 60 percent from the 398 defeated candidates; 64 percent of the 67 "new winners"; and 50 percent of the 367 incumbent winners. Democratic losers and new winners had slightly higher response rates (7 and 5 percentage points, respectively) than their Republican counterparts, but Democratic incumbents responded at a significantly lower rate (42 percent) than Republican incumbents (61 percent). For further details of the survey administration, see Robert J. Huckshorn and Robert C. Spencer, *The Politics of Defeat* (Amherst: University of Massachusetts Press, 1971), v-x.

14. Huckshorn and Spencer defined as "marginal" any district that appeared on two or more of three reference lists of competitive districts. These included the lists prepared by the National Republican Congressional Committee, the Democratic National Committee; and *Congressional Quarterly Weekly Report*, May 4, 1962, 690. A total of 84 districts satisfied this rule, and 44 losers and 18 winners in these districts returned questionnaires. For further details on this point, see Huckshorn and Spencer (1971), 6-12.

15. A "professional" manager has experience in previous campaigns and is a salaried member of, or paid consultant to, the campaign staff or a member of an incumbent's congressional staff; or the individual has been a manager for more than six years, whether or not compensated. An "amateur" manager is a manager or a candidate serving in that role who has little or no previous campaign experience or who is serving as a volunteer.

Chapter 3	Designing a Campaign Strategy

Political campaigning is still more art than science. Practitioners believe that their strategic decisions pay off at the polls, but to what extent they pay off is yet to be demonstrated. Nearly everyone agrees that money matters, and spending money is certainly one important form of strategic behavior. Other important decisions must be made, however, before much money is spent. Who among the district's citizens should be targeted? Which messages and themes should be emphasized? Which information vehicles should be used to transmit the messages? Explaining the development of these initial strategic decisions is the purpose of this chapter and the next.

The person occupying the pivotal role for developing and executing strategy is the campaign manager. There are three central elements that form the basis for a manager's strategic planning: a general theory concerning political campaigns and how they should be run, the realities of the current contest, and an evaluation of the candidate's chances of success. In the first place, a manager is responsible for the broad outline of the political campaign—a notion of what a campaign is, how it should be organized, and what tactics succeed under a variety of circumstances. The "working model" is based upon the managers' training and experience. In conjunction with a track record in past races, this model is what the candidates buy when they secure a manager's services. The manager's general theory of campaigns and elections has to be tempered by the realities of the current contest. Factors such as the nature of the constituency and the characteristics of the opponents provide a grounding for these theories in a specific electoral context. These two elements—theories of elections and district realities—are combined in assessing candidates' chances for victory: are they easy winners, uncertain combatants, or sure losers? They are also relevant to the campaign's ability to influence the size of the margin of victory. Ambitious incumbents may choose to flex their electoral muscles and run up the margin to demonstrate their suitability for higher office; the fear of losing may not affect all challengers, only those who want to make a career of politics. Together these three factors—theories, realities, and assessments—determine the strategy and suggest the tactics that can be used to implement it.

This chapter focuses on the first part of this sequence, the relationship among the managers' theories of election, district realities, and the managers' overall assessments of likely campaign success. It forges a link between the managers' assessments of their chances and their campaign strategies. The next chapter looks at the transformation of strategy into tactics.

The number of past studies of House campaigns is surprisingly small. They have tended to concentrate on a few cases (Clem, 1976; Fenno, 1978; Gore and Peabody, 1958; Jones, 1966), on races in a single state (Hershey, 1974; Kingdon, 1968; Leuthold, 1968) or on a subset of types of candidates (Fishel, 1973; Huckshorn and Spencer, 1971). Despite their limited scope, these early efforts provide valuable theoretical insights and initial direction to this study of congressional campaigns by highlighting two factors that are especially important to the development of campaign strategies: the candidate's party and its relation to the distribution of party preferences in the district and the candidate's status.

The Role of Party

A number of previous studies have reported substantial differences between Democrats and Republicans in their campaign beliefs, strategies, and patterns of resource allocations. John Kingdon, for example, reported dramatic party differences in the makeup of candidates' supporting coalitions and in the types of issue appeals they made. Most Democratic candidates in his study reported labor-oriented coalitions and tended to make liberal issue appeals, while Republican candidates had business-oriented group support and made conservative issue appeals.[1] More recent accounts of party activities have commented on the Republicans' greater use of direct mail techniques and the larger dollar amounts their candidates receive from their national committees.[2] Thus, partisan differences in campaigns are expected because of characteristic differences in the groups supporting Democratic and Republican candidates, in the general ideology of the candidates, and in the amount and types of outside resources available to Democratic and Republican campaigns.

Partisan campaign differences also derive from the different challenges Republican and Democratic incumbents face in their districts. There are more Democratic than Republican House incumbents. Moreover, although a number of Democratic incumbents run in overwhelmingly Democratic districts (in terms of the distribution of party identification), very few Republican incumbents run in overwhelmingly Republican districts. As members of the minority party, Republicans rarely can afford to appeal only to their own partisan supporters. To assemble winning coalitions, they need to broaden their appeal to independents and members of the opposite party as well. As a result, the campaign strategies of Republican incumbents tend to be more broadly targeted and more ambitious than those of Democratic incumbents. This explains why Marjorie Hershey found party differences in resource allocations: Republicans were (and still are) more likely than Democrats to use television advertising.[3]

The Role of Candidate Status

A second theme in past studies of congressional campaigns is candidate status. The incumbency advantage in House races obviously is important even if the explanations of the advantage have differed. Many scholars have concentrated on explanatory factors that come into play before the immediate campaign period: perquisites of office (Cover, 1977); positive media treatment (Robinson, 1981); opposition by weak challengers (Jacobson, 1981; Mann and Wolfinger, 1980; Ragsdale, 1981); constituent service (Fiorina, 1977); the declining importance of party identification as a cue for voters (Cover, 1977; Ferejohn, 1977); or positions on roll call votes (Fiorina, 1981; Johannes and McAdams, 1981).

In addition to all these factors, campaign activity also matters (Caldeira and Patterson, 1982; Jacobson, 1980). Gary Jacobson demonstrated that campaign spending, especially by challengers, translates into votes. Various campaign strategies affect whether the voters recognize candidates and how they evaluate them. Recognition and evaluation affect electoral outcomes. Because challengers and incumbents tend to start a general election campaign from very unequal positions in terms of their name recognition and accomplishments in office, their managers differ substantially in their beliefs and strategies for the campaign.

Theories and Realities in 1978

The theories of elections that managers bring to campaigns reflect the collected wisdom of their prior political experience. Some of it comes from formal schooling; instruction is available through colleges and seminars offered by the national political committees, but the most substantial source is on-the-job training in past campaigns. By the time managers were interviewed for this study, their initial theories already had adjusted to the realities of their particular 1978 races. They had views about who and what mattered to the election in their district, and these views reflected important district characteristics such as the basic distribution of partisanship.

Data based upon the sample of contested congressional races in 1978 show the variation in district realities that campaign managers faced. Because the study included only contested races, information was available from nearly equal numbers of Democrats and Republicans as well as nearly equal numbers of incumbents and challengers.[4] Of the sampled House contests, one-quarter (24 percent) were in districts where the distribution of party identification in the constituency was so lopsided that the normal vote advantage to the majority party was greater than 10 percentage points.[5] In normal vote terms, only 1 district was lopsided in favor of the Republicans, while 21 favored the Democrats. The distribution of party identification in the other 64 districts was fairly evenly divided between Republicans and Democrats.

In the recent past, however, many congressional districts with relatively close normal votes were in fact very safe races for the incumbents. In more than five in six (86 percent) of the races, the average votes of recent elections were lopsided. Of these districts where more than 55 percent of the vote was cast for one party, nearly twice as many favored the Democrats as the Republicans.

Virtually all of the managers knew of the relative strength of the two major parties in recent races for Congress in their districts. Many of them (58 percent) believed, however, that the relative strength of parties in their districts was changing, primarily toward greater competitiveness. Although much of this thinking can be traced to the perceptions of hopeful challengers, one quarter of the incumbents' managers also felt this way. There is no objective evidence that, based upon actual electoral outcomes, those districts that managers believed were becoming more competitive did in fact become more competitive between 1976 and 1978. Nevertheless, the expectations of change existed and contributed to feelings of uncertainty.

The realities of the candidates' party and status play an important role in the development of campaign strategy in conjunction with the theories that managers hold about who and what matters to electoral success. These factors influence the managers' assessments of their chances that, in turn, affect the strategy and how actively it is pursued. Campaigns are not necessarily designed to reach all district voters. Managers believe that certain individuals and groups are more important than others in building a winning coalition for their candidates and that certain factors are more influential than others. Because their resources are limited, they must target specific groups and select among other strategic alternatives. In the 1978 study, managers were asked several questions about who and what mattered to the campaigns in their districts.

Who Matters?

Most managers (72 percent) could identify specific local groups that were important to election outcomes in their districts.[6] By far, the most frequently mentioned type of local group was a union (48 percent), followed by black and Hispanic groups (18 percent), business groups (17 percent), and womens' groups (15 percent). Although there was no difference between Democrats and Republicans in their mentions of local minority or womens' groups, Democrats were more likely than Republicans (56 percent to 40 percent) to mention unions as important local groups. Virtually all of the Democrats who mentioned unions expected their support; only one-third of the Republicans who thought unions were significant in their districts expected to receive their support. On the other hand, Republicans were somewhat more likely than Democrats to mention business groups as important (21 percent to 13 percent). Nine in 10 of these Republicans and about one-half of the Democrats expected these groups to support their candidates.

These findings are consistent with previous studies that found different supporting coalitions for Democrats and Republicans, as well as prevailing beliefs about union and business sympathies.[7] These support groups are important because once candidates become elected representatives, they are assumed to be more accessible and responsive to those who are judged important to their reelection chances. When union and business interests clash, as they often do, Democrats and Republicans in the House can be expected to take different legislative and policy positions. They will react in accord with their different perceptions of important constituent groups and in response to past support in their electoral coalitions.

Party differences, however, do not tell the whole story. Incumbency also matters. Managers for incumbents were more likely to mention labor *and* business support than managers for challengers. Although the numbers are small and must be interpreted cautiously, it appears that Democrats expected support from labor regardless of their candidates' status, while Republican incumbents were considerably more likely to expect labor support than were Republican challengers. Similarly, Democratic incumbents were more likely than Democratic challengers to expect business support, while Republicans could expect it regardless of their candidates' status. Incumbents were supported financially by a larger number of political action committees (PACs) —groups of individual contributors from labor unions; corporations; or trade, membership, and health organizations—and with larger average contributions than were given to challengers. Most PACs strive to back winners; given the safety of their seats, it is no surprise to see incumbents reporting broader coalitions of supporters than the challengers report.

What Matters?

In addition to consideration of important groups, managers also bring to their campaign strategies theories about which factors influence the way people vote in their district. A number of measures available from the 1978 study provide insight into this aspect of the managers' theories of election. First, a set of questions asked the managers to assess several possible influences on the vote: the relative background and experience of the candidates, the incumbent's record, the candidates' partisan affiliations, national issues, other state and local races, turnout levels, party organization in the district, editorial endorsements, and President Jimmy Carter's performance in office.[8] The data in Table 3-1 present the results separately for managers of incumbents and challengers.

Several aspects of the information in Table 3-1 are striking. Managers for incumbents believed overwhelmingly in the importance of their candidates' background, experience, and record as members of Congress. Managers for challengers saw voter turnout as very important; they thought that low turnout would benefit the incumbent and that, therefore, to win they needed to mobilize their supporters to vote. Few managers for incumbents considered editorial endorsements or other state and local contests to be of great importance. The challengers' managers did not attach a great deal of significance to endorsements either, but they were more concerned than the incumbents about local party organizations and other state and local contests.

Even opposing managers running campaigns in the same district did not necessarily evaluate the significance of these factors in the same way. Fewer than one-half of the pairs of opposing managers agreed on the importance of most factors. Where they disagreed, managers for challengers generally attached less significance to their opponents' background and experience and more significance to voter turnout than did managers for incumbents.

With two interesting exceptions, party differences were relatively small once incumbency was controlled. More Democrats (57 percent) than Republicans (39 percent) regarded party as important. More Republicans than Democrats regarded national issues (45 percent to 30 percent) and Carter's performance (51 percent to 42 percent) as important. Both were engaging in some wishful strategic optimism. Democrats hoped for large turnouts of their party faithful. They knew that many of their congressional districts had more Democrats than Republicans among the potential voters. Their campaigns could concentrate on mobilizing regular party supporters, a strategy that is characteristic of the campaigns of candidates from the majority party in a constituency. For many Republicans, especially managers for challengers and for candidates in open races, their best hope lay in bringing important national issues, including the president's performance, to the voters' attention. Without issue voting, their candidates hardly could expect to overcome the party and experience advantages of their opponents. Because they were usually the candidates from the minority party in the district, their campaigns frequently had to be based upon efforts to convert people who normally identify with the other party. Issue-based

Table 3-1 Importance of Factors to the Vote as Seen by Managers for Incumbents and Challengers, 1978

	Incumbents (N=64)			Challengers (N=69)		
	Very Important	Somewhat Important	Not Important	Very Important	Somewhat Important	Not Important
Background and experience	88%	8	5	47%	38	16
Incumbents' voting records	80%	17	3	54%	25	21
Presidential performance	43%	—	57	45%	—	55
Party	42%	38	21	51%	29	19
National issues	30%	43	27	43%	42	14
Turnout	28%	6	66	78%	3	19
Party organization	21%	31	49	37%	29	34
State and local contests	13%	20	67	37%	32	32
Editorial endorsements	7%	39	54	10%	39	51

appeals are an important element in forging winning coalitions by this strategy.[9]

A second approach to understanding what managers believe matters in congressional elections is available in data from a series of open-ended questions about the strengths and weaknesses of their own candidates as well as their opponents. Some of the managers mentioned as many as 12 strengths and weaknesses for each candidate. The only interesting partisan difference was, once again, a tendency by Republicans more than Democrats to emphasize issues as a candidate strength. This was true across all three types of candidates—incumbents, challengers, and those running in open races. There were more substantial differences among managers according to the incumbency status of their candidates. Managers for incumbents emphasized the advantages of incumbency, name recognition, and voting record, in that order. Relatively few said that their opponents had any strengths, but those who did tended to notice well-financed challengers. The most frequently mentioned weakness in their own campaigns was that some incumbents spent too much time in Washington, D.C., and too little time in their districts. Their challengers were seen as much weaker, primarily because they lacked the experience of incumbency, name recognition, and money.

Managers for challengers saw their advantages in their issue positions and in their candidates' personal characteristics, such as energy, sincerity, and intelligence. They saw incumbency, name recognition, and money as their opponents' strengths and the lack of all three as their own weaknesses. Thus there was considerable agreement by opposing managers regarding the factors contributing to incumbent strength and challenger weakness. The main disagreement stemmed from a greater belief by the challengers' managers that their candidates' personal characteristics mattered and that their opponents were seriously vulnerable, primarily because of their voting records.

A third and final measure of what managers believe matters in congressional elections is based upon their ranking of three factors—party, issues, and candidate characteristics—as most and least important to voters in their district. Just over one-half of the managers (52 percent) considered candidate factors most important, followed by party identification (30 percent) and issues (18 percent). Roughly one in six regarded candidate characteristics as least important (16 percent), with the others splitting evenly between party affiliation and issues.

Which factor was considered most important depended in part on the type of district in which the manager was working. In districts with lopsided partisanship favoring one party or the other, more than twice as many managers as in close districts ranked party as the most important of the three factors, far outstripping issues and personal characteristics as considerations. In districts with closer normal votes, personal characteristics were the overwhelming choice, leaving party and issues each with only one-fifth of the first place rankings.

Assessments of Electoral Chances

Candidates in contested races can be categorized by their assessments of their chances of winning the election—whether they are confident or uncertain of the outcome.[10] Data are presented in Table 3-2 that show the relationship between uncertainty about the election and various politically relevant characteristics of the candidates and the district.

Although no managers of incumbents in 1978 expected their candidates to lose, one in four is classified as "Vulnerable" because he or she felt uncertain about the outcome and expected a potentially serious challenge. Overall, managers for Republican incumbents were more likely to feel uncertain about the outcome of their races (36 percent) than managers for Democratic incumbents (19 percent), a reflection of the closer normal vote situations Republican incumbents faced. This was especially so with the Watergate class of Democrats removed: other than those Democrats who were elected initially in 1974, very few Democratic incumbents had managers who felt vulnerable. Democrats elected first in 1974 ran in districts with unusually close (or even Republican) normal votes. Republicans and Democrats in districts with comparable partisanship were equally likely to feel uncertain about electoral results.

Although no managers of challengers expected to win easily, 61 percent were "Hopefuls" who felt they could win with effort. The remaining 39 percent ran their campaigns under the assumption that they would lose. Managers of Republican challengers were somewhat more likely than Democrats to be classified as "Sure Losers," once again reflecting the more lopsided partisan divisions in their districts.

In the open races most managers, all of the Democrats and two-thirds (64 percent) of the Republicans, felt uncertain about the outcome. The two Sure Losers were Republican candidates running in lopsided districts with Democratic normal votes.

Managers of established incumbents (those having served three or more terms) felt more comfortable than those of short-termers. During their tenure, most incumbents build reliable supporting coalitions by providing service to their constituents. These incumbents had access to resources that could be used to discourage serious primary challenges as well as serious general election challenges. Their obvious seniority, experience, and name recognition made most of them confident of success in 1978.

If Democratic challengers were facing long-term rather than short-term incumbents, their managers tended to be less hopeful. Whether they were running against long-term or short-term incumbents, the division of partisan-

Table 3-2   Managers' Subjective Assessments of Electoral Chances, by Candidate and District Characteristics, 1978

	Sure Winners	Vulner- ables	(N)	Hopefuls	Sure Losers	(N)
Candidate Status & Party						
Candidates in Open Races	10%	0		80	10	(20)
Democrats	0%	0		100	0	(9)
Republicans	18%	0		64	18	(11)
Incumbents	75%	25	(65)			
Democrats	81%	19	(43)			
Republicans	64%	36	(22)			
Challengers				61%	39	(71)
Democrats				66%	35	(29)
Republicans				57%	43	(42)
Length of Service						
Democratic Incumbents						
Long-term	91%	9	(21)			
Short-term	73%	27	(22)			
Republican Incumbents						
Long-term	69%	31	(16)			
Short-term	50%	50	(6)			
Democratic Challengers of						
Long-term Incumbents				58%	42	(19)
Short-term Incumbents				80%	20	(10)
Republican Challengers of						
Long-term Incumbents				61%	39	(23)
Short-term Incumbents				53%	47	(19)
Underlying Partisanship						
Safe Districts*	100%	0	(20)	39%	61	(20)
Relatively Competitive	65%	36	(45)	69%	31	(51)
Recent Electoral Outcome						
Safe Districts**	81%	19	(54)	55%	45	(60)
Relatively Competitive	45%	55	(11)	91%	9	(11)

* A long-term incumbent is one who has served 3 terms or longer, while a short-term incumbent served fewer terms.
** Safe districts are those where the vote (normal vote or recent electoral outcome) is greater than 55 percent in favor of the party of the incumbent. Relatively competitive districts are those with votes between 45 and 55 percent in favor of the party of the incumbent.

ship in their districts was in the close range. Therefore, the seniority of their Republican opponents was an important factor in assessing their chances. In contrast, many Republican challengers ran in strongly Democratic districts that showed no prospects for party turnover regardless of how long the incumbent had served. For them, the seniority of their Democratic opponents was irrelevant.

Although few managers, if any, expressed familiarity with the political science concept of the normal vote, they were well aware of the basic partisan tendencies of their districts. Managers were more likely to feel uncertain if they were operating in districts with normal votes near 50 percent than in districts with more lopsided underlying partisan advantages. All the managers of majority party incumbents in districts with lopsided partisanship were certain of victory, as opposed to 65 percent of those in districts with close partisan divisions. More than half (61 percent) of the managers for challengers in districts with lopsided partisanship were certain of defeat, as compared with one-third of those in districts with close partisan divisions.

The partisan division of the district's electorate is, of course, only one indication of how competitive congressional races may be. Some incumbents are able to win with large margins, even in places with relatively close divisions in partisanship. Election outcomes of the recent past also figured into the managers' assessments of chances for races involving incumbents and challengers. Managers for incumbents were more likely to feel certain of victory if they were running campaigns for candidates who had won by large margins in 1976 (81 percent) than if their candidates had won only narrowly last time (45 percent). Similarly, more managers for challengers were hopeful if the last House race in the district had been close than if the incumbent had won handily in 1976. This confidence or lack of it was felt by both Democrats and Republicans.

The roots of electoral uncertainty can be seen partly in unalterable realities such as the candidate's status or the underlying partisan division of the vote in the district. They also can be seen in the manager's theory of elections—the beliefs the manager holds about who and what will matter in the race. In response to an open-ended question about candidate weaknesses, substantially more of the Vulnerables than the Sure Winners saw the potential for an issue-sensitive and attentive public in their districts and believed issues to be important to the vote. Two-thirds of them (67 percent), as compared with only 16 percent of the Sure Winners, believed the level of turnout would be critical to their election chances.

Forty percent of the managers for incumbents in districts with close partisanship felt vulnerable, as compared with only 4 percent of those in districts with lopsided partisan distributions in their favor. Data presented in Table 3-3 show that both district realities (in the form of the underlying partisanship) and theories of election (in the form of managers' judgments about important factors in the election) contributed independently to uncertainty. Those managers who judged factors such as national issues and level of turnout as important were more likely to feel vulnerable than those who did not. Although fewer than one-quarter of the managers for incumbents judged national issues and voter turnout to be important factors in their races, those who did were acknowledging the significance of factors that are least easily controlled by the incumbent and most easily manipulated by the challenger. In contrast, other factors are either largely uncontrollable, such as partisan affiliation, or more clearly to the advantage of the incumbent, such as candidate background and experience. If managers both believed in the importance of issues and turnout and faced a closely divided electorate in terms of partisan preferences, they were highly likely (80 percent) to feel vulnerable in the race.

Managers for challengers, too, were guided both by district realities and their theories of election. In districts with close partisanship, 69 percent of the managers were hopeful, as compared with 48 percent of those in districts with lopsided, disadvantageous partisan distributions. In open-ended responses to a question about candidate weaknesses, Sure Losers acknowledged their minority party status as well as their sense that party mattered. Two-thirds of the managers for challengers believed in the importance of national issues and voter turnout, and those who thought this way tended to be Hopefuls more often than those who did not. Three-quarters of the managers who both ran in closely divided districts and saw issues and turnout as important were hopeful of staging an upset.

In summary, objective measures of candidate status and district safety are important in understanding uncertainty in the campaign. Most of the incumbents' managers tended to be confident of victory, but some felt vulnerable; most of the managers for candidates in open races were uncertain of the outcome; and most challengers' managers were hopeful, but a substantial number knew they would lose. The distribution of partisan affiliation varies across districts, and the closeness and direction of a district's partisanship affects feelings of vulnerability and hopefulness in a campaign. The differences between Democratic and Republican candidates in their campaign uncertainty are understandable once the differences in the partisanship in their districts are recognized.

Uncertainty about the electoral outcome often reflects obvious unalterable realities of the district. Sometimes, however, incumbents feel uncertain even when the objective indicators of campaign vulnerability used by political scientists show no cause for concern. In any given election, about 19 out of 20 incumbents seeking reelection will be returned to office. Whether uncertainty under these conditions results from perceptual distortions on the part of candidates or from poor choices of indicators by political scientists remains to be seen. In any case, it is the perception—whether or not it mirrors actual political reality—that is useful in understanding campaign behavior.[11] The candidates' uncertainty about their electoral chances is a third factor that affects how campaign strategies are planned and executed.

Two additional points warrant discussion before turning to campaign tactics. The first is an observation in the literature on campaigns that responses to questions about the most important factors affecting campaigns are not always what they seem. The second is a further elaboration of the importance of issues in congressional elections.

Table 3-3   Assessments of Electoral Chances by District Realities and Managers' Theories of Elections, 1978

	Percentage of Incumbents Who Feel Vulnerable	
	Normal Vote*	
	Lopsided	Close
National Issues and Turnout**		
Neither is important	0% (21)	23% (27)
Both are important	20% (5)	80% (10)

	Percentage of Challengers Who Feel Hopeful	
	Normal Vote	
	Lopsided	Close
National Issues and Turnout		
Neither is important	25% (8)	57% (14)
Both are important	60% (15)	74% (31)

* A lopsided normal vote is greater than 55 percent in favor of the party of the incumbent. The N's indicate the number of managers for incumbents and challengers in close or lopsided districts who responded both to the questions about assessments of chances and important factors in the race.
** The original questions were as follows: How much will the vote for Congress in your district be affected by national issues — very much, quite a bit, somewhat, not very much, not at all? Do you think that the outcome of the election this year in this district is at all dependent on the level of voter turnout? (Yes, Depends, No). The category "Both are important" comprises a "high" answer on one item and at least a "moderate" answer on the other. Otherwise the issues and turnout variable was coded "Neither is important."

Congratulations/Rationalization

John Kingdon examined the responses to questions about three important campaign factors in his postelection study in Wisconsin (Kingdon, 1968). Based on observed differences between the responses of winners and losers, Kingdon suggested the existence of a "congratulations-rationalization" effect: winners exaggerate the importance of candidate factors and losers exaggerate the importance of "blind party loyalty." His explanation of postelection differences in candidate perceptions was that winners and losers shift their assessments in different directions once they know the election outcome. To see whether perceptions do indeed shift, a panel design is necessary to allow comparisons of the pre- and postelection perceptions of the same people. The 1978 study incorporated such a panel design: 134 managers were asked to rank the same three factors—party, national issues, and candidate characteristics—both before and after the election.[12]

First, a look at only the managers' postelection perceptions in 1978 showed differences between incumbents and challengers that are very similar to those Kingdon found in his study of Wisconsin races. These differences were apparent, however, before the election as well, and the shifts that occurred are not in the expected direction. The data in Table 3-4 present the results by candidate status and by uncertainty of election outcome. After the election, more than one-half the managers for challengers, as compared with only 21 percent of the managers for incumbents, believed that party had been the most important factor in their races. Even before the election, however, party was seen as the most important factor by more managers for challengers than managers for incumbents.

More dramatic differences are apparent in Table 3-4 when candidates are distinguished further in terms of their uncertainty about electoral outcomes. Not all challengers (or losers in Kingdon's terms) shifted to party explanations of their defeat. Hopefuls, not the Sure Losers, show the largest pre- to postelection difference. Managers of Sure Losers acknowledged even before the election that they would lose because they knew that partisan affiliations in their districts made a win highly unlikely. In contrast, the managers who were Hopefuls were optimistic before the election in part because they thought that party factors were relatively unimportant. For some of them, their experience in the campaign proved otherwise. By the postelection interview, 42 percent of the Hopefuls ranked party as the most important factor in their race, half again as many as in the early campaign period. Most Sure Winners, confident that their incumbent candidates would emerge victorious, believed that candidate factors were most important; so did the Vulnerables who managed campaigns for incumbents but were concerned about the outcome of their races.

The actual shifts in the responses of particular individuals who were interviewed both before and after the election are shown in Table 3-5. Most incumbents and 7 of 10 Sure Losers chose the same factor as most important in both the pre- and postelection interviews. Only one Vulnerable shifted pre- to postelection in his judgment about which factor was most important in his race. Relatively few Sure Winners shifted either; those who did shifted toward candidate-based factors. Consequently, there appears to be little indication that winners changed their minds as they congratulated themselves for their victories. On the other hand, nearly one-half (47 percent) of the Hopefuls changed their minds, and most of their shifts were toward acknowledgment of the significance of party factors: 14 percent of the managers shifted from candidate characteristics to party and an additional 11 percent shifted from issues to party.

But what of rationalization? Greater shifts by Hopefuls than by Sure Losers are consistent with the idea of rationalization. Greater rationalization would be expected from those surprised by their defeat than by those anticipating defeat all along. Additional evidence, however, suggests that

Table 3-4 Preelection and Postelection Comparisons of Most Important Factors by Candidate Status and Assessments of Electoral Chances, 1978*

	Preelection			Postelection			
	Party	Issues	Candidate	Party	Issues	Candidate	(N)
Status							
Incumbents	21%	16	63	21%	13	66	(56)
Challengers	41%	20	39	51%	10	39	(59)
Candidates in open races	32%	21	47	68%	0	32	(19)
Assessments of Chances							
Incumbents							
Sure Winners	22%	16	62	20%	11	69	(45)
Vulnerables	18%	18	64	27%	18	55	(11)
Challengers							
Hopefuls	28%	25	47	42%	17	42	(36)
Sure Losers	61%	13	26	65%	0	35	(23)

* Respondents who were interviewed both before and after the election and for whom an assessment could be ascertained.

Table 3-5 Consistency in Factor Rankings Before and After the Campaign by Assessments of Electoral Chances, 1978

Assessments of Chances	Consistent Responses	Shifting Responses by Type					
		Party to Candidate	Party to Issues	Candidate to Party	Issues to Party	Candidate to Issues	Issues to Candidate
Incumbents							
Sure Winners	84%	4	0	2	0	2	7 (45)
Vulnerables	91%	0	0	9	0	0	0 (11)
Challengers							
Hopefuls	53%	8	3	14	11	6	6 (36)
Sure Losers	70%	13	0	4	13	0	0 (23)

learning is a more appropriate explanation than rationalization for the shifts. If rationalization were causing Hopefuls to adjust their perceptions after they lose, then they should be shifting toward party regardless of the realities of their election contest. In the majority of cases, however, the Hopefuls' managers who shifted were in charge of campaigns in lopsided districts for the partisan underdog. Hopefuls in districts with traditionally close divisions in the partisan vote did not shift toward "blind party" explanations. Moreover, if the incumbent opponents of those hopeful managers shifted in their judgments, they too shifted toward party. Because they won, and by even larger margins than in 1976, these managers had nothing to rationalize. Looked at in these ways, shifts in factor rankings over the course of the campaign appear to indicate that managers learned about electoral realities in the districts where they were running campaigns.[13]

Do Issues Matter?

The data presented above show that few managers regarded issues as the most important element in their campaigns. This fact may discourage those who see properly functioning democratic elections as those in which opposing candidates clarify their substantial differences on important issues so that citizens can vote their issue preferences. Discouragement is probably unwarranted. While few managers judged issues to be the most important factor, by no means did they view them as unimportant. Only 20 percent indicated that national issues were unimportant according to the data in Table 3-1, a proportion that compares favorably with turnout, party organization, other state and local races, and editorial endorsements.

Managers also were asked how many of their districts' residents were really interested in and kept up to date on issues. Although relatively few managers saw issue interest as widespread, two-thirds of them thought 20 percent or more of their district residents were sensitive to issues. As others have pointed out, what matters to campaigns (and to the behavior of elected officials while in office) is not whether a majority of constituents care about issues at any particular time, but whether an attentive public can be *made to care* (Jackson, 1973). In particular, the question is whether an attentive public will notice issues and become active (or inactive) based upon the candidates' positions on them (Fiorina, 1974; Mayhew, 1974). Most managers believed there was a small but significant attentive public in their districts and, therefore, the potential existed for issue interest to grow.

In sum, important party differences in the managers' theories of elections appeared in their perceptions of who and what mattered to the outcome of elections in their districts. Democrats acknowledged their support from organized labor, Republicans their support from business. Democrats emphasized the importance of voter turnout and partisan factors, while Republicans emphasized national issues and Carter's performance.

Status differences were even more pronounced. Incumbents anticipated having broader supporting coalitions than challengers, partially muting expected partisan differences in support from business and labor. Managers, especially those for incumbents, recognized the potential issue sensitivity of an attentive public in their districts, although they rarely ranked issues as the most important factor in the election. Virtually all managers recognized the advantages of incumbency, but substantial numbers of the managers for challengers believed they could overcome this problem through campaign effort. Their losses carried with them lessons about the limits of campaign effects, especially in places characterized by a lopsided partisan electorate.

The theories that managers hold regarding who and what matters to campaign success vary according to the particular situations they face. Are they Democrats or Republicans? Are they managing for an incumbent or challenger or in an open race? What is the partisan makeup of the district? These district realities and the managers' perspectives on what matters to the election lead to overall assessments of likely success or failure in the race. One important finding that emerges from the study of House races in 1978 is that the campaign manager's uncertainty about how the election will turn out is much more central to our understanding of political campaigns than has been recognized previously.

Notes

1. See Kingdon, 1968, 48.
2. Herbert E. Alexander, *Financing Politics: Money, Elections, and Political Reform,* 3d ed. (Washington, D.C.: CQ Press, 1984), 71-72.
3. See Hershey, 1974, 91
4. In the preelection survey with 153 of 172 managers interviewed, there were 81 Democrats and 72 Republicans—64 managers for incumbents, 69 managers for challengers, and 20 managers in open races. In the postelection survey, 158 managers were interviewed: 82 Democrats and 76 Republicans—68 managers for incumbents, 69 managers for challengers, and 21 managers in open races.
5. The precise derivation of the normal vote measure is described in detail in the Appendix.
6. The exact question was worded as follows: "Other than the parties, are there any particular individuals or local groups who are important in determining the outcome of this election?" (If yes) "Who are they? Which of these groups do you expect to support your candidate? Which groups do you expect to support your opponent?" Managers could name up to five different individuals or groups.
7. Using different question wordings and different aggregation rules, Kingdon reported much sharper party differences in the same direction in the makeup of supporting coalitions for candidates in Wisconsin. See Kingdon, 1968, Chap. 3.
8. Questions were worded as follows: "How much will the vote in this district be affected by the relative background and experience of the two candidates?" The question on

presidential performance took a different form: "Do you think that the performance of President Carter in his first two years of office will be an issue in this campaign, or not?"

9. Three of the possible influences shown in Table 3-1 were included both in the 1958 postelection representation study reported in Stokes and Miller (1962) and in the 1978 postelection survey of managers. Because of shifts between .pre- and postsurvey responses, discussed in detail below, the appropriate comparisons with Stokes and Miller's data come from the 1978 postelection questions. Despite minor variations in wording of questions between the two studies, differences in types of respondents (candidates in 1958, managers in 1978), and 20 years of elapsed time with attendant developments, the 1978 assessments of important factors were remarkably similar to those in 1958. Eighty-five percent of the incumbent candidates in 1958 said that the candidate's record and standing were very or quite important, as compared with 88 percent of the 1978 managers for incumbents. Thirty-six percent of the challengers in 1958 regarded the incumbent's record and standing as important, as compared with 41 percent of the 1978 managers for challengers. The changes that have occurred—a decline of more than 10 percent in the number who see party identification and other state and local races as important—are consistent with the decline in the importance of partisan cues and the growth of individual candidate-based campaigns that occurred over the intervening 20 years. See Donald Stokes and Warren Miller (1964).

10. Questions were worded as follows: "In this year's election, would you say that one candidate has a much better chance of winning, or would you say both candidates have a good chance of winning? If the election were held today, which candidate do you think would win? Would it be a close election or not close at all? On election day, do you think (same candidate) will win? Now let's think about your opponent. How much money will it cost (him/her) to run a winning campaign in this district? Do you think (he/she) will be able to raise it?" The self-described "Sure Winners" and "Sure Losers" expected the outcome to be lopsided. Those who anticipated that the outcome would change due to their campaign efforts, that the eventual outcome would be close, or that their opponent might raise enough money to win were labeled either "Vulnerable" or "Hopeful" depending on whether they were managers for incumbents or challengers. According to Jacobson (1981), the 1978 sample of congressional districts actually "exaggerates the strength of incumbents and the weakness of challengers." Consequently, the 25 percent figure from the sample is probably a low estimate of the proportion of vulnerable incumbents in the 1978 House races as a whole.

Huckshorn and Spencer (1971) also used a measure of the challengers' assessments of their chances in the election. None of the candidates was certain of victory, while 55 percent said their chances were "good" or "fair," and 45 percent thought their chances were remote or nil.

11. See Fenno, 1978, 806; Miller, 1964; Kingdon, 1968.

12. See Kingdon, 1968, Chap. 2. Kim and Racheter used a pre-post questionnaire design to explore this same question. They found little evidence of congratulations-rationalization using Kingdon's approach, but substantial evidence using a modified approach. See Kim and Racheter (1973).

13. Actually some managers were learning, some others were probably rationalizing, and some were doing both. Additional study is needed to sort out the details of this relationship. However, the commonly held notion of rationalization clearly is insufficient to account for interesting preelection differences and for most of the shifts pre- to postelection.

| Chapter 4 | Developing Campaign Tactics |

Candidates employ very different campaign tactics depending on how certain they are of victory or defeat. The managers' assessments of their candidates' chances have important consequences for the development of a campaign strategy and the tactics used to implement it. The relationship between these assessments and three particular aspects of campaign tactics are addressed here: the characteristics of the electorate in the district targeted for campaign appeals, the substance of the appeals, and the methods used to collect information from voters during the campaign.

Targeting the Electorate

In every campaign, the basic strategy requires mobilizing a candidate's partisan supporters to vote. A significant imbalance in party identification in a district may enable the incumbent to continue to hold office and to deter any serious challenge. But many campaigns also try to attract independent voters and to convert adherents of the other party. Political campaigns are not necessarily designed to reach every voter. Using finite resources, candidates try to reach enough voters to build a winning coalition. One of the important elements of campaign tactics is deciding who will be targeted.

Scope of Targeting

In 1978 managers were asked before the election about their targeting strategies.[1] In response, 28 percent said they planned to target only their own supporters; 32 percent said they would concentrate on independents, too; and 40 percent expected to have to convert voters of the opposite

Table 4-1   Targeting Constituents by Dominance of the Candidate's Party in the District, 1978

	Mobilize Supporters	Appeal to Independents & Supporters	Appeal to Everyone/ Convert Other Party	
Majority Party Candidate*	64%	18	18	(22)
Close Division	26%	36	39	(109)
Minority Party Candidate	0%	27	73	(22)

* Majority party candidates ran in districts with a normal vote more than 55 percent in favor of their party. Close candidates ran in districts with a normal vote between 45 percent and 55 percent in favor of one party. Minority party candidates ran in districts with a normal vote less than 45 percent in favor of their party.

party or appeal to everyone in their district to win.

The breadth of campaign targeting was expected to vary according to whether candidates were of the majority or minority party in their districts. Minority party candidates must appeal beyond their own partisan supporters if they hope to attract enough votes to win. The data in Table 4-1 show that most managers of candidates from the majority party (64 percent) appealed only to their own partisan supporters. The managers in districts with a close partisan division tried a variety of techniques, and those working with minority party candidates broadened their appeals beyond traditional partisan supporters to include independents and supporters of the other party as well.

The Role of Uncertainty

The partisan division of voters in the district, however, is not the only factor that affects the breadth of targeting. Previous campaign studies have found that uncertainty plays a role as well. Both John Kingdon and Richard Fenno, for example, suggested that incumbents who are uncertain of victory appeal to a larger set of citizens and groups in their districts, while those confident of winning can afford to concentrate on a narrower group of supporters who compose their "reelection constituency." According to this point of view, the uncertainty that Vulnerables experience should lead them to broaden their targeting to be certain of reaching enough voters in the district to win.

As the data in Table 4-2 show, Democrats behaved as expected. Their Sure Winners concentrated on mobilization strategies, focusing only on traditional partisan supporters, while Democratic Vulnerables broadened their appeals to include independents as well. Even in places with evenly

Table 4-2 Targeting Constituents by Managers' Assessments of Electoral Chances and Party, 1978

	Mobilize Supporters	Appeal to Independents & Supporters	Appeal to Everyone/ Convert Other Party	
Incumbents				
Sure Winners				
Democrats	57%	23	20	(35)
Republicans	14%	7	78	(14)
Vulnerables				
Democrats	13%	63	25	(8)
Republicans	14%	14	72	(7)
Challengers				
Hopefuls				
Democrats	16%	63	21	(19)
Republicans	21%	25	54	(24)
Sure Losers				
Democrats	30%	40	30	(10)
Republicans	13%	31	56	(16)
Candidates in Open Races				
Democrats	33%	44	22	(9)
Republicans	18%	27	55	(11)

divided partisanship, one-half of the Democratic Sure Winners were content to target only their own partisan supporters. Republicans, however, did not follow suit. Uncertainty was unimportant to their targeting strategies. Regardless of their assessments of their chances, they broadened their targeting to build or maintain winning coalitions. Virtually all Republican incumbents—Sure Winners as well as Vulnerables—ran in districts with close normal votes. Perhaps Republicans tend to see themselves as candidates of the national minority party and plan accordingly, even in places where they do not suffer serious disadvantages in terms of partisan preferences.

As expected, challengers and candidates in open races broadened their targeting beyond their traditional partisan supporters, but Democrats once again differed from Republicans. Democrats believed they could build a winning coalition with their own partisan supporters plus some independents. Republicans were more likely to try to convert people of the other party as well, especially in strongly Democratic districts. Even in districts that were closely divided in partisan terms, Republican challengers were more likely than Democratic challengers to rely on conversion strategies.

In sum, uncertainty did lead to broader targeting strategies for Democratic incumbents, but Republicans targeted broadly regardless of their assessments of their electoral chances. Minority party candidates—whether challengers, participants in open races, or the few incumbents who ran in districts with voters predominantly of the other party—tended to target broadly.

Campaign Appeals

A second type of tactical decision concerns the kinds of appeals candidates decide to use to generate support. Political scientists are interested for two reasons in the messages candidates choose to convey and the positions they take on important issues. The first is a fundamental desire to understand how campaigns are fought and won and the strategic role of issues in them. The second is a desire to trace the extent to which the winners' issue positions during the campaign show up later as recorded votes in Congress. Before the 1978 election, managers were asked which messages they planned to communicate to the voters.[2] Nearly 9 in 10 mentioned one or more issue messages, and two-thirds mentioned one or more messages about their candidates' characteristics. Relatively few (9 percent) mentioned their party affiliation.

After the election, managers were asked whether their campaigns had emphasized the qualities of their own candidates, their opponents' weaknesses, both, or neither. Following conventional wisdom, incumbent campaigns stressed their candidates' virtues and ignored their opponents entirely. Challenger campaigns went on the attack, more than one-half of them stressing their opponents' weaknesses. Democratic challengers emphasized their opponents' weaknesses even more than their own candidates' strengths, while Republicans tended to do both.

Convergence Theory

Based on the relative strengths of the candidates, these general message appeals were strategic and probably had little potential spillover to representational behavior. Candidate stands on specific issues are of greater interest in that regard. Previous studies have addressed the effects of electoral competitiveness on the positions that candidates take on issues. In brief, the theory of convergence suggests that competition leads candidates to take intermediate positions with respect to the distribution of district opinion as they try to build winning coalitions (Downs, 1957; Page, 1978). This perspective leads to the expectation of small differences between the positions of opposing candidates in competitive districts. In noncompetitive districts, however, the opportunity exists for the candidates' own views or the views of other interests to draw candidates' issue stands away from the center and therefore away from each other.

John Jackson and Morris Fiorina refined this argument by pointing out that under certain circumstances candidates will not take intermediate positions with respect to a distribution of citizen preferences on an issue (Fiorina, 1974; Jackson, 1973). Candidates avoid the middle when citizens disagree about the issue and those on one side care about their position much more than those on the other side. In such circumstances, candidates generally will position themselves near the intense minority. In competitive situations, both candidates face the same distribution of citizen preferences weighted by issue salience, and, other things being equal, both candidates tend to side with intense minorities and therefore to position themselves near each other.

In contrast to the convergence theory, Samuel Huntington proposed in his revised theory of American party politics that candidates in noncompetitive districts would be quite similar in their issue positions, while candidates in competitive districts would be quite different. Competition, according to Huntington, would lead candidates to "attempt to win elections by mobilizing a high degree of support from a small number of interests rather than by mustering a relatively low degree of support from a large number of interests." [3] In competitive districts, therefore, candidates would be expected to diverge as each attempts to build a winning coalition based upon different parts of the constituency. As Fiorina pointed out, the proper test of Huntington's revised theory is a comparison of the policy positions of pairs of opponents in competitive and noncompetitive districts.

Such evidence is scant. Most studies of issue positioning fall into the "constituency influence" genre and compare Republican with Democratic officeholders in the aggregate, rather than pairs of opponents within districts. An exception is Warren Miller's study of candidates in the 1958 election. Using attitudes on the social welfare issue, he reported average differences in issue positions for pairs of opponents in safe and competitive House races. Counter to convergence theory and apparently supportive of Huntington's revised theory, Miller found that candidate differences within districts were "heightened when electoral competition is keen and reduced under single party domination of congressional electoral politics." [4]

A Current Perspective

The 1978 study included questions that permitted an analysis of the relationship between electoral competition and the candidates' positions on selected national issues. Managers were treated as informants who were knowledgeable about their candidates' issue stands. They were asked about their candidates' positions on five separate issues. [5] The positions of pairs of opponents then could be compared to see whether candidates converged or diverged with competition. Each district was designated as

Table 4-3 District Competitiveness, Candidates' Party, and Issue Positions, 1978

Competitiveness and Party	Issues				
	Guarantee Jobs	Help Minorities	Preferential Treatment	Recession-Inflation*	U.S./ U.S.S.R.
Positions of Candidates					
Democrats					
Noncompetitive**	3.3 (23)	2.7 (23)	3.7 (24)	4.3 (22)	3.3 (24)
Competitive	3.7 (23)	2.8 (23)	3.4 (22)	4.0 (23)	3.8 (24)
Republicans					
Noncompetitive	5.7 (21)	4.5 (20)	5.7 (21)	5.0 (16)	5.0 (20)
Competitive	5.2 (23)	4.1 (23)	5.2 (23)	5.2 (22)	4.7 (23)
Distances between Candidates					
Competitiveness					
Noncompetitive	3.1 (17)	2.6 (16)	2.8 (18)	1.6 (13)	2.5 (17)
Competitive	1.6 (23)	1.8 (23)	2.1 (22)	1.6 (22)	1.5 (23)

Note: Position entries are mean positions of candidates on 7-point scales according to the managers. Distance entries are mean distances between candidate and opponent on 7-point scales. N's are shown in parenthesis for each question.

* The ends of the recession-inflation scale have been reversed to correspond to the other four scales so that smaller numbers indicate liberal responses and larger numbers indicate conservative responses.

** Competitive districts include those where both managers were uncertain about the outcome. Noncompetitive districts involve contests between Sure Winners and Sure Losers. Mixed districts are omitted.

competitive or noncompetitive based on the managers' paired assessments of their chances of winning the election. Noncompetitive races were contests between Sure Winners and Sure Losers; competitive races pitted two uncertain managers against each other. Mixed cases (one certain and one uncertain manager) were eliminated.

Table 4-3 presents the findings on candidate issue positions and the distance between opposing candidates in competitive and noncompetitive races. As expected, Republicans were consistently on the conservative side of each issue (scores greater than four on a scale of one to seven); with one exception, Democrats were consistently on the liberal side (scores less than four). The mean distance between candidate and opponent positions was greater in noncompetitive than competitive races for four of the five issues, tending to support the convergence theory view and to draw the generality of Miller's 1958 findings into question.[6] The exception was the recession-inflation question, which warrants additional attention.

The recession-inflation issue was by far the most salient one in 1978. Opinion was tilted heavily toward the need to fight inflation. More than one-half of the managers interviewed (57 percent) cited inflation as the most important problem facing people in their districts; only 11 percent mentioned unemployment. Other economic concerns, including taxes, were mentioned by 14 percent, and fewer than 2 in 10 managers mentioned any of the other possibilities, ranging from housing to crime to government performance. Inflation also was a preoccupation of the voters, named by 54 percent of those interviewed in the 1978 American National Election Study as the most important problem facing the country. It was mentioned as the most important issue in their congressional district races by 14 percent of those ANES respondents who identified any issue at all; another 3 percent mentioned the recession.

Although the recession-inflation issue was the most prominent in 1978, its seven-point scale was also the least valid.[7] Approximately 50 percent more managers were unable or unwilling to place their candidates on that scale than on the other four scales. Managers' side comments indicated that a number of them rejected the forced-choice premise upon which the recession-inflation scale was based. Even in 1978, and certainly since, a number of managers subscribed to the notion that inflation and recession can occur together and should be addressed simultaneously. Although this exception is tantalizing, the measurement is sufficiently questionable to discourage overinterpretation.

Overall the findings in Table 4-3 are most compatible with the convergence theory. They differ from what Miller found in 1958 and what Huntington predicted based upon his revised theory. Miller acknowledged that his 1958 findings might be peculiar to the policies or time period studied (Miller, 1964), and perhaps they were. A more satisfying test of these ideas would incorporate systematic evidence on the distribution of opinion in the district electorate as well as more detailed information about the candidates' perceptions of opinion in their districts.

The test also would include repeated measures of the stands candidates take on important issues to see whether they, especially incumbents, actually shift their positions as a strategic response to more or less competitive situations or whether the challengers who are recruited in competitive races tend to differ less from their opponents on issue stands than the challengers who run in lopsided contests. If the former is true, then incumbents are reacting strategically to competition in their district. If the latter is true, the strategic behavior is that of the challengers and their party.

One final note on issue positions and district competition is worth mentioning. Fiorina has argued that noncompetitive districts are homogeneous places with regard to important issues, places where incumbents (and challengers) easily can identify district preferences and represent them all. In contrast, competitive districts, according to Fiorina, are heterogeneous places where potential voters disagree on important issues; consequently, in competitive districts incumbents (and challengers) can appeal only to a limited part of the constituency at once. In competitive districts the distance between the candidates' issue positions should be greater than in noncompetitive districts, in Fiorina's view. For him, what drives the process of candidates' positioning themselves on issues is the homogeneity or heterogeneity of constituent opinions rather than the competitiveness of the race. The data in Table 4-3 do not support this notion, however. Further testing of this idea requires adequate samples of constituent opinion on important district issues, together with measures of candidate positions and competitiveness. To date, such data have not been available. If Fiorina is correct, the stands candidates take on issues will not shift strategically during the campaign in response to stronger opposition.

Information Gathering in the Campaign

A third important element of campaign tactics is deciding which techniques are effective for learning what the people think. The need for political intelligence is common to all campaigns. In some, knowledgeable local party people serve as the major source of information. Other ways to learn what potential voters are thinking include conducting opinion polls; reading mail, newspaper columns, and letters-to-the-editor; and conversing with voters. Voter opinions about issues and candidates are used strategically to plan and target campaign materials. Feedback from the constituency also may alter candidates' views and elected officials' behavior. Consequently, more rather than less information gathering generally is regarded as desirable in a democratic system. If campaign situations and activities lead officials to become better informed about citizen views, then the functioning of representative rule should be enhanced.

In her study of the 1970 Wisconsin races, Marjorie Hershey found that electoral uncertainty produced greater candidate effort in seeking voter opinion through the use of polls, canvassing, and other information-gathering techniques. The implication is that vigorous challenges and the uncertainty they produce for incumbents are important to democracy because, among other things, they encourage officials to pay attention to the citizenry. The irony for Hershey was that nearly all of the incumbents in the Wisconsin races she studied felt very certain they would win. Consequently, those candidates most likely to occupy public office in Wisconsin were not pushed by uncertainty to seek information from their constituents.[8]

In 1978 managers were asked how much they depended on each of six possible sources of information for learning what the people in their districts thought about the major issues of the campaign. Managers' responses emphasized both personal contacts and opinion polls. The data in Table 4-4 show that virtually every manager (90 percent) relied upon meeting voters; most also relied on polls. Overall, the use of opinion polls in 1978 was much

Table 4-4 Sources of Campaign Information by Candidate Status and Assessments of Electoral Chances, 1978

	Personal Contacts	Polls	Mail	People in Party	Media Editorials	Letters to the Editor	(N)
Candidate Status							
Incumbents	91	74	54	29	22	6	(65)
Challengers	90	61	18	31	25	17	(71)
Open races	90	80	20	25	15	10	(20)
Assessments of Chances							
Sure Winners	92	69	58	25	23	0	(48)
Vulnerables	87	87	33	40	20	7	(15)
Hopefuls	88	63	19	30	19	9	(43)
Sure Losers	92	58	19	35	35	31	(26)

Note: Cell entries are the percentage who report using a particular technique to gather information either "very much" or "quite a bit."

higher than observed in past studies, a sign of the increasing professional-ism and sophistication of congressional campaign techniques.

There were no consistent differences between Republicans and Demo-crats, and few between incumbents and challengers, in their use of most means of information gathering. On average, the managers reported conducting two surveys during the campaign. Candidates in open races conducted a slightly higher number of polls, as did vulnerable incumbents, especially Republicans. Sure Winners and Sure Losers relied the least on polling information, conducting fewer than one survey per campaign on average. Of all the sources of information shown in Table 4-4, successful polling requires the most independent effort by the campaign and offers the most systematic feedback. The data on polling are consistent with Hershey's earlier findings about the relationship between uncertainty and information gathering.

In addition to personal contacts and polls, managers for incumbents, especially Sure Winners, also relied on mail from voters. Most challengers could not depend on this information source because they received so little of it. Material in the media—whether editorials or letters to the editor—was seen as an important source of information by fewer than one-quarter of the managers.

In sum, three elements of campaign tactics—targeting the electorate, taking positions on issues, and gathering information from constituents—are indeed related to the candidates' party, status, and uncertainty about electoral results. Uncertainty is, in turn, a consequence of the political realities of the race, such as the closeness of the partisan division in the dis-trict and the manager's beliefs about what matters in winning elections there. Understanding the manager's views provides important additional information beyond the standard objective measures of safety for those interested in explaining the various forms of campaign tactics that can be observed.

It is not enough to talk of winners and losers, incumbents and challengers, or Democrats and Republicans. Knowing if an incumbent's manager feels certain of victory or vulnerable and knowing if a challenger's manager is hopeful or sure of losing tells us a great deal about how vigorous the race is likely to be, how broad a targeting strategy to expect, which fac-tors are likely to be emphasized, how much of a choice the electorate can expect on important issues, and even which techniques are seen as effective for the important job of learning what the voters think.

Notes

1. Questions were worded: "Candidates rarely have the time and money to reach every qualified voter in the district and, therefore, they usually concentrate only on some of them. Which types of voters is this campaign concentrating on? Is your campaign targeted mostly at getting out your own supporters, attracting independents, or converting members of the other party to vote for your candidate?" Managers could indicate one, two, or all three possibilities or offer a fourth targeting strategy in an open-ended response.

2. The question was worded: "Could you tell me what major messages you plan to communicate to the voters in this campaign?" Managers could mention up to five separate messages, each of which was coded in detail on four content dimensions: candidate characteristics, issues, partisan references, and other. Issue-based campaigns mentioned only issue messages or no more than one nonissue message along with two or more issue messages.

3. See Samuel Huntington, 1950, 660-677.

4. See Warren Miller, 1964, 359.

5. The issue questions took the form of seven-point scales as follows: "Some people feel that the government in Washington should make every possible effort to improve the social and economic position of blacks and other minority groups. Others feel that the government should not make any special effort to help minorities because they should help themselves. Where would you place your candidate on this scale? Where would you place your opponent? Where would you place most people in this district?" The other four issue questions posed choices ranging from: 1) government effort to see that everyone has a job and good standard of living to government's letting every person get ahead on his own; 2) preferential treatment for women or minorities to an individual's ability and experience should be the only consideration for hiring; 3) government should solve inflation even if it means higher unemployment to the reverse; 4) United States should do more to improve relations with the Soviet Union to the United States has gone too far.

6. Campaign managers saw the distances that way as well: in safe races, managers perceived greater issue distance than in competitive races. Managers consistently believed that the opponent was more distant from their own candidate than was indicated by the difference between the two managers' separate reports on their own candidates' positions.

7. We appreciate Donald Kinder's assistance in suggesting this possibility.

8. See Marjorie Hershey, 1974, 19-39.

Patterns of
Campaign Receipts

Money is the grease for the wheels of a successful congressional campaign. Candidates spend money to make themselves known, to communicate their positions on the issues in an effective manner, and to organize campaign events that generate news coverage and stimulate members of the electorate to vote. Cash and credit alone cannot ensure electoral success; but most campaign activities cost money, and some cost a great deal. The average House campaign now costs more than $200,000, and a few very expensive races cost millions.

Any discussion of the effects of campaign funding must address a number of important concerns. An imbalance in financial support between opposing candidates increases the likelihood that the bigger spender will win. Inequities in securing and spending money also have important consequences for the quality of our representatives, for the vitality of political campaigns, and for the quality of the discussion and debate of issues associated with them. Most critical are concerns about the quality of candidates who can and cannot afford to run for office and the influence of special interests on candidates who depend on them for contributions.

Detailed analysis of congressional campaign budgets began only in the early 1970s with the passage of the Federal Election Campaign Act of 1971 (FECA) and its amendments. For some time there had been a good deal of normative debate on the appropriate levels of public and governmental involvement in the financing of elections. Yet very little of the debate was informed by relevant, systematic data on actual receipts and expenditures, particularly in elections below the presidential level.

The Watergate affair stimulated the reform of campaign finance practices and procedures. One consequence has been better information about where money comes from and where it goes. The FECA required for the first time that candidates for federal office report their total receipts and disbursements, details of individual expenditures, and some specific data about certain contributors. For congressional races, these data were first reported to the Clerk of the House and Secretary of the Senate and then eventually to the Federal Election Commission (FEC). Since 1972 these data have come under increasingly intense scrutiny by public interest groups, the media, and political scientists.

The following three chapters examine the role of money in congressional campaigns. They rely upon two special data bases that provide a detailed description of congressional campaign expenditures. This chapter begins with a review of the sources of campaign funds and the general patterns of raising money in congressional campaigns in the 1970s, and three central findings are highlighted. First, incumbents generally raise more money than challengers, although that is not always the case. Second, federal election reforms have had important consequences for campaign finance. They have limited the size of political contributions by wealthy individuals and have stimulated the growth of political action committees (PACs). Third, Republican candidates continue to have an advantage over their Democratic counterparts in terms of the quantity and quality of support they receive from their national party.

Campaign Finance Reform

The excesses of the Watergate period that began with the "dirty tricks" of the 1972 presidential campaign provided the final impetus for enacting legislation to regulate campaign finance. The principal focus of this legislation was on presidential elections, although it included provisions related to contests for the U. S. Senate and House of Representatives. Successive amendments strengthened the reporting and disclosure requirements of the law, most significantly by establishing and providing legislative guidance to the Federal Election Commission.

The history of the legislation and its consequences for presidential elections—particularly its public financing provisions—are covered in great detail in several sources (Alexander and Haggerty, 1981; Alexander, 1984). For other federal offices, the FECA required candidates and their principal campaign committees to report their total expenditures; the date, amount, and purpose of each individual expenditure of $100 or more; and the full name, mailing address, occupation, and principal place of business of each contributor. The legislation also required that, during the course of the campaign, periodic reports of this information be filed in the states as well as with a designated federal official.

The FECA has been amended three times since 1971. In 1974 the Federal Election Commission was established, and the reporting requirements were revised to include quarterly submissions of data as well as those 10 days before an election and 30 days after.[1] The law also established spending limitations for Senate and House campaigns, but they were overturned in a legal challenge that went all the way to the Supreme Court (*Buckley v. Valeo*). The Court decided that congressional candidates did not have to abide by these limitations because they did not receive any federal funding.[2] Although the 1976 amendments had no consequence for congressional elections, the 1979 amendments were concerned with several "housekeeping" functions in the law and were designed to simplify reporting requirements. Candidates who were unable to raise and spend any significant amount of money ($5,000 or less) were exempted. Candidates no longer had to report itemized expenditures below a $200 limit or independent expenditures on behalf of another candidate below $250.[3]

Even before the FEC was fully functioning, Herbert Alexander and his Citizens' Research Foundation, Congressional Quarterly, and Common Cause—a public interest group active in election reform—tabulated and released information on congressional receipts and expenditures. Today the FEC collects and disseminates these data, and its staff issues a full range of press releases and special reports. Much of the research on campaign finance relies heavily on these FEC materials.

Raising Money for the Campaign

Research related to patterns of campaign financing has been motivated by concerns about the role of special interests in American politics, raising the prospect of public financing as an alternative to private fund raising. Attempts to enact public financing for House and Senate candidates have been noticeably ineffective in the Congress,[4] but many states have passed laws that provide at least partial funding for such races, as well as for other statewide offices (Jones and Miller, 1982). The debate over public financing has been accentuated by the rise of PACs, which have replaced state and local parties as the major institutional source of public campaign funds. As candidates have turned increasingly to organizing their own campaigns, especially to secure their party's nomination for the general election, they have had to seek money and other types of resources outside of the formal structure of their party.

A substantial literature supports the notion that the private financing of elections is detrimental to the fundamental tenets of democracy (Adamany, 1972 and 1975; Alexander, 1984; Fleishman, 1976; Heard, 1960). Although this view is not universally held and some of the effects it describes may be inadvertent, it suggests that the high costs of campaigns and the need to raise these funds solely from individual contributors tend to dissuade qualified people from running for public office. Furthermore, the high costs of privately financed campaigns increase the potential influence of wealthy individuals and special interest groups, and conceivably they foster improper behavior in office by successful candidates who are indebted to their financial supporters and inclined to repay them with special favors.

There has been surprisingly little systematic research on the effects of private financing of congressional elections on the representational behavior of officeholders and resulting public policy. What have been studied are the patterns of contributions and the reasons for contributing. Candidates who are perceived to have the best chance of winning are much more likely than their opponents to receive substantial contributions (Jacobson, 1978). Not all contributions or independent expenditures, however, go to Sure Winners. Groups with ideological interests tend to contribute to candidates in close races, including challengers who may be able to use additional money to affect the outcome (Welch, 1979). Some individuals contribute because they want to bet on a sure thing; others give money simply because it represents an important form of political participation for those who can afford it (Dawson and Zinser, 1976). Some forms of giving, therefore, add to a race's competitiveness, while others merely increase the front-runner's advantage.

Understanding the relationship between contributions and competitiveness is even more complex than discerning the reasons for giving and the patterns of contributions. Do popular perceptions of a candidate's chances result in more contributions, or does successful fund raising increase his or her chances? Or both? Overall, the perceived front-runners, especially incumbents, have a much easier time raising funds than their challengers. Incumbents raise more money earlier in the campaign and get off to a faster start. This quick start usually works to increase the inherent advantages with which they begin. Much of their fund-raising success is due to previous contact with supporters from earlier campaigns and the successful maintenance of good relationships with contributors.

To understand the effects of money in current campaigns and to trace changes in the patterns of contributions, it is useful to distinguish among three sources of funds. One is money obtained from individual contributors, limited to $1,000 per individual in the primary race and another $1,000 in the general election campaign.[5] A second source of funding is PACs. The third source of support is the political parties. Party support comes in three forms: direct contributions in cash to the candidate's principal campaign committee, coordinated expenditures made on behalf of the candidate, and in-kind contributions of services that can be used in the campaign but do not involve direct transfers of money.

Data are presented in Table 5-1 that show the changing sources of campaign funds in recent congressional elections. Total receipts have risen dramatically since the 1977-1978 election cycle, just about doubling in both the House and Senate. Contributions from individuals provide most of the

Table 5-1   Sources of Campaign Funds in Recent Congressional Elections by Candidate Characteristics, 1977-1982 (in millions)[a]

| | Net Receipts[b] | Individual Contributions[c] | PACs | Major Party | |
				Contributions	Expenditures[d]
Type of Candidate					
Senate					
1977-1978	$ 66.0	$ 55.9 (84.7%)	$ 8.9 (13.5)	$1.2 (1.8)	$ 2.9
1979-1980	$ 76.9	$ 59.8 (77.8%)	$15.9 (20.7)	$1.2 (1.6)	$ 6.6
1981-1982	$117.2	$ 94.3 (80.5%)	$21.7 (18.5)	$1.2 (1.0)	$11.0
House					
1977-1978	$ 92.2	$ 64.4 (69.8%)	$22.9 (24.8)	$4.9 (5.3)	$ 1.4
1979-1980	$124.6	$ 84.1 (67.5%)	$36.0 (28.9)	$4.5 (3.6)	$ 2.5
1981-1982	$185.0	$121.7 (65.8%)	$57.6 (31.1)	$5.7 (3.1)	$ 6.0
Candidate Status					
Incumbents					
1977-1978	$ 75.0	$ 53.9 (71.9%)	$18.8 (25.1)	$2.3 (3.1)	$ 1.5
1979-1980	$106.8	$ 72.1 (67.5%)	$32.5 (30.4)	$2.2 (2.1)	$ 1.6
1981-1982	$166.2	$109.1 (65.6%)	$54.0 (32.5)	$3.1 (1.9)	$ 5.4
Challengers					
1977-1978	$ 46.2	$ 37.0 (80.1%)	$ 7.0 (15.2)	$2.2 (4.8)	$ 1.8
1979-1980	$ 67.4	$ 51.4 (76.3%)	$13.4 (19.9)	$2.6 (3.9)	$ 5.5
1981-1982	$ 80.3	$ 62.7 (78.1%)	$15.0 (18.7)	$2.6 (3.2)	$ 7.6
Open seats					
1977-1978	$ 37.0	$ 29.4 (79.5%)	$ 6.0 (16.2)	$1.6 (4.3)	$ 1.0
1979-1980	$ 27.4	$ 20.5 (74.8%)	$ 6.0 (21.9)	$ .9 (3.3)	$ 1.9
1981-1982	$ 55.8	$ 44.3 (79.4%)	$10.3 (18.5)	$1.2 (2.2)	$ 3.9
Party					
Democrats					
1977-1978	$ 76.2	$ 57.3 (75.2%)	$17.1 (22.4)	$1.8 (2.4)	$ .3
1979-1980	$102.0	$ 73.7 (72.3%)	$26.8 (26.3)	$1.5 (1.5)	$ 1.4
1981-1982	$156.1	$111.7 (71.6%)	$42.8 (27.4)	$1.6 (1.0)	$ 2.9
Republicans					
1977-1978	$ 80.8	$ 61.8 (76.5%)	$14.7 (18.2)	$4.3 (5.3)	$ 4.0
1979-1980	$ 98.1	$ 69.0 (70.3%)	$24.9 (25.4)	$4.2 (4.3)	$ 7.6
1981-1982	$145.6	$104.0 (71.4%)	$36.4 (25.0)	$5.2 (3.6)	$14.0

[a] These data are taken from three Federal Election Commission press releases: "FEC Releases Final Report on 1977-1978 Financial Activity of Non-Party and Party Political Committees," April 24, 1980; "FEC Releases Final PAC Report for 1979-80 Election Cycle," February 21, 1982; "FEC Releases Data on 1981-1982 Congressional Spending," May 2, 1983.

[b] For 1977-1978 and 1979-1980, these totals have been adjusted for transfers between multiple committees for the same candidate, but the FEC in early 1984 had not completed this task for 1981-1982. These adjustments can be substantial for some senatorial campaigns, but they have been less than 1 percent in past House campaigns. The sum of the sources of funds does not equal total receipts because of cash-on-hand (surpluses) at the end of the campaign. These data are only for candidates who ran in the general election.

[c] These totals are the difference between net receipts and contributions from major parties and PACs. This difference is actually composed of contributions from individuals, loans from individuals or banks, contributions and/or loans from the candidate, interest income, and refunds and rebates.

[d] Coordinated expenditures by the major parties on behalf of candidates are not included in their receipts, but they nevertheless represent a major and growing source of campaign funds.

money. In the Senate, individuals provide about 80 cents of each dollar, while in the House, individuals' contributions represent less than 70 cents.

Because there are many fewer candidates for the Senate than the House in any election year, these total receipts translate into much higher average receipts for Senate than for House candidates. The large amounts of money raised by Senate campaigns often are invested to yield interest payments that can constitute a substantial source of additional income, and they are included in the "Individual Contributions" shown in Table 5-1. Furthermore, Senate candidates are more likely to use their personal wealth in their campaign effort, either in the form of loans or contributions. These amounts vary substantially depending on who is running in a given election. Mark Dayton, a 1982 Democratic candidate for a Minnesota seat, contributed $5,673,298 of his own money and made or guaranteed loans for an additional $1,253,500 to his campaign in an unsuccessful effort to unseat a first-term Republican incumbent, Sen. David Durenberger.

During this same period, the major parties maintained their cash contributions at a steady level (which is nevertheless a declining portion of an ever-increasing pie), but their coordinated expenditures on behalf of candidates increased markedly. Contributions from PACs also increased sharply: overall, the amount of money they provide has more than doubled. House candidates now receive almost one-third of their money from PACs; Senate candidates get almost one-fifth.

These campaign funds are not evenly divided among the candidates, however. Incumbents are clearly advantaged. They receive about one-half again as much money from individual contributors as challengers and more than twice as much from PACs as challengers. The proportion of the total money that incumbents received from individuals has declined since 1977-1978 because of the great increase in contributions from PACs. Across these three elections, the dollar value of the contributions of PACs to incumbents tripled; in the 1981-1982 election, PACs gave $54 million to incumbents. Their funding of challengers doubled in the same period, but the total value of those contributions stood at only $15 million.[6]

Of the two major parties, the Republicans clearly offer more financial assistance to their candidates. Their national committees have mastered the art of raising money through organized appeals and then redistributing it to their congressional candidates. By 1981-1982, the Republicans were contributing more than three times as much money to their candidates as the Democrats ($5.2 million to $1.6 million); Republicans were spending almost five times as much as the Democrats on behalf of their candidates ($14.0 million to $2.9 million).

Data are presented in Table 5-2 on the average receipts from these same sources for House candidates in 1982. Across the board, Republican candidates received more money than Democrats from individual contributions and in direct contributions and coordinated expenditures from other

Table 5-2   Average Receipts from Various Sources for House Candidates, by Selected Characteristics, 1981-1982[a]

	Total Receipts[b]	Individual Contributions[c]	PACs	Major Party Contributions	Major Party Expenditures[d]
Incumbents					
Democrats	$269,801 (218)	$166,112	$101,864	$ 1,824	$ 1,184
Republicans	$304,759 (168)	$187,274	$104,471	$13,014	$12,236
Challengers					
Democrats	$128,714 (166)	$ 89,385	$ 36,364	$ 2,964	$ 1,918
Republicans	$130,303 (176)	$ 97,539	$ 23,977	$ 8,787	11,052
Open Seats					
Democrats	$269,462 (51)	$191,361	$ 74,986	$ 3,115	$ 2,209
Republicans	$329,661 (51)	$238,060	$ 73,684	$17,917	$25,018

a These data represent sources of primary and general election campaign receipts, excluding loans, for candidates who ran in the general election. The data are taken from "FEC Releases Data on 1981-82 Congressional Spending," May 2, 1983.

b This figure is inflated somewhat because amounts transferred from one of a candidate's committees to another within a campaign are counted multiple times. For past House races, this adjustment has been less than .5 percent.

c These totals are the difference between total receipts and contributions from the major parties and PACs. This difference is actually composed of contributions from individuals, loans from individuals or banks, contributions and/or loans from the candidate, interest income, and refunds and rebates.

d Coordinated expenditures by the major parties on behalf of candidates are not included in their receipts.

party committees. The average Republican incumbent had total receipts that were about $35,000 greater than the average Democratic incumbent. Most of the difference came from the fact that the Republican received $21,000 more than the Democrat from individual contributions, as well as $11,000 more from the party. In addition, Republicans benefited from a further $11,000 advantage in coordinated expenditures by their party committees that is not included in the "Total Receipts" figure. Republican and Democratic incumbents received about equal amounts of money from PACs, more than $100,000. For challengers, the total receipts for Republicans and Democrats were virtually identical. On the one hand, the Republicans received almost three times as much from their national party as the Democrats did from theirs and $8,000 more in individual contributions. On the other hand, the Democratic challengers raised about $12,400 more on average than Republicans from PACs. For the challengers, the widely noted Republican advantages in direct mail solicitation were offset by the equally well-recognized support received by Democrats from organized labor PACs.

In open races, where the average total receipts were comparable to those for incumbents, candidates raised "only" about $75,000 from PACs (about $25,000 to $30,000 less than the incumbents), but their receipts from individual contributions were much higher. The average Republican received more than $43,000 in assistance from the national party, while the Democratic counterpart received only about $5,300. Republican candidates in open races received more financial support on average than Democrats from every source except PACs.

The FECA and its amendments were proposed to mitigate the negative effects of unrestricted private financing of elections. Controlling the campaign contributions of wealthy individuals was a central legislative purpose. Alexander (1984) reported that, in the period just prior to enactment, from one-half to three-quarters of the groups he defined as "centimillionaires" (people with personal fortunes of $150 million or more) and the "newly rich" (people in 1973 with personal fortunes of $50 million or more accumulated since 1968) donated large amounts to political campaigns. Obviously, the 1974 amendments restricted the size of individual contributions by the wealthy. Not only are they now limited in what they can give to each candidate, but also they are limited to $1,000 in independent expenditures on behalf of a candidate and to $25,000 in total contributions in any year to all candidates.

Little is known about the individuals who contribute to congressional candidates today. One citizen in 10 makes contributions to candidates for federal office, apparently for a variety of reasons: feelings of a community obligation, desire to make a difference in the outcome of the election, and efforts to influence policies of government (Powell, 1980). By giving to candidates in open races, contributors provide money for the massive spending strategies in those typically hard-fought contests. By giving to incumbents more often than challengers, individual contributors usually add to the advantages incumbents already enjoy.

Somewhat more is known about the patterns of giving by PACs and national parties. Because the size of these contributions has grown dramatically over the recent past and the patterns have important consequences for the competitiveness of congressional races, each is discussed in some detail below.

Funding from Political Action Committees

By pooling funds, PACs maximize the impact of relatively small contributions from individuals with similar interests. These committees were organized initially by labor unions as a means of collecting voluntary political contributions independent of their dues structure. With the FECA amendments of the 1970s, the doors were opened for corporations to solicit money from their employees and stockholders; in practice, they concentrate only on their executives and administrative personnel (Alexander, 1983).

One way to assess the influence of PACs is to review the numbers that contribute and the size of the contributions to various types of candidates. In the sample of competitive 1978 races, the managers reported, on average, that 26 PACs contributed $25,695 to their campaigns, or about $1,000 each. Managers for incumbents reported the strongest financial support from PACs, although Republicans on average received smaller contributions from twice as many PACs (66) as Democrats (33). When managers felt their incumbents were vulnerable, they were likely to turn to a wide variety of PACs for help. Vulnerables raised more than twice as much PAC money from almost three times as many PACs as did Sure Winners. Challengers received less money than incumbents. The average PAC contribution to incumbents and challengers was in the same range, but many fewer PACs decided to back challengers. Those that did tended to favor Hopefuls over Sure Losers by more than 10 to 1.

Type of PAC. Different types of PACs give money to different types of candidates, and these patterns are obscured when only total PAC contributions are examined. The FEC classifies PACs as those representing corporations; labor unions; trade/membership/health organizations that are not unionized, such as real estate agents and doctors; other nonconnected groups; cooperatives; and nonstock corporations. Information is presented in Table 5-3 that shows the aggregate contributions to congressional candidates by these various types of PACs since the 1977-1978 election cycle. While the increased level of contributions has kept pace with inflation, a larger proportion of the money has been going to House races. In 1979-1980, for the first time, *corporate* PACs became the largest source of these funds for House candidates—they contributed almost $19 million dollars in 1981-1982, as compared with the contributions by labor PACs of slightly

Table 5-3   Total PAC Contributions by Type to House and Senate Campaigns, 1977-1982[a]

	Total PAC Contributions	Type of PAC					
		Corporate	Labor	Nonconnected	Trade/Membership/Health	Cooperative	Non-stock Corporation
Type of Race							
Senate							
1977-1978[b]	$10.10	$ 3.60	$ 2.80	$ .70	$ 2.80	$ .20	$ .03
1979-1980[c]	$17.33	$ 6.93	$ 3.82	$1.86	$ 4.14	$ .34	$ .24
1981-1982[d]	$22.35	$ 8.54	$ 4.83	$ 3.30	$ 5.00	$ .42	$ .26
House							
1977-1978	$25.00	$ 6.10	$ 7.40	$2.10	$ 8.60	$ .70	$ .10
1979-1980	$37.88	$12.25	$ 9.39	$3.08	$11.73	$1.03	$ .40
1981-1982	$60.76	$18.83	$15.33	$7.39	$16.72	$1.68	$ .80
Candidate Status							
Incumbents							
1977-1978	$20.00	$ 5.75	$ 6.05	$ .73	$ 6.76	$ .64	$ .07
1979-1980	$33.54	$10.86	$ 9.38	$1.56	$10.19	$1.11	$ .44
1981-1982	$54.81	$19.85	$11.48	$4.88	$16.03	$1.73	$ .85
Challengers							
1977-1978	$ 7.78	$ 2.07	$ 2.24	$1.25	$ 2.13	$ .08	$ .02
1979-1980	$14.48	$ 5.94	$ 2.21	$2.46	$ 3.66	$ .09	$ .12
1981-1982	$16.02	$ 3.63	$ 5.58	$3.73	$ 2.84	$ .15	$ .09
Open seats							
1977-1978	$ 7.43	$ 2.00	$ 2.00	$ .80	$ 2.40	$ .20	$ .03
1979-1980	$ 7.20	$ 2.39	$ 1.62	$ .92	$ 2.02	$ .17	$ .07
1981-1982	$12.28	$ 3.90	$ 3.11	$2.09	$ 2.85	$ .23	$ .12
Party							
Democrats							
1977-1978	$19.90	$ 3.70	$ 9.80	$ .70	$ 5.00	$ .60	$ .10
1979-1980	$28.90	$ 6.87	$12.36	$1.46	$ 6.98	$ .90	$ .33
1981-1982	$45.10	$ 9.38	$19.06	$5.44	$ 9.26	$1.33	$ .62
Republicans							
1977-1978	$15.34	$ 6.10	$ .60	$2.10	$ 6.30	$ .20	$ .04
1979-1980	$26.22	$12.29	$ .84	$3.44	$ 8.87	$ .47	$ .30
1981-1982	$37.99	$17.99	$ 1.09	$5.24	$12.45	$ .78	$ .44

[a] These are contributions only to campaigns of candidates seeking office in the indicated year and exclude contributions to retire past debts. They are reported in millions of dollars.

[b] These data are taken from "FEC Releases Final Report on 1977-1978 Financial Activity of Non-Party and Party Political Committees," April 24, 1980.

[c] These data are taken from "FEC Releases Final PAC Report for 1979-80 Election Cycle," February 21, 1982.

[d] These data are taken from "FEC Releases Data on 1981-1982 Congressional Spending," May 2, 1983.

more than $15 million. Corporate PACs gave almost twice as much to Senate candidates in that period as did labor PACs.

The advantages enjoyed by incumbents in PAC contributions are striking. Their support has increased more than two and one-half times since 1977-1978, from $20 million to almost $55 million. This increased support has come disproportionately from corporate and trade/membership/health PACs, while the support of labor PACs has not quite doubled. PAC support for challengers and candidates for open seats also has increased, but not so dramatically. In fact, support for challengers from corporate and trade/membership/health PACs actually declined between 1979-1980 and 1981-1982. Challengers' contributions from labor PACs more than doubled over the same period, making labor an increasingly important source of challenger support.

Party and Status. Support for candidates according to their party affiliation is characteristically different by type of PAC. Almost two dollars out of three from corporate PACs go to Republican candidates, while 95 cents of each labor dollar go to Democrats. Although Democrats received about as much money from labor PACs ($19 million) as they did from corporate and trade/membership/health PACs, Republican candidates received about 30 times as much ($30 million) from these sources as from labor PACs.

The combined effects of a candidate's status and party are shown in Table 5-4, which presents average contributions by type of PAC for House candidates in 1982. For both Democratic and Republican incumbents, the average levels of PAC contributions were about equal, but the Republicans received almost one-half of their money from corporate PACs and another 38 percent from trade/membership/health PACs. For the Democrats, labor PACs were the largest givers, although contributions from corporate and trade/membership/health PACs also were significant.

For Democratic challengers, on the other hand, two-thirds of their PAC support came from labor unions, while Republicans received almost nothing. Corporate PACs contributed about nine times as much to Republican as to Democratic challengers, but this amount did not offset the substantial giving by labor PACs to Democrats. For candidates in open seats, the patterns of giving by party were similar. Democrats received much more from labor PACs than Republicans, but here this difference was offset by strong Republican support from corporate and trade/membership/health PACs.

Most political action committees, like individuals, tend to contribute to the candidates who have the best chance of winning. As a result, incumbents and candidates in open races are their primary beneficiaries. They receive from three to four times as much in contributions as the challengers. But there are important differences among types of PACs in their patterns of giving. Labor PACs contribute disproportionately to Democrats; corporate and trade/membership/health PACs give most of

Table 5-4 Average Contributions to House Candidates from Various Types of PACs, by Selected Characteristics, 1981-1982[a]

	Total PAC Contributions	Type of PAC					
		Corporate	Labor	Non-connected	Trade/ Membership/ Health	Cooperative	Nonstock Corporation
Incumbents							
Democrats	$101,864 (218)	$26,869	$35,424	$ 9,049	$24,779	$3,951	$1,793
Republicans	$104,471 (168)	$48,646	$ 3,413	$ 8,029	$39,628	$3,277	$1,477
Challengers							
Democrats	$ 36,364 (166)	$ 1,098	$24,438	$ 6,581	$ 3,591	$ 408	$ 249
Republicans	$ 23,977 (176)	$ 9,532	$ 51	$ 6,907	$ 7,254	$ 113	$ 119
Open Seats							
Democrats	$ 74,986 (51)	$ 9,501	$40,458	$10,738	$11,603	$1,874	$ 807
Republicans	$ 73,684 (51)	$32,698	$ 1,518	$13,137	$24,805	$ 986	$ 541

[a] These data represent the sum of contributions from all PACs for candidates who ran in the general election. Both their primary and general election activities are included. These data are taken from "FEC Releases Data on 1981-82 Congressional Spending," May 2, 1983.

their funds to Republicans. Labor PACs support Democrats generally whether they are incumbents, challengers, or candidates in open races. Corporate and trade/membership/health PACs use a much more targeted approach. They concentrate on Republicans who have a reasonable chance of winning, and they support probable Democratic winners as well. These patterns result in keeping the open races quite competitive and generally providing large financial advantages to the incumbents of either party.

Support from Political Parties

Candidates for the House can receive several types of financial assistance from their respective parties at the national, state, and even local levels.[7] This assistance can be direct cash contributions to the candidates or the provision of "in-kind" services such as polling or assistance in producing ads, which are assessed at their "fair market value." There is a $5,000 limit on these contributions, but this applies separately to each distinct party organization and separately to primary and general elections. Although parties are understandably reluctant to pick sides in many primary contests, they can contribute to the elimination of a successful candidate's debts after the primary is over. Contributions also take the form of coordinated party expenditures in the general election on behalf of candidates, subject to a $20,000 limitation in House races.

Republican Party Advantage. The Republican party, particularly at the national level, has been more successful at raising money than the Democratic party. The Republicans outperform the Democrats by providing much more assistance to their candidates in the form of coordinated expenditures. The Republicans have targeted funds to races where they will do the most good, particularly to open seats and to Republican challengers in the most competitive districts. This aid more than offsets the dollar advantages that Democratic candidates, especially incumbents, have in PAC receipts from labor unions.

The Republican party advantage comes primarily from a larger, more stable national staff that can successfully coordinate its activities across elections (Kayden, 1980). Direct mail has been the source of the money, with Republicans taking particular advantage of the reduced postage rates offered by amendments to the FECA signed into law after the 1978 election (2.7 cents per letter for the parties rather than the 8.4 cents for third-class mail). As a result, they offer a greater range of programs and services to their congressional candidates than the Democrats. These services include seminars on campaigning and fund raising; technical assistance with accounting and legal issues; use of mailing lists; shared research, including polls; and party-oriented advertising in the mass media (Sabato, 1981). Although there are signs of growing Democratic party strength—a larger professional staff, more successful fund-raising efforts, new training courses

for candidates and campaign workers—the Republican party edge probably will persist for some time (Bonafede, 1983).

These shifting financial fortunes of the national parties and the trickle-
down effects to congressional candidates have helped Republican candidates disproportionately to date. For example, both the National Republican
Congressional Committee (NRCC) and the National Republican Senatorial
Committee (NRSC) have assembled election returns and voting records of
members since the 1960s. The Republicans were also the first to conduct
postelection studies of the electorate to assess what happened in the
electorate during the past campaign. These various historical data sources
provide background information helpful for developing current campaign
strategy. The Republicans also maintain lists of political consultants and
PACs who have assisted in past campaigns.[8]

Another important Republican advantage is in the production of
advertising. The NRCC maintains its own in-house media production
capability, which is regarded as one of the best of its kind in the country.
The NRCC can produce a complete broadcast advertising package for a
House candidate for less than $5,000; the committee can also do the media
buying to place the ads if the candidate wants. It produced more than 300
commercials in the 1980 campaign.[9] The NRCC also produces and runs
generic advertising in support of the party and its policy positions without
any reference to specific candidates. The Democrats are trying hard to
catch up here as well, planning a national advertising campaign in 1984
(Bonafede, 1983).

The parties also produce print material for use by local newspapers in
the form of regular press releases. Again the Republicans have refined this
technique to an art by generating standard copy and then inserting into the
text the name of a Democratic incumbent who has voted in opposition to
the administration. Small newspapers in the congressional district frequently
run this material without any change. Because no Republican candidate is
mentioned in the press release, the NRCC does not have to report this effort
to the FEC, nor count it against its contribution limitation.

The managers' reports of direct financial assistance and in-kind
services from their parties in 1978 demonstrate the clear advantages of
Republicans across all types of candidates. Information is presented in
Table 5-5 that shows the proportion acknowledging the receipt of money
and a variety of in-kind contributions by party and status. Whether they
were managing campaigns for incumbents, challengers, or candidates in
open races, the Republicans were more likely to say that they received
money from their national committee, and greater proportions of Republican
incumbents and candidates in open races also acknowledged receiving
money from other campaign committees outside the district.

Among all the candidates, 23 percent indicated they received in-kind
services in the form of opinion polls and surveys. But 70 percent of the

Table 5-5 Support for Congressional Candidates from Their Party, in Cash and In-kind Contributions, 1978[a]

	Received Money from[b]		Received In-kind Contributions in the Form of[c]				
	National Committee	Other Campaign Committees	Polling	Targeting/ Research	Media	Literature Distribution	Printing
All Candidates	29% (151)	51% (151)	23%	18%	15%	13%	5% (157)
Incumbents							
Democrats	32% (40)	44% (41)	9%	9%	4%	9%	5% (44)
Republicans	54% (22)	81% (21)	13%	0%	22%	4%	4% (23)
Challengers							
Democrats	18% (27)	42% (26)	15%	22%	15%	26%	0% (27)
Republicans	36% (42)	38% (42)	38%	33%	33%	19%	10% (42)
Candidates in Open Races							
Democrats	50% (10)	54% (11)	18%	18%	9%	0%	0% (11)
Republicans	90% (10)	90% (10)	70%	30%	30%	10%	10% (10)

a The entry in each cell is the percentage of managers responding affirmatively that they had received such money or in-kind help.

b The questions were worded:
  Did your campaign receive any money from the (Republican/Democratic) national committee?
  Did your campaign receive any money from other (Republican/Democratic) campaign committees outside the District?

c The question was worded:
  In addition to money, campaigns also receive contributions in the form of services which have to be reported to the Federal Election Commission. For each of the following services, please tell me if your campaign received this type of in-kind help. Media production and publicity? Opinion polls and surveys? Printing services? Literature distribution? Targeting and research?

Republican candidates in open races said they received this form of help compared with 18 percent of the Democrats, and 38 percent of the Republican challengers reported such assistance, while only 15 percent of their Democratic counterparts did. These same Republican candidates also were more likely to indicate help in the form of targeting and research, and they were two to five times more likely to report receiving assistance with media production and publicity than were Democratic candidates of equivalent status.

Nationalization of Campaigns. One consequence of these activities on the part of both parties has been the nationalization of important kinds of campaign efforts. The parties have shifted from providing voter-centered to candidate-centered services (Gibson, Cotter, Bibby, and Huckshorn, 1982). Common themes are stressed in congressional races across the country, and common techniques are used widely, making their development more cost effective. Some observers speculate that the increased influence of the national party in campaigns may enhance party control over those who seek office and the party loyalty of elected officials. If so, this enhanced control is more likely in Senate than House contests because the restrictions on party contributions to the latter are much more stringent (Conway, 1983).

The provision of advertising services by in-house staffs at the national committees is important for three reasons. First, good commercial operations are so scarce that some candidates would be unable to acquire these services otherwise. Second, ads with central themes can be produced more economically if they are done centrally, with low marginal costs for each candidate-specific variant. The savings, which are passed on to the candidates, provide an indirect subsidy for House candidates: the cost that is charged against the party's contribution is lower than the fee a commercial firm would charge. The party can provide more value and still keep within the dollar limitations on contributions imposed by law. Third, this form of production tends to standardize content and to increase the presentation of national themes in local contests.

Fund raising is a major preoccupation of candidates in contemporary congressional campaigns. The costs of campaigning have escalated dramatically over the past few election cycles and show no signs of leveling off. Individual contributors still provide the bulk of what is required to finance congressional contests, but wealthy donors are restricted in the amounts they can give. Concerns about the implications of private financing have shifted away from wealthy individuals to PACs, which have grown in number, size, and importance.

Party differences in fund raising remain quite striking. Republicans have mastered the art of direct mail, using it to raise large sums of money from individuals. They also attract the financial support of corporate and trade/membership/health PACs so long as candidates appear to have a chance of winning. The Republican party nationally has developed impressive in-house capabilities to strengthen campaigns. Meanwhile, the Democrats still benefit from the support of organized labor, which many feel far exceeds in value the dollars contributed by labor PACs. If they are likely winners, Democratic candidates also win the support of other PACs as well. The national Democratic party is actively developing its own direct mail, training, and advertising capabilities in an effort to catch up with the Republicans. Although the effects of a trend toward greater national party influence over campaigns are yet to be demonstrated, they are potentially significant and warrant close attention in the future.

The amounts that candidates raise to fund their campaigns obviously is closely related to what they spend. There are differences, however, between what is accumulated and what is spent, and it is the latter that is more significant for how campaigns are waged and with what results. Moreover, the timing of expenditures and their allocation are as important as their overall magnitude. The next chapter turns to patterns of spending in House campaigns.

Notes

1. A brief summary of the current law and the commission's role in enforcing it can be found in *The FEC and The Federal Campaign Finance Law.* (Washington, D.C.: Federal Election Commission).
2. With the availability of matching funds in the primaries, adjusted for the size of individual state's electorates, and fixed expenditures covered entirely by public funds in the general election campaign, presidential candidates were not given judicial relief.
3. In practice, however, perusal of expenditure reports filed by candidates shows that the common practice is simply to transfer all of their principal committee's checkbook entries to the FEC forms.
4. The latest failure in the 97th Congress is described in Dennis Farney and Albert R. Hunt, "Backers of Public Funding of House Races Drop Idea, Will Seek New Curb on PACs," *Wall Street Journal* (September 16, 1983), 6.
5. The restriction on individual contributions can be circumvented somewhat by contributions from multiple members of the same family, without any questions asked about where the money for the contributions came from.
6. Some PACs make expenditures that are completely independent of individual candidates. These expenditures have been increasing rapidly, by 146 percent between the 1979-1980 and 1981-1982 cycles. The $5.75 million spent most recently is a function particularly of which senatorial seats were at stake. Most of the money (80 percent) was spent to advocate the defeat of candidates, and almost all of that ($3.04 million) by the National Conservative Political Action Committee (NCPAC). The main target of these efforts in 1981-1982 was Sen. Edward M. Kennedy, D-Mass. He had $500 spent on his behalf and $1,146,135 spent in opposition to his reelection. For a brief summary of the major efforts in 1981-1982, see "Independent Spending Increases," *Record* (Washington, D.C.: Federal Election Committee, December 1983), 8-9.

7. Local party organizations, most typically at the county level, have to demonstrate independence from the state party to have their contributions qualify as separate. The FEC has specified these conditions in its advisory brief known as the Iowa Opinion. See Xandra Kayden, "The Nationalization of the Party System" in *Parties, Interest Groups, and Campaign Finance Laws*, ed. Michael J. Malbin (Washington, D.C.: American Enterprise Institute for Public Policy Research, 1980), 257-282.

8. This discussion is informed by personal communications with William Sweeney of the Democratic Congressional Campaign Committee and Linda DiVall of the National Republican Congressional Committee. We are grateful for their time and assistance; the synthesis of their commentary is, of course, the authors' responsibility.

9. Larry J. Sabato, *The Rise of Political Consultants* (New York: Basic Books, 1981), 292.

Patterns of
Campaign Expenditures

Chapter 6

Understanding the causes and consequences of campaign spending requires a fairly detailed description of how money is spent. Most previous research has focused on aggregate levels of campaign spending, without appropriate attention to how those resources were allocated. By studying the detailed expenditure reports the candidates are required to file with the Federal Election Commission (FEC), it is possible to characterize overall spending patterns for different kinds of candidates.

Four important findings from this analysis are presented below. First, incumbents not only raise more money but also usually spend more than challengers on their campaigns, although there are interesting exceptions. Second, Republican candidates for the House tend to spend more than Democratic candidates of equal status. Third, many incumbents raise and spend money all through the two-year interelection period, sometimes using surpluses from their last campaign, while most challengers are unable to spend money earlier than the general election campaign. Finally, there are systematic variations in the ways candidates spend their money.

Levels of Spending
In Congressional Races

Determining how much is spent in congressional races is a complicated undertaking. It requires initial measurement decisions about which spending and which candidates should be counted, and results differ depending on how these decisions are made. If total spending is measured over the entire two-year interelection period, for example, then the spending advantages of

Table 6-1   Average Total Receipts and Expenditures for All . . .

| | 1976[a] | | 1978[b] | |
	Receipts	Expenditures	Receipts	Expenditures
U.S. House				
Incumbents	$ 91,094	$ 79,837 (385)	$ 120,596	$ 111,247 (379)
Challengers	$ 49,600	$ 48,945 (370)	$ 55,039	$ 54,430 (458)
Open Seats	$117,310	$114,869 (105)	$ 162,503	$ 159,466 (131)
Democrats	$ 80,965	$ 74,757 (433)	$ 114,228	$ 108,502 (426)
Republicans	$ 77,440	$ 71,945 (390)	$ 111,632	$ 107,011 (384)
Others	$ 13,006	$ 12,955 (37)	$ 4,265	$ 4,226 (158)
U.S. Senate				
Incumbents	$677,278	$649,801 (24)	$1,322,450	$1,341,942 (22)
Challengers	$440,461	$433,263 (24)	$ 355,925	$ 351,941 (59)
Open Seats	$768,996	$756,951 (16)	$ 521,492	$ 508,000 (30)
Democrats	$590,300	$569,902 (33)	$ 744,997	$ 730,454 (37)
Republicans	$628,014	$616,501 (30)	$1,147,784	$1,151,407 (33)
Others*	$809,346	$802,928 (1)	$ 12,593	$ 12,293 (41)

[a] "House Races: More Money to Incumbents," *Congressional Quarterly Weekly Report*, October 29, 1977, 2299-2311; "Money, Incumbency Failed to Guarantee Success in 1976 Senate Races," *Congressional Quarterly Weekly Report*, June 25, 1977, 1291-1294.
[b] "Candidates' Campaign Costs for Congressional Contests Have Gone Up at Fast Pace," *Congressional Quarterly Weekly Report*, September 29, 1979, 2151-2163.

incumbents over challengers appear much greater than if spending is measured only during the general election campaign. Or, if average expenditures are calculated based on every candidate who ever filed, their spending appears substantially lower than when averages are based on only those who made it to the general election ballot or those in contested races. In what follows, several widely accepted conclusions about spending in congressional races are reexamined using alternative measurement approaches. In some cases, the conclusions are confirmed and even strengthened. In others, the conclusions require significant qualification.

Spending in All Races

Three widely accepted generalizations about campaign finances are that incumbents spend more than challengers, that candidates in open races spend even more than incumbents, and that the costs of campaigning have been increasing—particularly in the area of media expenses—more rapidly than general inflation. Data are presented in Table 6-1 that illustrate these points. They show the average total receipts and total expenditures for all House and Senate candidates from 1976 to 1982. These data are aggregated for the two-year period leading up to each election from reports the

... Candidates in U.S. House and Senate Races, 1976-1982

1980[c]		1982[d]	
Receipts	Expenditures	Receipts	Expenditures
$ 180,000	$ 162,884 (398)	$ 285,015	$ 263,464 (386)
$ 61,716	$ 60,942 (603)	$ 74,825	$ 74,082 (594)
$ 171,358	$ 166,886 (92)	$ 228,242	$ 225,030 (134)
$ 142,229	$ 133,105 (430)	$ 215,921	$ 202,962 (435)
$ 154,712	$ 145,415 (403)	$ 230,242	$ 221,256 (395)
$ 4,279	$ 4,200 (260)	$ 618	$ 604 (284)
$1,351,688	$1,314,098 (26)	$1,871,212	$1,796,192 (30)
$ 425,411	$ 407,855 (71)	$ 526,977	$ 523,161 (68)
$ 445,700	$ 437,755 (26)	$1,576,675	$1,554,230 (16)
$1,166,758	$1,141,202 (35)	$1,885,082	$1,824,367 (33)
$ 994,362	$ 971,502 (36)	$1,657,268	$1,631,275 (33)
$ 5,821	$ 5,764 (52)	$ 6,251	$ 6,093 (48)

[c] "Will Money Preserve GOP Gains of 1980?" *Congressional Quarterly Weekly Report,* April 10, 1982, 814-823.

[d] "FEC Release Data on 1981-82 Congressional Spending," press release, May 2, 1983.

* Not reported on a comparable basis in 1976.

candidates' principal campaign committees filed with the FEC. This form of calculation *underestimates* the receipts and expenditures for competitive races because it includes both minor party candidates who generally ran low-level campaigns and some incumbents who were unopposed and therefore usually spent relatively little.

These data show quite clearly the disparity in resources between major and minor party candidates and between incumbents and challengers, as well as the high level of resources required to contest an open House seat. They also show the rapid rate of increase in campaign spending over time, although that rate is higher for incumbents than for challengers. The most significant relationship in the data for all races is the incumbents' advantage in spending substantially more than challengers. During this period, incumbents outspent challengers, on the average, in the range of 63 to 167 percent, and the rate has been increasing. Average expenditures by House incumbents in 1982 were unusually high, however, because of redistricting that forced some gerrymandered incumbents to run against colleagues. In the most extreme case, Barney Frank, a Democrat, spent $1,502,581 to defeat Margaret M. Heckler, a Republican, who spent $966,621 for the redrawn Fourth District in Massachusetts.[1] Average expenditures by incumbents in 1984 are not expected to increase so dramatically over their 1982 levels. House incumbents' surpluses of receipts over expenditures have been growing as well, approaching $18,000 on average in 1980 and $22,000 in 1982.

Conventional wisdom holds that Republicans have an even greater advantage because of national party giving on the Senate side. For example, in 1980 Paul Gann, the Republican candidate in California, received $521,755 from his national party—the most of any candidate— while his opponent, Sen. Alan Cranston, received $26,180 from his.[2] Cranston's allotment was about two-thirds of the largest contribution ($39,940) the Democrats gave to any candidate in that year. In 1982, fighting to maintain their newly gained majority, the Republicans spent twice as much in support of their incumbents as the Democrats, although they had only about half as many incumbents, and Republicans spent more than six times as much as the Democrats on their challengers' efforts. Republicans also spent five times as much in the open races.[3]

On the other hand, Republicans do not always have the edge in Senate campaign spending. Over time, the average expenditures by party in senatorial races fluctuate considerably, depending on both the size of the constituencies in those states with Senate races and the number of incumbents each party has running for reelection. The size of a state's constituency has a great deal to do with a candidate's ability to secure funds: it determines the size of the pool of potential contributors and the amount the national party can contribute under the FEC's rules and regulations. Because Senate incumbents are substantially more successful than challengers in capitalizing on the full pool of potential contributors in their state, the party with the greater number of incumbents running in large states shows a surge in average contributions and expenditures and tends to outspend the other party. Taking these factors into account, the Republican senatorial candidates in the general election outspent their Democratic opponents by substantial amounts in 1978, and the Democrats were slightly in the lead in 1980.

Campaign activity in statewide races can have important consequences for House races in the same state. Occasionally campaign costs and information are shared, and successful get-out-the-vote efforts can benefit all of the candidates of one party. Therefore, heavier spending by one party in Senate races should not be overlooked in terms of its potential significance for House campaigns.

Spending in Contested Races

A somewhat different picture of expenditure levels is seen by looking at races where two major party candidates are contesting a congressional seat. The data in Table 6-2 show average campaign expenditures in the contested races for the U.S. House, by party and candidate status, from 1976 through 1982. The table presents two interesting pieces of informa-

Table 6-2   Average Campaign Expenditures by U.S. House Candidates in Contested Races by Party and Incumbency Status, 1976-1982

	Incumbents	Challengers	Open Seats
1976			
Democrats	$ 79,100 (208)	$ 44,646 (121)	$144,060 (50)
Republicans	$ 90,184 (121)	$ 55,484 (208)	$ 97,687 (50)
1978			
Democrats	$111,424 (200)	$ 70,947 (109)	$212,671 (52)
Republicans	$138,765 (109)	$ 73,043 (200)	$192,514 (52)
1980			
Democrats	$166,190 (209)	$ 68,767 (127)	$189,022 (54)
Republicans	$190,729 (127)	$111,149 (209)	$204,511 (54)
1982			
Democrats	$242,242 (163)	$116,141 (152)	$266,264 (51)
Republicans	$264,566 (152)	$126,173 (163)	$324,462 (51)

Note: Includes candidates with major party opposition only and excludes races in 1982 where incumbents faced each other because of redistricting.

Sources: These data were compiled by Gary Jacobson from data supplied by Common Cause (1972 and 1974) and the Federal Election Commission (1976-1980).

tion. First, the costs of campaigning are escalating across the board. The average expense of an incumbent's or a challenger's campaign roughly tripled between 1976 and 1982. The cost of open races increased as well. Second, Republican advantages are apparent for incumbents and challengers, but the most notable surge is seen in Republican spending in open races: in 1976 and 1978 Republicans trailed Democrats in spending, but by 1980 Republican candidates in open races moved ahead; by 1982 they widened their dollar lead even more. In open races, where there is no incumbency advantage, the greater fund-raising capabilities of the National Republican Congressional Committee, combined with greater sophistication of their direct mail appeals have resulted in a substantial Republican dollar advantage for their candidates.

The effect of aggregating across all House races—even just the contested ones—also is deceptive. Contested races vary in terms of competitiveness, and competition affects not only the total amount spent but also the size of the gaps between Republicans and Democrats and between incumbents and challengers. To demonstrate these relationships, it is necessary to shift the analysis to a sample of races in 1978 for which adequate indications of competitiveness are available.

In addition, patterns of spending are different for the entire two-year interelection period and the latter part of that period, which can be considered the general election campaign. What follows compares these two periods in terms of total spending and looks at levels of spending for different types of candidates.

Spending and Candidate Uncertainty

The aggregate data compiled by the FEC and presented in their standard reports mask distinctions between general election campaign activity and efforts leading up to it. Because the FEC data are aggregated to total receipts and expenditures, they also fail to provide information about *intracampaign* allocations of funds, either by function or over time. As part of the study of the 1978 congressional races for the House, a series of reports that candidates submitted to the FEC were analyzed to determine how much money was spent in general election campaigns, in what ways, and by what types of candidates.[4]

For the 167 campaigns in which interviews with the managers were obtained, every expenditure that was reported was recorded in terms of the date, type, and amount.[5] The data in Table 6-3 show average expenditures of $100,932 from January 1, 1977, through December 31, 1978, in the races in the sample.[6] The average general election campaign expenditure in the sample was $59,664.[7] The average difference of $41,268 represents expenditures before July 1, or in a primary battle, or both. Therefore, only about $6 in $10 of the average major party candidates' expenditures occurred during the general election period.

Overall, candidates in open races were by far the biggest spenders, with average total expenditures of $203,840 and late campaign expenditures of $111,231. These amounts were greater than what the average incumbent and challenger combined spent. Large pre-July expenditures by candidates in open races reflect the intensity of primary battles that many of them faced to secure the nomination. These primaries often are highly competitive because of the opportunity presented by a congressional race with no incumbent running. Incumbents, on the other hand, appear to have outspent challengers of the other party dramatically in the early part of the two-year period and by relatively less late in the general election campaign.

The data also show interesting differences in the timing of expenditures associated with party, candidate status, and the managers' perceptions of their chances in the election. Republicans who faced tight races, either as vulnerable incumbents or hopeful challengers, spent more money before the general election than their Democratic counterparts. The assistance of their national party organization and their sophisticated fund-raising skills gave them an early edge in terms of campaign activity.

The data in Table 6-3 also permit comparisons of the expenditure levels of candidates who vary in their status and their uncertainty about electoral

Table 6-3   A Comparison of Average Total Campaign Expenditures and Post-July General Election Expenditures for Major Party Candidates in a Sample of Competitive 1978 House Races, by Candidate Characteristics

	FEC-Reported Two-Year Expenditures	Post-July General Election Expenditures	Pre-July and/or Primary Expenditures
All Candidates	$100,932	$ 59,664	$ 41,268 (167)
Incumbents			
Democrats	$ 92,030	$ 51,657	$ 40,373 (45)
Republicans	$138,190	$ 83,102	$ 55,088 (26)
Challengers			
Democrats	$ 67,931	$ 46,695	$ 21,557 (29)
Republicans	$ 59,468	$ 37,095	$ 23,141 (45)
Open Seats			
Democrats	$218,390	$102,380	$116,010 (11)
Republicans	$189,290	$120,082	$ 69,208 (11)
Incumbents vs. Challengers			
Sure Winners			
Democrats	$ 71,862	$ 33,038	$ 38,824 (35)
Republicans	$ 86,659	$ 55,742	$ 30,917 (14)
Vulnerables			
Democrats	$163,030	$116,750	$ 46,280 (8)
Republicans	$185,280	$106,090	$ 79,190 (7)
Hopefuls			
Democrats	$ 81,911	$ 58,632	$ 23,279 (19)
Republicans	$ 94,650	$ 58,405	$ 36,245 (25)
Sure Losers			
Democrats	$ 41,368	$ 24,014	$ 17,354 (10)
Republicans	$ 19,086	$ 12,764	$ 6,322 (18)
Open Seats			
Sure Winners			
Democrats	—	—	—
Republicans	$185,110	$100,690	$ 84,420 (2)
Hopefuls			
Democrats	$232,570	$111,630	$120,940 (9)
Republicans	$238,240	$156,620	$ 79,690 (7)
Sure Losers			
Democrats	—	—	—
Republicans	$ 16,222	$ 15,646	$ 576 (2)

outcomes. Several conclusions are warranted. First, incumbents who were vulnerable spent a great deal of money both before and during the general election campaign. Not surprisingly, they spent considerably more than incumbents who were certain of victory. Second, Hopefuls outspent Sure Losers. The Hopefuls' total campaign effort, using the metric of expenditures, was comparable to that of the Sure Winners. Third, most Republicans raised and spent more than Democrats with equivalent electoral prospects, with the exception of Sure Losers.

Although there is a limited number of cases, there also appears to be a relationship between perceived likelihood of success and the spending behavior of candidates in open races. The biggest spenders were those who thought they could win but knew it would take some effort. They spent more than candidates in open races who felt sure of winning. But even in open races, some candidates have no expectation of winning. Just because a seat has fallen vacant through death or retirement does not guarantee a competitive race; the underlying partisanship in the district obviously plays an important role, and, where it is lopsided in favor of one candidate, the other may have no realistic chance. The spending behavior of these underdogs corresponded directly to the challengers who also were certain of defeat.

Although the data in Table 6-3 show that the average incumbent outspent the average challenger, regardless of party, they do not tell us whether incumbents always outspent their particular challengers. In fact, they did not. Sure Winners consistently outspent their Sure Loser opponents, on average by more than $20,000. When there was some perception of a competitive race, however, Republicans generally outspent Democrats, irrespective of status. As expected, Republican Vulnerables consistently outspent Democratic Hopefuls, by an average of about $43,000. More surprisingly, Republican Hopefuls also outspent Democratic Vulnerables, on average by approximately $22,500, although a few Democratic Vulnerables outspent Republican Hopefuls. In open races Republicans also outspent their opponents. While the average Republican advantage was more than $32,500, differences in candidate spending ranged from a $6,535 advantage for the Democrat to $75,867 for the Republican. Sure Winners tend to have an easy time with money, regardless of party, but a sense of competition stirs the Republicans to extra effort. Part of the Republican candidates' success in raising money can be attributed to their own skills, but a good measure also is due to the success of the National Republican Congressional Committee in helping its candidates.

Consequently, the accepted wisdom that incumbents spend more than challengers does not always hold. Competitiveness and money go together, especially for Republicans. Most incumbents are Sure Winners whose spending appears much more modest once the relatively few high-spending Vulnerables are considered separately. Nevertheless, Sure Winners apparently spend enough. They outspend their opponents and see no need to raise or spend any more. Most challengers are Hopefuls, and their spending appears more robust once the low-spending Sure Losers are treated separately. Hopefuls spend more than confident incumbents. If they benefit from Republican fund-raising skill, Hopefuls outspend their opponents even when running against vulnerable incumbents.

How much money a campaign spends is an important indication of its vitality. How the money is allocated among various types of campaign activities, especially late in the campaign, reveals strategic behavior in greater detail. During the general election campaign, the candidates square off against each other, and the level of their activity generally is great enough to attract the attention of the electorate. The analysis of resource allocations that follows is based upon expenditures in the period after July 1, when the bulk of most candidates' money is spent.

Allocating Campaign Money

Although candidates were required to report only expenditures of $200 or more, in practice they appear to have transcribed for the FEC all of the checkbook entries of their principal campaign committees. As a result, an extremely detailed record is available for analysis of patterns of resource allocation within campaigns from July 1, 1978, to the end of the year. This record provides information about *where* the money went. For the first time, a candidate's total expenditures can be broken down and described in terms of the distribution of dollars to politically meaningful campaign functions. Not only can patterns be examined for the different types of candidates—by partisan affiliation, status, and type of contest—but other measures, such as perceived chances of winning and the strategic plans of managers, also can be incorporated into the analysis.

Information is presented in Figure 6-1 depicting the allocation of funds in the late campaign period for the average 1978 congressional campaign. The largest single set of expenditures in the average congressional campaign was for advertising and media expenses, almost 60 cents of every dollar. The next greatest expenses were for staff salaries (16.1 percent) and for running an office (7.6 percent). Approximately equal amounts were devoted to financial transactions such as opening bank accounts or paying filing fees, expenses of individual campaign staff members such as meals or transportation, and organized campaign events such as dinners, rallies, and parties. Relatively modest expenditures (2.7 percent) were devoted to research functions, including polling, precinct maps and voter lists, clipping services, and subscriptions to local newspapers and magazines.

When these data are presented separately for incumbents, challengers, and candidates in open races, the slices of the pie show striking uniformity in the *relative* allocations by candidates.[8] Given their different circumstances, this similarity is quite surprising. For example, with greater name recognition problems and broader targeting strategies, challengers might be expected to rely more heavily than incumbents on mass media appeals. In fact, this expectation is borne out when incumbents are distinguished further according to the managers' assessments of their electoral chances.

Data are presented in Figure 6-2 that illustrate relative allocations in

Figure 6-1 Relative Allocation of Average Total Expenditures in House Races, 1978

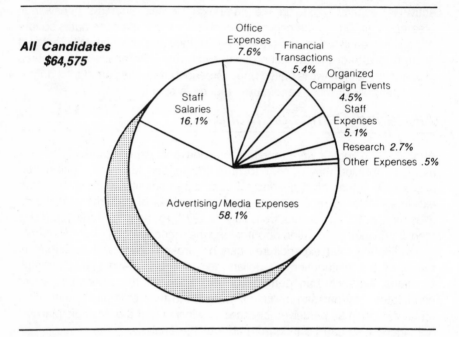

All Candidates
$64,575

Office Expenses 7.6%

Financial Transactions 5.4%

Organized Campaign Events 4.5%

Staff Expenses 5.1%

Research 2.7%

Other Expenses .5%

Staff Salaries 16.1%

Advertising/Media Expenses 58.1%

races involving incumbents and challengers, this time distinguishing between candidates in terms of their perceptions of their chances of winning. Sure Winners spent the least in proportional terms (51 percent) on the media. They were already well known in their districts; they targeted more narrowly on their partisan supporters, and, therefore, they had less to gain from extensive media use. On the other hand, challengers and vulnerable incumbents relied more heavily on the media in an effort to target broadly in their districts.

Because of the importance of expenditures for media and voter contact in the campaign, these expenditures have been broken down further. The information in Figure 6-3 shows the allocation of these expenditures in the average campaign in 1978. The total amount involved was $36,643, and more than two-thirds of it was allocated to three categories of expenditures—printing costs (32.6 percent), the preparation and placement of television commercials (23.4 percent), and the other undesignated advertising expenses (22.7 percent). A considerable amount was allocated to newspaper ads (8.7 percent) and radio spots (6.5 percent). Very little was devoted to outdoor advertising, movies, photos, and other miscellaneous advertising expenses.

Figure 6-2   Relative Allocation of Average Total Campaign Expenditures by Assessments of Electoral Chances, 1978

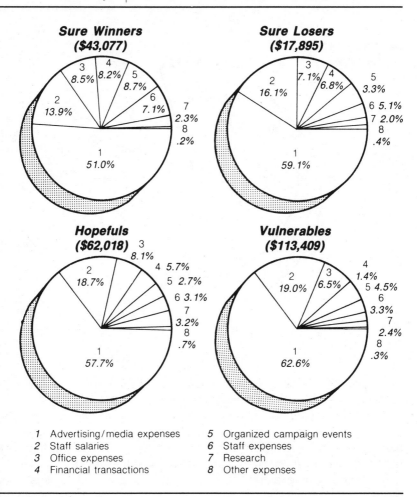

Sure Winners
($43,077)

3   8.5%   4   8.2%   5   8.7%
2   13.9%   6   7.1%   7   2.3%
8   .2%
1   51.0%

Sure Losers
($17,895)

3   7.1%   4   6.8%
2   16.1%   5   3.3%
6   5.1%   7   2.0%
8   .4%
1   59.1%

Hopefuls
($62,018)   3   8.1%

2   18.7%   4   5.7%   5   2.7%
6   3.1%   7   3.2%
8   .7%
1   57.7%

Vulnerables
($113,409)

2   19.0%   3   6.5%   4   1.4%   5   4.5%
6   3.3%   7   2.4%
8   .3%
1   62.6%

1   Advertising/media expenses
2   Staff salaries
3   Office expenses
4   Financial transactions
5   Organized campaign events
6   Staff expenses
7   Research
8   Other expenses

The patterns of allocation again look strikingly similar for incumbents, challengers, and candidates in open races, taking differences in absolute expenditures into account. The pie charts presented in Figure 6-4 illustrate these similarities clearly, with some notable exceptions. Spending for printing continues to consume the bulk of the candidates' budgets. Incumbents allocated relatively smaller amounts of their money to television (20.2 percent) compared with 25.6 percent for challengers and 26.4 percent for candidates in open races. Because of the difference in the size of their budgets, however, incumbents actually spent more for TV ads, on average, than their challengers. Incumbents also were more likely to allocate

Figure 6-3   Relative Allocation of Average Media Expenditures in House Races, 1978

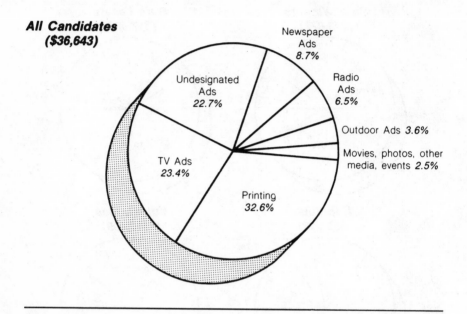

All Candidates ($36,643)

- Newspaper Ads 8.7%
- Radio Ads 6.5%
- Outdoor Ads 3.6%
- Movies, photos, other media, events 2.5%
- Printing 32.6%
- TV Ads 23.4%
- Undesignated Ads 22.7%

money to newspaper ads (10.9 percent) than either challengers (8.2 percent) or candidates in open races (5.4 percent).

These spending decisions are shown even more clearly in the pie charts in Figure 6-5 where allocations are given for incumbents and challengers according to their managers' perceptions of their chances. How money was allocated differed strikingly for candidates with different expectations about the outcome. For example, the Sure Winners allocated unusually large proportions to printing (37.6 percent) and to newspaper ads (18.2 percent). They preferred to devote their effort to mobilizing partisan supporters. They felt confident of their name recognition as compared with their opponents' and had less interest in relying on untargeted advertising vehicles such as television and undesignated advertising expenditures. As expected, Democrats, because of their narrower targeting strategies observed in Chapter 4, fit this pattern even more closely than Republicans.

In contrast, the Vulnerables allocated relatively large portions of their media dollars to broad advertising alternatives. The undesignated advertising expenditures, which consumed 30.2 percent of the Vulnerables' media dollars, went to professional advertising specialists who purchased a variety of carefully selected media outlets. Vulnerables in particular were more likely

Figure 6-4   Relative Allocation of Media Expenditures in House Races
by Candidate Status, 1978

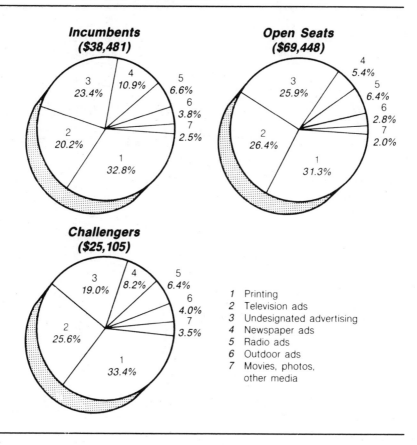

Incumbents
($38,481)

3 23.4%
4 10.9%
5 6.6%
6 3.8%
7 2.5%
2 20.2%
1 32.8%

Open Seats
($69,448)

3 25.9%
4 5.4%
5 6.4%
6 2.8%
7 2.0%
2 26.4%
1 31.3%

Challengers
($25,105)

3 19.0%
4 8.2%
5 6.4%
6 4.0%
7 3.5%
2 25.6%
1 33.4%

1   Printing
2   Television ads
3   Undesignated advertising
4   Newspaper ads
5   Radio ads
6   Outdoor ads
7   Movies, photos,
    other media

to employ advertising agencies (71 percent) than were Sure Winners (40 percent), Hopefuls (38 percent), or Sure Losers (23 percent). In addition, the Vulnerables allocated another 24.3 percent of their funds to television, amounting to about $17,240 on average. Hopeful challengers also allocated substantial portions of their media budgets to printing (34.9 percent), television ads (24.7 percent), and other undesignated advertising expenditures (21.2 percent). Their overall media budgets on average were only one-half the size of the Vulnerables', and those of the Sure Losers were only one-seventh the size. While the relative allocations to TV by the Sure Losers were high (36.3 percent), the absolute amount of money involved was only about $3,850 on average. They had little to spend overall, but what they had went into broad targeting efforts to reach all potential voters in their districts. These choices reflect the narrow targeting strategies that incumbents

Figure 6-5 Relative Allocation of Media Expenditures in House Races by Assessments of Electoral Chances, 1978

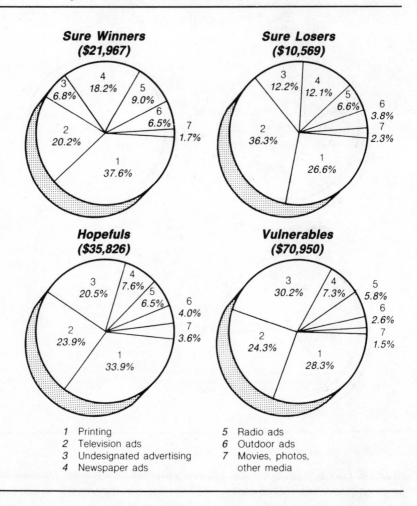

1 Printing
2 Television ads
3 Undesignated advertising
4 Newspaper ads

5 Radio ads
6 Outdoor ads
7 Movies, photos, other media

employ and their preference for relying on techniques that permit greater control over the distribution of their campaign messages.

Challengers and candidates in open races spend nearly every dollar they raise. Incumbents spend most of their campaign money, but not all of it, unless they feel threatened by a serious challenge.

Highly aggregated data mask substantial differences in spending by different kinds of candidates. Overall, incumbents spend more than challengers, but those who are certain of victory actually spend less, on average, than challengers who are hopeful of winning. Republicans have a spending edge where they feel there is some real chance of electoral success. Their highly professionalized fund-raising operations, together with a growing level of contributions from corporate PACs, translate into Republican dollar advantages in close races.

Although patterns of allocation appear similar for incumbents, challengers, and candidates in open races, interesting allocational differences become clear once candidates are distinguished according to the competitiveness of their races. Candidates who try to win over independents and convert members of the other party, as well as to mobilize their own partisan supporters, target the district broadly. They turn to the media, especially to broadcasting. Those content to concentrate on mobilizing partisan supporters rely more heavily on organized campaign events.

Candidates' assessments of their chances are related to their levels of general election expenditures and to their strategic decisions about how the money should be spent. Given their lower capacity to accumulate funds, challengers who allocate money in the same ways as their incumbent opponents merely allow themselves to be outspent across the board. By shifting their allocation patterns in response to their particular targeting strategies and name-recognition needs, challengers can close the gap in certain spending areas. To develop a more complete understanding of the candidates' resource allocations, the spending behavior of pairs of opposing candidates must be analyzed. Only in this way can the marginal effects of money on votes be understood. A model of these effects is presented in the next chapter.

Notes

1. "Big Spenders: Financing Congressional Races," *National Journal,* October 30, 1982, 1860.
2. *Congressional Quarterly Weekly Report,* November 1, 1980, 3235.
3. "FEC Reports Republicans Outspent Democrats by More than 5-to-1 in '82 Elections," Federal Election Commission Press Release (Washington, D.C.: Government Printing Office, April 26, 1983).
4. Time series of the quarterly flow of expenditures from the candidates' designated primary or general election campaign committees were recorded from computer printouts of the E Index of Receipts and Expenditures prepared by the FEC. Furthermore, all Schedule B's for Itemized Expenditures were retrieved from microfilm that contained general election expenditures for the period from July 1, 1978, to the end of the campaign. This screening of reports was conducted to eliminate variations in the candidates' participation in primary contests and the strength of opposition encountered there, rather than to deny the importance of early spending in primaries.
5. The candidates filing the reports indicated whether these were primary or general election expenditures. Each line on the report page became a data record in the file, and more than 22,000 records in all were coded and keypunched.
6. Compared with an average expenditure of $107,843 among all of the 810 major party candidates who ran in 1978, the sample races tend to be somewhat less robust and

active—as measured by level of spending—than the entire group. There were 19 candidates who filed only interim reports with the FEC or none at all because their total expenditures did not meet the minimum requirement of $5,000. They were recorded as effectively spending nothing.

7. This figure is actually the sum of the average amounts spent on various items. Although it varies slightly from the average total expenditures, its use makes the subsequent calculation of percentages more straightforward in the pie charts showing resource allocations.

8. Because the total budgets were quite different in size, differences in the actual amounts spent were quite large. While all three types of candidates devoted equal allocations to advertising and media expenses (between 57 and 59 percent), challengers spent an average of $26,539, while incumbents spent $38,480 and candidates in open races spent $69,448.

The Strategic Uses of Money

Chapter 7

The amount of money available to a candidate is sometimes not so important as the timing of its receipt. Particularly in the nascent stages of a candidacy, money is needed to establish an organization, to begin advertising and establish name recognition, and to develop a popular perception of viability. If this effort is successful, additional funds will flow to the candidate; if not, campaign activity will stall from a lack of financial resources.

Once money flows into the candidate's campaign chest, there are many ways it can be allocated—to buy skills, to stage events, to disseminate messages, to mobilize supporters, and to raise more money. Sometimes greater sums of money are raised and spent than seems necessary to defeat a particular opponent, and sometimes money is spent long before the opponent is known. Besides using money to help win general elections, candidates use it to discourage opponents from entering the race in the first place and to further other political ambitions. One year's campaign has consequences for future contests; an accumulated string of substantial victories can create an image of invincibility that reduces the burden of subsequent campaigns by discouraging serious challenges. Large margins of victory also can enhance the winners' political careers by making them attractive candidates for higher office. These strategic uses of money are analyzed in this chapter.

Preemptive and Reactive Spending

As Gary Jacobson (1978) alerted us, high expenditures by congressional candidates are not necessarily associated with large electoral margins. Challengers who spend more do better; but incumbents who spend more actually do worse than those who spend less. Incumbents who spend large sums do so in response to serious opposition. The concept of "reactive spending" reflects an incumbent's efforts to raise and spend more money in response to stronger, better financed challengers.

The vulnerability an incumbent feels reflects much more than a specific challenger, however. Candidates' assessments of their chances also reflect the realities of the district, including the composition of the constituency, recent electoral outcomes, and the candidates' own strengths and weaknesses. Today incumbents assemble campaign war chests earlier and in larger amounts than in the past. These funding patterns raise new questions about the strategic use of campaign funds because not all of this money is being expended in the traditional general election campaign period in response to a known opponent.

Incumbents clearly have the ability to spend "preemptively" to structure the nature of the contests they will face (Goldenberg, Traugott, and Baumgartner, 1983). They time their fund raising across the full two-year electoral cycle, capitalizing on the symbolic importance of large cash balances and surpluses from previous campaigns. They have the potential to use early money to affect decisions about who their challengers might be—in the context of the current race as well as in future races.

Preemptive fund raising and spending involve accumulating cash in anticipation of a serious challenge, often when the specific challenger is unknown, as well as spending money in advance of the general election campaign to dissuade serious challengers. Some candidates spend preemptively to ensure their success in the current campaign. By the general election period, reactive spending may be unnecessary because potentially strong opponents have dropped out of the primary race in the face of large sums of money stockpiled by an apparently invincible incumbent. There is no reason to assume that incumbents are disinterested in who their challengers will be or that they will sit back to find out who will be the most "worthy" opponent the opposition can find.

Although the concept of preemptive behavior by congressional candidates is intriguing, it has received limited empirical attention. Until recently, too narrow a definition of campaign activity has restricted the view of how campaign funds are used. The process of continuous campaigning by incumbents is now more clearly understood (Fenno, 1978). Of equal significance has been a measurement problem. Information on campaign expenditures over time is needed to study preemptive behavior. For some time, the Federal Election Commission reported only two-year expenditure totals, and these have been the data employed in most analyses. Now the FEC reports on campaign receipts and expenditures by time period, making possible the preliminary analysis of preemptive behavior.[1]

Taking advantage of this opportunity, the research reported here rests on three sets of analyses. The first, which must remain essentially descriptive, investigates the patterns of fund raising and expenditures across the entire length of the interelection period from January 1, 1977, to December 31, 1978. Additional information would be needed on the composition and changing character of the pool of potential challengers over time to understand fully the consequences of incumbents' spending behavior for the quality of challenges they face. The second part of the analysis tests a model of incumbent spending that incorporates both the ideas of response to district competitiveness and reaction to behavior by the challenger. This analysis is based on a congressional district-level comparison of the spending behavior of pairs of incumbents and challengers. The third approach analyzes deviant cases of incumbents who spend much more or less than predicted.

Taken together, the results enhance our understanding of the uses of money in congressional campaigns. They also suggest fruitful avenues of further research on the effects of money on the outcome of congressional elections and additional considerations to be accounted for when debating changes in the current system of funding congressional elections.

Patterns of Spending Over Time

The importance of the strategic use of campaign funds is highlighted when patterns of campaign spending are viewed over time. As the costs of campaigning have increased, so have the candidates' (particularly incumbents') capacities to raise funds. While some may complain about the effort involved in soliciting funds, they nevertheless demonstrate increasing success, as measured by receipts. In fact, very few incumbents run campaigns with a deficit any longer, and many enjoy substantial surpluses. In the 1978 sample, only 4 incumbents had a deficit greater than $5,000; 24 essentially broke even relative to their costs (plus or minus $5,000). Thirty had small surpluses between $5,000 and $20,000, and 17 had surpluses greater than $20,000.[2]

One of the advantages that many incumbents have is the availability of funding early in the two-year cycle. With surpluses from the previous race and early contributions to the current one, they can pace themselves better across the campaign and exert an influence on the nature of the opposition they eventually will face. When candidates' spending data are assembled by quarter across the entire two-year interelection period, they present a picture of the candidates' financial activity that is quite different from what might be expected based only on the information on their total expenditures.

Such data for the 1978 preelection cycle are presented in Table 7-1. They show quite clearly that much of the advantage incumbents have over challengers in spending money occurs early in the campaign. Thirty cents of

Table 7-1 Mean Expenditures Over Time for House Candidates, by Status, 1977-1978

| | 1977 | | | | | 1978 | | | | Two-Year Total |
	1st Qtr	2d Qtr	3d Qtr	4th Qtr	1977 Total	1st Qtr	2d Qtr	3d and 4th Qtr (July 1-)	
Incumbents (N=71)	$3,956 3.7%*	$3,985 3.8	$3,382 3.2	$5,847 5.5	$17,170 (16.2)	$ 6,183 5.9	$11,561 10.9	$ 70,731 67.0	$105,645
Challengers (N=74)	0 —	0 —	$ 41 0%	$ 909 1.3	$ 950 (1.3)	$ 1,957 2.9	$11,221 16.6	$ 53,663 79.2	$ 67,791
Open Races (N=22)	0 —	$ 411 0.2%	$1,252 0.6	$5,075 2.6	$ 6,738 (3.4)	$18,838 9.7	$43,356 22.4	$124,801 64.4	$193,733

* Percentages represent proportion of two-year total budget spent in each quarter.

every dollar incumbents eventually spent was allocated before July 1 of the election year, and almost twenty cents was spent before April 1. These average expenditures by incumbents were more than 10 times as much as challengers spent during the same period. More than one-half of the edge that incumbents had over challengers in total dollars spent occurred before the challengers had begun spending any substantial amount of money on their campaigns.

Incumbents allocated one-sixth of their total expenditures long before they knew whether they would face opposition or who the challengers would be. And early spending was not simply a necessity for those facing primary opposition: incumbents spent early whether or not they ran in a primary. The challengers spent virtually all their money (96 percent) in the last nine months of 1978, and four-fifths of that after July 1. Challengers commonly were most concerned about the general election period. They knew precisely whom they had to beat and they raised and spent all they could in their uphill efforts.

Candidates for open seats, like incumbents, spent a considerable portion of their total two-year dollars before July 1 of the election year. Unlike incumbents, however, they spent heavily in the first and second quarters of 1978, improving their name recognition and contesting what were often hard-fought primaries in an effort to secure their party's nomination. In 1977 they spent proportionately about the same as challengers, although they had six times as much money available. Overall the expenditures of candidates in open races in the two-year period were the highest, averaging almost twice as much as those of incumbents and three times as much as challengers.

Why did incumbents spend so much money so early in the campaign, in a pattern that clearly did not represent a reaction to the behavior of their challengers? One answer seems to be that they spent the money because they had it and were using it to dissuade serious challengers. They spent *preemptively* rather than *reactively*.

The candidate-selection process differs for incumbents and the challengers who eventually face them. For some challengers, there is potentially a long road to the nomination that may include competing with other candidates for the right to oppose the incumbent. In other contests, because of the relative strength of the incumbent, the opposition party may have to recruit a challenger if none volunteers. For incumbents, on the other hand, the path to renomination usually is completely within their control. In most cases, they only have to decide whether to run again and the place on the ballot is theirs. But they may have additional motives that influence their campaign behavior, particularly early in the cycle. They may be insecure in their position and feel the need to start early, with the intent of scaring off more serious challenges. For them, an early investment may pay off later in an easier general election contest.

Vulnerability and Early Spending

Incumbents may feel vulnerable at any time during the two-year interelection period. Assessing their vulnerability vis-à-vis their next challenger may be impossible right after reelection, but candidates do have information about the potential for a serious challenge.[3] For one thing, an incumbent may feel vulnerable, even after a winning campaign, because of a close division of partisan support in the district. Among candidates contesting districts with a relatively close partisan division, average spending prior to July 1 was $35,969, or 13 percent more than the average level in districts that were not so close. Data are presented in Table 7-2 that illustrate the relationship between early spending and the partisan division in the sample of districts. Spending in the early stages of the two-year period appears to reflect the vulnerability of an incumbent to a serious challenge because of a close distribution of partisanship, indicating strong potential support for the out-party.[4] Even so, the amount spent before July by incumbents in districts with closely divided partisanship was a smaller proportion of their total spending because they intensified their effort considerably after July, spending more than twice as much as safer incumbents.

Another indicator of safety for any incumbent is length of service (Cover, 1977). The very fact of successive reelections reinforces feelings of safety. Data are presented in Figure 7-1 that illustrate quite clearly the relationship between early spending and total spending by incumbents and their challengers, controlling for the incumbent's length of service. Total expenditures are greatest among the most junior members, primarily as a reflection of the amounts they spent before July 1. With the exception of the Watergate class of 1974, the data show that incumbents' overall expendi-

Table 7-2 Mean Expenditures Over Time for Incumbents by Potential Challenge, 1977-1978

	Pre-July 1978	After July 1, 1978	Total*
Partisan Division in the District			
Close** (N=51)	$35,969 29%	$88,021 71	$123,990
Not close (N=20)	$31,727 44%	$40,127 56	$ 71,854

* For the ease of calculating percentages, this total is the sum of the two means.
** Districts with a close partisan division are those between 45 percent and 55 percent in favor of one party.

Figure 7-1   Average Total Campaign Expenditures and Post-July General Elections Expenditures, for Incumbents and Challengers, by Number of Terms Served, 1978

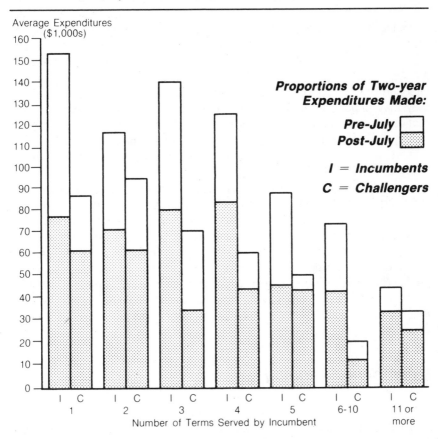

tures decline with their length of service. Much of this decline comes from reduced spending in the early period. These data suggest that short-term incumbents engage in preemptive spending because they have the most to gain by affecting the selection of their opponent.

Spending money early in the election cycle is only one manifestation of preemptive behavior. Another is raising money early. Large cash balances can make incumbents appear invulnerable and discourage potential opponents. If candidates raise and spend only what they feel they need at the time, there should be a relatively high and constant correlation between receipts and expenditures over time and across types of candidates. In fact, this is not the case. Although candidates tend to spend most of what they accumulate by the end of the campaign, the relationship between getting and spending is not strong in the early part of the cycle, especially for incumbents. Incumbents consistently underspent relative to their resources through July 1978. Only in the last six months of the campaign was their spending highly related to available cash. Challengers, on the other hand, more consistently spent what they collected.[5]

Incumbents may raise money early simply to get it over with or because it is easier before potential contributors are solicited by others, without any intention of publicizing their stockpile to discourage strong challengers. Or they may engage in strategic fund raising for preemptive purposes. Their motives require further study. Regardless of their intentions, that early money almost certainly acts to discourage potential challengers if they know it is there. A definitive demonstration of those effects awaits systematic study of the preprimary period.

The data that are available on spending over time suggest that react've spending is not the only explanation of candidates' resource allocations. There are strategic uses to which money can be applied other than defeating a particular general election opponent. The data suggest strongly that money can be raised and spent preemptively to dissuade serious challengers, especially by incumbents uncertain about their electoral prospects. By segregating and then analyzing these *early* expenditures, it is possible to pursue more directly the consequences and significance of reactive spending in the general election period, when the incumbents know who their opponents will be.

Incumbent Spending

During the general election period, incumbents raise and spend money in response to the seriousness of their challenge. Conceptually, there are two important parts to this response. One includes variables dealing with the characteristics of the district; the other, with the characteristics of the two candidates. Incumbents from districts historically hostile to their party are likely to spend more money, regardless of their challenger, than those from districts with more support for their party. In addition, during the general election period, incumbents also respond to what their specific challengers spend. Regardless of district properties, high-spending challengers induce incumbents to follow suit. This is the kind of spending that Jacobson has termed "reactive spending."

A simple model with three independent variables captures these concepts and uses them to explain spending by incumbents during the general election. The first is a normal vote estimate of the strength of the incumbent's (and challenger's) partisan support in the district. The normal vote incorporates the realities of district's partisanship that set the parameters for the nature of the challenge, largely independent of and uncontaminated by campaign effects in previous elections. The second measure is the challenger's general election expenditures in the post-July 1 period. This amount represents the cue for reactive spending in the model. The third measure is an assessment that the incumbents or their managers make regarding their vulnerability.

This measurement is taken late in the campaign period and reflects the managers' overall assessments of electoral chances in light of the characteristics of both the district and the specific opponent.[6] Its inclusion in the model is an acknowledgement that incumbents tend to spend more when they *feel* vulnerable even though the obvious objective measures of safety do not indicate that they should.

This model treats incumbents as responding to two important but distinct stimuli. One is the race at hand. They raise and spend money in reaction to the expenditures of the challenger as well as in response to their general feelings of vulnerability in this campaign. The other is the competitiveness of their district. Incumbents representing districts historically sympathetic to their own party spend significantly less money than those from more competitive districts.

The results suggest a base estimate of about $44,000 for incumbent expenditures in the post-July 1 period in 1978, had there been no uncertainty about the outcome or reactive spending. From this base, incumbents who felt vulnerable were likely almost to double their expenditures, spending an added $41,000. Furthermore, incumbents were likely to spend an additional 25 cents for every dollar spent by the challenger and almost $2,000 less for every percentage point advantage they have in the partisan division in the district, regardless of perceived vulnerability.[7] This three-variable model explains 56 percent of the variance in incumbents' expenditures.[8]

Money is used strategically by House incumbents as they campaign continuously over the two-year interelection period. During the first 18 months of their term, some incumbents spend liberally as they attempt to dissuade potential challengers from announcing their candidacies. To the extent that they succeed, these early expenditures are extremely important in determining incumbency return rates.

The model above shows that spending during the general election period also represents strategic responses by incumbents to their vulnerability and to their opponents' spending behavior. It accounts for more than half of the variance in incumbent spending. Although part of the unexplained variance in incumbent spending undoubtedly is due to measurement error, an examination of deviant cases—those in which actual expenditures were under- or overestimated to a considerable degree—offers clues about additional factors that may affect how much incumbents spend, clues that provide guidance for future research.[9]

Overspenders and Underspenders

Eight incumbents in the sample overspent substantially by amounts that were $30,000 or more above what was predicted by the model. None was a moderate overspender. Three incumbents underspent substantially, and ten were moderate underspenders, in the range of $20,000 to $30,000. Information available in *The Almanac of American Politics* and other publicly available sources provides further insight into the spending strategies and motivations of congressional candidates. Two types of situations appear to encourage overspending, and two types appear to encourage underspending. Below, each type is described in terms of particular cases.

Overspending for Career Advancement

Incumbents who are planning to seek higher elective or party office try to demonstrate their money-raising and vote-getting abilities. In 1978 three incumbents spent large sums on their reelection campaigns—many times what their opponents spent—even though there was never the slightest doubt they would win.

These candidates were maximizing their percentage of the vote against opponents who everyone knew from the outset would lose. One raised his 60 percent share of the vote in 1974 to 66 percent in 1976 and to 70 percent in 1978. He raised and spent more than $100,000, running an active campaign that sent out a half dozen mailings and placed advertisements in more than a dozen district newspapers and on eight radio and two television stations. Two years later, he ran successfully for the Senate.

A second safe incumbent also was maximizing his 1978 vote percentage. Although he was unopposed in the primary, he raised $80,000 by primary time and stockpiled the funds for general election use. In the general election campaign, he spent $150,000—more than ten times what his opponent spent. He had an additional $40,000 available that he never got around to using. He improved his 51 percent victory margin in 1974 (an impressive feat for a Republican newcomer that year) to 56 percent in 1976 and to 75 percent in his landslide 1978 win. Two years later, he also ran successfully for the Senate.

If reactive spending and incumbent vulnerability were adequate explanations of incumbent spending, the third big spending safe incumbent would have been a very low spender indeed. He was first elected in the 1950s and has won easily ever since in his strongly Democratic urban district. In 1976 he rolled up an 81 percent vote share after spending only $50,000. Two years later he outspent his opponent 30 to 1 and won with 86 percent of the vote. This incumbent already was a member of the House leadership, but his electoral security, seniority, and relative youth put even higher leadership positions within his reach.

Aspirations for higher party or elective office explain high levels of expenditures by some incumbents who are electorally safe. They may spend to demonstrate their campaign skills or to impress colleagues or interest groups with their electoral security. They may try to devastate their current challengers to discourage future challenges, freeing themselves for a while to concentrate on House business or concerns outside their districts. They also may contribute some of their receipts to other candidates' campaigns to establish political debts for future use.

Counteracting Scandal

Some incumbents feel especially vulnerable because of unusual circumstances, such as scandal, surrounding their candidacies, and there is evidence to suggest that they should be concerned (Peters and Welch, 1980). The dichotomous measure of vulnerability incorporated in the model is inadequate to capture the extra burden of personal scandal that leads some incumbents to outspend their opponents by substantial sums. They see heavy spending as necessary to ensure victory, but even if victory is certain, candidates in traditionally safe districts want to return to comfortable margins of victory sufficient to discourage future challenges.

Many of these candidates were secure before personal incidents became public. These incidents might involve anything from traffic accidents to public drunkenness to disclosures about their sexual behavior and preference. If they can muster sufficient funds to weather the first challenge after the public becomes aware of the scandalous incident, they usually can hold on to their seats. This effort may mean unusually high levels of spending for the next one or two elections, however, to regain a strong sense of security.

Involuntary Underspending

One obvious reason why some incumbents underspend is their inability to raise additional funds. Although most studies on campaign finance give the impression that incumbents have only to ask—that their ability to raise money is virtually unlimited—this impression is misleading when the amounts required are exceptionally large or when the incumbent's fund-raising skills are limited. Some incumbents secure office after defeating the previous incumbent in an upset, often because the vote was against the incumbent rather than for the eventual winner. Sometimes, this victory is linked to an incident of scandal that occurred late in the campaign and from which the former incumbent could not recover by election day.

In succeeding elections, particularly in safe one-party districts with strong machines, the new incumbent may find it suddenly very difficult to raise substantial amounts of money. Such first- or second-termers may be vulnerable and require relatively large amounts of money, but the district realities and unusual circumstances surrounding their initial victories may preclude obtaining adequate funding. In 1978, one incumbent faced a challenger who spent more than $300,000 in his primary and general election campaigns. The incumbent's staff found it difficult to raise amounts even approximating those available to his opponent. His campaign spent $80,000, three-quarters of it post-July. The election was a cliff-hanger; the incumbent won by only 4,000 votes. In 1980 he lost to the same opponent by a slim margin. In their rematch, the challenger raised more than $1 million, while the incumbent was able to increase his spending to only $120,000.

Confident Underspending

Incumbents sometimes feel so safe that they allow their challengers to outspend them. The usual reason for their confidence is the lopsided composition of a district's electorate. In strongly Democratic or Republican districts, challengers can spend a great deal without stimulating equivalent expenditures by majority party incumbents. The incumbents underspend when campaign intelligence and polling results indicate they need have no cause for concern.

Underspending also is likely in districts where challengers spend large amounts of money on television ads in markets that are not cost effective. Secure incumbents, with the benefit of experience and good information, may discount their challengers' behavior as wasteful and choose not to follow suit. In 1978 an incumbent in an urban district with favorable partisanship was challenged by an independently wealthy opponent. The challenger spent thousands of dollars on television ads that reached many people outside of the district. Judging the challenger's tactics as ineffectual, the incumbent did not bother to raise and spend all the available money.

Occasionally favorable poll results lull incumbents into unwarranted confidence. In 1978 one incumbent allowed himself to be outspent by a challenger who succeeded in winning. The incumbent could have raised more money but did not try because his surveys showed him as a comfortable winner. By the time the poll results changed, it was too late to raise enough money and buy sufficient media time to reverse his downward trend.

The role of money in congressional campaigns is neither simple nor direct. Incumbents accumulate money and spend some of it even before their challengers are known, and the effects of these campaign war chests on the eventual strength of the challengers are still unknown. It is plausible to assume that incumbents are concerned about who their challengers will be and that incumbents act strategically in ways that will enhance their security by discouraging serious opposition. Gary Jacobson and Samuel Kernell

(1982; also Jacobson, 1981) suggest that national economic conditions early in the election year affect strategic calculations of potential challengers—that strong challengers choose to run when those economic conditions portend a national shift in their favor and to avoid running when national trends will hurt them. Surely these strategically sophisticated challengers also judge carefully the vulnerability of their opponents, including the amount of money available and already in the bank, as they make the decision about whether the time is propitious for a successful challenge. Of course, once the opponent is known, incumbents react by raising and spending more money in response to well-financed challengers. Reactive spending has been documented in the general election period, but it probably also occurs in primary races.

Although clearly important, the concept of reactive spending alone does not account for all of the systematic variation in amounts incumbents spend in their general election campaigns. Some incumbents spend more than anticipated and others less, in response to the spending of their opponents. Feelings of vulnerability, based on the underlying level of potential support for the opposition party or caused by other special circumstances surrounding the race, lead incumbents to spend more. A careful examination of deviant cases suggests that aspirations for higher elective or party office also may lead incumbents to spend more heavily than anticipated. They may spend less than expected if they have difficulty raising money or if they are confident of winning. A full model of incumbent expenditures awaits a systematic inquiry designed to test these ideas.

Notes

1. The data on receipts and expenditures over time were assembled from the series entitled "Candidate Index of Supporting Documents— (E)." This is a summary of each candidate's dollar totals of receipts and expenditures with an indication of the election type, general or primary, as recorded by the candidate.

2. For a discussion and examples of large surpluses in the 1982 elections, see Kenneth Noble's article in the New York Times, "Some in House Using Excess Cash for Expensive Living," April 5, 1983.

3. While there are no comparable data for 1978, Huckshorn and Spencer (1971, 57-58) reported that 6 percent of the 1962 House losers had announced their candidacies between the 1960 election and the end of the year, and another quarter in 1961. During the first quarter of 1962, almost one-half of the Republicans (44 percent) and one-third of the Democrats (37 percent) announced. By July 1, 94 percent of the Republican losers and 93 percent of the Democratic losers were announced candidates. Furthermore, the candidates who announced in 1961 generally did better at the polls, in terms of proportion of the votes cast.

4. Objective indicators of vulnerability, such as the partisan division in the district, inevitably fail to capture the full range of factors that incumbents consider as they assess their chances of winning. Some incumbents feel vulnerable even though they appear to be safe to everyone else. A preferable measure would be their perceptions of vulnerability, taken early and often

to track changes and their consequences for strategic behavior. Unfortunately, the only such measure available in 1978 was taken late in the campaign period and reflects only imperfectly the perceptions of vulnerability early in the race. Nevertheless, uncertainty late in the campaign is related to early campaign spending. Most incumbents who felt vulnerable in October 1978 probably also felt that way earlier and spent heavily in anticipation of a tough race.

5. The correlation (Pearsonian r) between incumbents' spending and available cash was .5 in the first six months of 1978. It rose to .9 in the last six months of 1978. For challengers, however, the correlation was .7 for the first six months of 1978 and .9 in the post-July period.

6. In this case, the measure distinguishes only between incumbents who are Sure Winners or Vulnerables. With more refined measurements, it should eventually be possible to discriminate more finely along a dimension of vulnerability.

7. The full results of the three-variable regression equation are as follows:

	Regression Coefficient	t-ratio
a	44.10	
Challenger's Expenditures	.251	2.8
Incumbent's Vulnerability	41.12	3.3
Normal Vote Estimate	−1.77	−2.2

The equation is based upon complete data for 63 pairs of candidates, and the R^2 = .56.

8. This model performs better than Jacobson's seven-variable model. Jacobson's analysis was based on 305 incumbents who faced opposition, while the sample used in this study comprises 71 districts with complete data necessary to test the model. Jacobson's model explains 44 percent of the variance in incumbent spending in the sample, compared with 35 percent for all races. For a detailed presentation of these results, see E. Goldenberg, M. Traugott, and F. Baumgartner, "Preemptive and Reactive Spending in U. S. House Races," presented at the 1983 annual meeting of the Midwest Political Science Association.

The measures used by Jacobson in his seven-variable model of reactive spending can be improved to enhance his model's predictive power. With two adjustments in measurement—the use of only general election expenditures and a normal vote estimate of party strength in the district—the predictive power of Jacobson's model of reactive spending is increased by one-third, from 44 percent to 58 percent. The results increase the importance of reactive spending as an accurate description of the behavior of House incumbents during the general election campaign.

9. There are various sources of measurement error. One is the measure used to capture general election expenditures. That measure includes only spending made after July that was designated by the campaign as for the general election. By using the July 1 cutoff date, we can be fairly certain that the challenger is known and reactive spending is possible. On the other hand, many primaries are over before July and some pre-July expenditures are actually general election spending. Nevertheless, the choice of July 1 as the beginning date for general election expenditures does not appear to cause any serious methodological difficulty. Alternative equations were run predicting 1978 general election expenditures where the measure captured all such expenditures after January 1, 1978, and the results were virtually identical to those reported here. A more significant potential source of error is the FEC's reliance on the campaign's designation of expenditures as "primary," "general," or "other." The meaning of these designations is not always clear. Just before the primary, spending is attributed to the primary. But what is spent long before the primary, as well as after the primary, is attributed typically to the general election. By including in the regression models only what is designated as a post-July general election expenditure, we sometimes underestimate an incumbent's or a challenger's expenditures. The larger lesson here is that campaigns do not always distinguish between primary and general election spending, and

perhaps we have to broaden our view beyond specific campaign periods to look at the flow of money throughout the campaign as a whole. To do so requires detailed data on the amounts and purposes of expenditures over time, and that demands significant data collection and coding resources.

A third source of measurement error is the estimate of the district's normal vote. Because adequate survey results were not available from each of the districts of interest, the normal vote had to be estimated through regression techniques, as described in the Appendix. Overall, this estimate has proved to be quite successful for systematic analysis, but errors in an estimate for specific districts may contribute to a few large residuals.

Finally, the measure of uncertainty employed in the equation is dichotomous although there is obviously great variation among candidates in terms of how uncertain they feel, and any one candidate's level of uncertainty may vary across the course of the campaign.

The Information Environment

Chapter 8

The campaign period provides an important opportunity for voters to collect information about elected officials and those seeking office. During the campaign, candidates attempt to communicate with the electorate in three ways. The first is to have personal contact with as many voters as possible. This technique is very effective, but the candidate's time is perhaps the most limited campaign resource in a constituency of any reasonable size. The candidate has to rely, therefore, on what others, a few senior staff members and groups of volunteers, can do. Using surrogates for the candidate is the second means of contacting the voters. In many districts, however, these two types of personal contact are not sufficient to deliver appeals to large segments of the constituency. The candidate must rely upon a third way of spreading messages to the voters—mass communications.

Candidates prepare their own messages and stimulate news coverage as well. Together these messages form the information environment for potential voters. There is substantial variation in the quantity and quality of information voters receive during the campaign. Describing and explaining that variation is the purpose of this chapter.

How well the candidates communicate with the electorate affects not only the election outcome but also the level of political information voters have before they make their choices. By now it is a generally accepted fact that few voters are well informed about candidates for most public offices. The level of information is lower in congressional than in presidential campaigns, and voters know substantially less about candidates for the House than the Senate.[1] After the 1978 election, a national sample of voters was shown the names of the candidates for the House in their own districts and the candidates for Senate in their states. They were asked if they recognized these candidates and, if so, how they felt about them and whether they had learned anything about them during the campaign. Although most voters could recognize and evaluate the incumbents in both the Senate and the House, many more could recognize and rate the Senate challenger than the House challenger.[2] Fewer than half the respondents remembered learning anything at all about the House challenger in their district (Abramowitz, 1980; Hinckley, 1980).

These kinds of findings provide no comfort to those who subscribe to a vision of voters making reasoned and rational choices between competing candidates. A traditional interpretation of democratic theory would lead one to expect that voters would become knowledgeable about *both* candidates before voting. For people to cast informed votes on the basis of their policy preferences, they need to know what the candidates stand for. People who cannot even recognize or express an opinion about one of the candidates hardly approach anyone's ideal of informed participants in the political process.

On the other hand, perhaps the ideal is unrealistic and unnecessarily demanding. Voters may not require a great deal of specific information about candidates or issues to make sensible voting choices, as long as they have general information and can apply general rules.[3] For example, voters may use party affiliation as a general indication of whether one candidate is more likely than another to represent their preferences. As long as voters can pull the party lever in the voting booth, recognizing the candidate's name is not essential. Moreover, even if most voters are uninformed, some incumbents may be concerned that small, but active, groups of voters will be alerted to policy stands they oppose. If at least some attentive citizens are well informed and have the potential of alerting others about sharp policy differences on important issues, should they develop, then the prospect of policy voting can encourage candidates to anticipate and reflect their constituents' views even before the election occurs (Fiorina, 1974; Key, 1966; Kingdon, 1968).

Both these arguments acknowledge the reality that most voters have little specific information about House candidates and offer perspectives that attempt to reconcile that reality with a properly functioning democracy. Both arguments have merit as well as limitations. For some voters, general information is not enough. Occasionally, voters need and seek additional information about candidates beyond their party or demographic characteristics. Furthermore, for candidates to continue to worry about voters becoming informed in the future, there must be some credible possibility that this might happen. For these reasons, it is important to understand what information is available to voters in the district, should they seek it. As long as information is available, poorly informed voters present a less serious problem to democratic theory.

Unfortunately, the prospect of the voter obtaining ample information is unlikely. According to Richard Stout, House contests are especially low in priority for media coverage because reporters are unimpressed with the importance of individual representatives. He wrote, "A House member is not directly responsible for running the town, city, county or state nor, for that matter, the federal government; after all, he is just one of a ruly mob of 435." [4] A number of congressional scholars also point to the scarcity of news coverage of the typical House campaign. They speculate that the media attention given to House races is so meager when compared with Senate contests that voters have little opportunity to become informed about House candidates (Abramowitz, 1980; Goldenberg and Traugott, 1979; Hinckley, 1980; Mann and Wolfinger, 1980). The reason cited most frequently for sparse coverage of House races is the poor overlap of congressional district and media market boundaries. If the media's disinterest in House campaigns is as universal as these scholars suggest, then news coverage is unlikely to provide adequate information even to interested voters.

As a description of the average set of circumstances, these observations are correct. However, House races vary considerably in terms of their vitality, and districts vary in terms of how closely they overlap media markets. It is certainly worth investigating whether mass media coverage of House races is always skimpy and under what circumstances coverage is more extensive.

Even if coverage is ample in quantity, its poor quality may still leave voters relatively uninformed. Thomas Mann and Raymond Wolfinger (1980) noted that few voters have any specific information on the issue positions of House candidates or the voting records of incumbents. [5] If candidates purposely obscure their issue positions in public statements and reporters allow that to happen, then little specific information becomes available. Benjamin Page's study of presidential candidates since 1932 found that their policy stands were "infrequent, inconspicuous and unspecific." [6] Unless it became necessary, presidential candidates avoided making clear statements about issues so they would not alienate potential voters who might disagree with them. Nevertheless, Page found that sometimes clarity became unavoidable and that extensive media attention to what candidates say could contribute to greater issue clarity. [7] Thomas Patterson (1980) echoed these findings in his study of the 1976 presidential campaign.

Although it is clear by now that generalizations derived from studies of presidential campaigns do not always apply to congressional races, some candidates for the House may also engage in the "art of ambiguity." House campaigns vary considerably on nearly every important dimension, one of which is the clarity of the candidates' issue positions. Either greater competition or greater news attention could lead to greater clarity. If incumbents perceive their challengers as threats or if reporters are aggressive in pushing candidates to be specific, incumbents may have to engage in more issue discussion and policy clarification than they would otherwise. At the same time, incumbents who do not face serious challenges may feel less pressure to run issue-oriented campaigns.

Even if candidates are clear in their issue statements, media coverage still may not reflect it. Communications scholars have accused the mass media of emphasizing the "horse race" aspects of campaigns to the neglect of discussions of substantive issues, whether or not candidates tried to generate issue coverage.[8] Therefore, it is also worth examining the kind of news appearing in the media. Do news stories emphasize the same themes that candidates try to stress in their campaigns? Does heavier coverage include more issue discussion or merely more campaign hoopla?

These questions are addressed below. The first part of this chapter concentrates on the information generated by campaigns. It looks at what the candidates try to present and how they try to present it. How do information strategies vary as a consequence of the type of race and the district setting? Which strategies are considered most effective? Which messages do different types of campaigns try to convey?

Although campaigns can shape part of the information that reaches potential voters during the weeks preceding election day, the dissemination of some information is largely beyond a campaign's control. Reporters and editors produce mass media content in the form of news coverage that is sometimes at odds with campaign intentions. Only citizens who are active and interested in politics read the materials produced by the campaign. Most people do not. For them, coverage in the mass media is much more important. The second part of this chapter focuses on the content of campaign coverage in the mass media. How much information is available in the media about the candidates and issues in House races? How and why do districts vary in the amount of campaign news available to readers of major daily newspapers? The translation of campaign themes into news is far from automatic, raising additional questions of importance. How does the content of news stories differ from the themes that campaigns try to present? How do opposing candidates fare in their treatment in the press? Can citizens reasonably be expected to become well informed about the candidates and issues in House races?

Information Techniques

Conveying campaign messages to win votes is the central activity of political campaigns. Information is shaped by the campaign staff with an eye toward reassuring traditional partisan supporters, wooing independents and supporters of the other party, and stimulating generous giving by financial contributors. To these ends, advertising is purchased, literature prepared, direct mail written, speeches carefully crafted, and endorsements and news coverage sought. The average congressional campaign in 1978 spent 60 percent of its budget on advertising and most of the remaining 40 percent on other ways of disseminating campaign messages. Choosing the methods to spread the word represents another important dimension of campaign tactics.

Dissemination Techniques

Campaigns use a variety of techniques for sending messages to potential voters, techniques that vary in terms of the degree of control the campaign exercises over message production and message distribution (Figure 8-1). For example, the mass media provide opportunities for the campaign to piggyback on already existing distribution networks, but these opportunities carry with them limited control over who receives particular messages. By placing advertisments or seeking news coverage in small-town newspapers, campaigns can target people in particular geographic areas; by advertising in ethnic or special-interest newspapers or on radio programs with well-defined audiences, campaigns can target people with similar interests. On the whole, however, the mass media—especially television and metropolitan newspapers—reach a highly diverse audience; they fall at the low end of the scale in terms of campaign control over the distribution of messages. Campaign strategies that rely on the mass media tend to target broadly in the district. If increasing the familiarity of a candidate's name in the district is the first priority of a campaign, then broad mass media appeals are often the most effective approach.

Within the category of limited control over distribution of messages, the candidates' control of the content of messages varies from high for the content of advertisements to low for the content of news, endorsements, and opinion columns. Campaigns often stage events to attract positive attention in the news, and they issue press releases with suggested story wordings. But reporters and editors decide what to cover and how to cover it. Journalistic norms of balance encourage reporters to seek out the views of a candidate's opponent so that they can be incorporated into the story. Consequently, campaigns that prefer great certainty about and control over the content of messages usually turn to paid advertisements rather than news stories.

Some strategies call for highly targeted appeals with significant campaign control over the distribution of messages. Candidates often tailor their messages for specific segments of the district's population. The candidate does not necessarily shift position on the same issue for audiences with different preferences but targets a particular audience by making appeals only on the issues of concern to them. After all, most citizens have short attention spans where political information is concerned. Crafting a message about some issue of special concern to a group of people offers a better

Figure 8-1 Campaign Control Over Production and Distribution of
Information

Campaign Control
over Production

Low   High

	Low	High
Low	News Endorsements Opinion columns	Advertisements in newspapers, on radio or TV Billboards Yardsigns
High	Government pamphlets Gospel tracts	Newsletters Direct mail Issue papers

Campaign
Control
over
Distribution

---

chance of capturing citizen attention and leaving a favorable impression.

The best techniques for highly targeted appeals are newsletters, direct mail, and campaign handouts. Developing mailing lists can be a burden, but today campaigns can buy lists along with direct mail expertise. The growing popularity of direct mail specialists attests to the desirability of more personalized and targeted messages in House campaigns (Sabato, 1981).

Control over distribution does not always imply campaign control over production as well. The content of direct mail correspondence, newsletters, and position papers is carefully managed by the campaign. But other materials sent to potential voters under the candidate's name, such as government publications or "gospel tracts," obviously are produced else-where.[9] Campaigns can be selective and choose to send out only those publications with which their candidates agree, but selectivity does not yield enough control over content to allow explicit credit taking by candidates for government programs.

The major advantage of using existing distribution networks, such as television or daily newspapers, is their wide reach. Advertisements and news stories in these media can be seen by large numbers of potential voters without the problems associated with separate mailings or door-to-door deliveries. The advantage of having little control over content is greater credibility with the citizenry. News content is not as suspect as the obviously self-interested products of a campaign organization. However, not all races are likely to attract news attention or to find television or daily newspaper advertising affordable. If district boundaries do not parallel media market boundaries closely, then advertising can be costly and highly inefficient. If the media's attention is divided among several congressional races within the broadcast or circulation area, then news coverage of any one race is likely to be limited. Even in good media markets with relatively abundant news coverage of the House race, however, most campaigns also turn to controlled alternatives to convey specific messages to particular segments of the electorate.

After the 1978 elections, managers were asked which of eight different information dissemination techniques they had used in their campaigns. Their responses, shown in Table 8-1, compare the frequency of use of the various techniques. Virtually every campaign relied on personal contact with the voters and the use of campaign literature. Campaign buttons and newspaper advertising were nearly as popular, and direct mail and radio were used in two-thirds of the races.

All of these techniques except for direct mail have been standard fare in House campaigns for years. Since Richard Viguerie built his direct mail empire during the 1960s, the use of direct mail in campaigns for national office has grown dramatically. As a means of sending campaign messages, it offers substantial advantages. Both message content and distribution can be carefully controlled. Advances in computer technology make the maintenance and manipulation of mailing lists relatively easy and inexpensive. With little effort, letters can be personalized, addressed, sorted, and bundled so that they qualify for inexpensive postal rates. Over time, direct mail has assumed more importance as a way for House campaigns to reach potential contributors and voters, and this trend probably will continue.

Substantial differences in the use of these eight techniques can be seen when campaigns are distinguished according to the candidates' incumbency status and the managers' overall assessments of electoral chances. If the outcome was in doubt, more effort was devoted to spreading campaign messages. Candidates in open races tended to use all eight techniques, including direct mail, radio, television, and billboards as well as the vehicles commonly used by all other campaigns. Among incumbents, Vulnerables tended to use a greater variety of techniques than Sure Winners, with especially large differences for the more expensive alternatives of television advertising and direct mail. Similarly for challengers, Hopefuls tended to use more information dissemination techniques than Sure Losers. Except for

Table 8-1 The Use of Information Dissemination Techniques by Candidate Status and Assessments of Electoral Chances, 1978*

Candidate Status and Party	Personal Contact	Campaign Literature	Buttons	Newspaper Ads	Direct Mail	Radio Ads	TV Ads	Bill-boards	N
All candidates	95	92	80	78	70	65	44	35	(149)
Incumbents									
Sure Winners	91	80	74	74	54	60	26	26	(46)
Vulnerables	100	100	94	88	100	81	75	44	(16)
Challengers									
Hopefuls	98	95	93	80	80	73	53	38	(40)
Sure Losers	88	92	58	65	46	42	27	15	(26)
Candidates in Open Races	100	100	90	82	85	77	69	61	(21)

* Cell entry is the percentage who mentioned using the technique in the campaign.

billboards, each of the other techniques was used by nearly every Vulnerable's campaign, and most Hopefuls used every technique except television and billboards.

How Important Is Television?

Perhaps the most unexpected finding is the relatively infrequent use of television advertising in House races. The modern fascination with political advertising on television, especially in presidential and statewide races, and the visibility given to several well-financed but atypical congressional races each term can create the impression that television is the communication vehicle of choice in all congressional races. Television was mentioned as the most effective means of getting information to the voters by 25 percent of the managers, a greater number than cited any other technique except personal contact, which was referred to by 33 percent. Yet, the data in Table 8-1 show that fewer campaigns used television than any other of the eight techniques, save billboards.

Over time, advertising on television has become more common in congressional races, but there are still many places where it remains too inefficient a means of reaching district voters. The quality of a district's television market affects a manager's judgment about the effectiveness of television as a campaign technique and, therefore, the likelihood that television advertising will be used. To identify other factors that influence a manager's view of television, the effects of market quality, in terms of cost effectiveness, must be understood.[10]

The 86 competitive districts in the 1978 sample included places with considerable variation in media market structures. A summary measure was created to capture the quality of a district's television market. Because television is a useful campaign vehicle only where the broadcast signals get to potential voters, the more people in a district who can view a station, the better the station's *reach* in that district. Television reach, one indicator of advertising desirability, was measured as the proportion of the total district population that lived within a given television market, commonly referred to as its Area of Dominant Influence (ADI). If everyone in a district could tune in to television stations in a market, then the stations' reach was a perfect 100 percent. Other things being equal, the better the reach, the better the district's television market for political advertising.

Of course, other things rarely are equal. In particular, television stations that reach most potential voters in a district often reach many people outside the district as well. Reaching more people is an advantage for product advertising, but candidates targeting their constituencies must reach the right people. Advertising rates are determined by total audience size, and the cost of reaching district voters through television advertising can be quite high when the signal area is much larger than the congressional district. The TV market's *efficiency* is defined as the ratio of its audience size to the district's population in the signal area. From the perspective of the political campaign, a good television market is one that reaches a significant portion of a district's population for relatively little cost. Therefore, a district's television market *potential* was measured as the number of households in the district that could be reached by a television station divided by the cost of an average advertisement on that station.[11]

Not all the people who live within a signal area actually tune in to a station when a political ad is running. At any particular time, many television sets are turned off, unwatched, or tuned in to different channels. The market potential measure indicates how many people could see an advertisement, not how many actually do. Campaigns must run many spot advertisements on several different stations to reach all of the television households in the district. Therefore, the market potential measure is useful solely to compare the advertising possibilities across different districts: the larger the number, the higher the market potential of the television market. According to this measure, quality varied from a low of 756 households per average advertising dollar in the New York City area to a high of 33,300 in a less urban area of the state.

Table 8-2 shows the median proportion of a district's population that could be reached, the cost of advertising on stations in the best ADI in the district, and the television market potential for various types of districts. In highly urban places, television reach in any one congressional district is excellent, but signals also are available to large numbers of viewers living in other districts. Consequently, advertising there is inefficient because it costs a great deal and the signal reaches many people who live outside the district. In districts that are 90 percent or more urban, the television market quality is relatively poor: typically only 1,452 district households can be reached per unit of advertising cost. That is, if every television set in an average urban district happens to tune in to the same channel at the precise moment when a 30-second campaign advertisement appears, then 1,452 households are reached per advertising dollar. Rural areas have poorer reach, but cost is sufficiently low to make television quality better than in urban locations. In districts that are less than one-half urban, only 48 percent of the households can be reached in the best television market, but more than five times as many households (7,920 compared with 1,452) can be reached per average advertising dollar as in the urban districts. Television advertising is a better buy in rural areas. To afford it in urban places, campaigns need plenty of money.

Substantial regional differences exist in television advertising costs, which follow from differences in population densities. The Border States and the South enjoy low-cost television markets with high advertising potential compared with districts in the West and New England.[12] The location of the district has other implications as well. Candidates in districts with

Table 8-2   Television Market Characteristics by District Location and Type, 1978*

	Reach (%)	Cost ($)	Market Potential	(N)
Percent Urban				
Less than 50%	48	11	7,920	(33)
50% to 89%	100	19	7,826	(15)
90% and more	100	124	1,452	(38)
Region				
New England	100	140	1,286	(23)
Midwest	100	21	4,660	(26)
South, Border	90	18	8,800	(19)
West	100	57	3,216	(18)
Partisan Division				
Close	89	20	5,891	(63)
Lopsided	100	123	1,463	(23)
Type of Race				
Democratic Incumbent	100	42	4,186	(45)
Republican Incumbent	74	23	2,974	(29)
Open	100	22	7,071	(11)

* Cell entries are the median percentage of district population reached (Reach), the median dollar cost per rating point of an average prime time 30-second spot (Cost), and the median number of households in the district reached per average dollar cost (Market Potential). The use of medians is dictated by skewed distributions of these measures across the sample of 86 competitive districts.

lopsided partisan divisions, disproportionately located in big cities, tend to run in poorer television markets than candidates in districts with more evenly divided partisanship. Although the poor television markets obviously did not cause districts to become lopsided in the first place, markets with low advertising potential close off one important technique that challengers in these kinds of races might use to campaign effectively.

As expected, the potential of the television market in a district was important to campaign managers as they decided whether to buy television time as part of their advertising strategies. The data in Table 8-3 show that the better the potential, the more TV time was purchased. Candidates purchased significant amounts of TV time only in the districts that fell in the best television markets. This kind of race supports the conventional wisdom about the importance of television in congressional contests.

For open races, the potential of the market alone provided an excellent clue to whether television was judged effective and would be used in 1978. For races with incumbents and challengers, market potential mattered, but so did assessments of campaign chances. Vulnerables and Hopefuls were more likely than Sure Winners or Sure Losers to rely on television advertising

Table 8-3 Television Use by Candidate Status, Assessments of Electoral Chances, and TV Market Potential, 1978*

	TV Market Potential					
	Low (N=31 districts)		Medium (N=26 districts)		High (N=29 districts)	
	Used TV Ads	Judged TV Most Effective	Used TV Ads	Judged TV Most Effective	Used TV Ads	Judged TV Most Effective
Candidate Partisan Affiliation						
Democrats	3	0	52	13	70	36
Republicans	7	4	54	35	79	59
Candidate Status and Assessment of Electoral Chances						
Sure Winners	0	0	43	7	50	0
Vulnerables	0	0	100	33	100	78
Hopefuls	23	8	62	23	71	53
Sure Losers	0	0	29	40	63	50
Candidates in Open Races	0	0	83	33	100	70

* Cell entry is the percentage who used television advertisements or who judged television to be the most effective means of reaching voters in the district. Thirty-one congressional districts had low television market potential, defined as 2500 households or fewer which could be reached per average advertising dollar; 26 districts fell into the medium range of between 2500 and 7500 households per average advertising dollar; and 29 congressional districts had high television market potential where over 7500 households could be reached per average advertising dollar.

in the campaign, so long as the market potential was even moderately conducive to the purchase of air time. For challengers, the use of television advertising in markets with moderately good potential depended on the availability of adequate campaign funds. Hopefuls, as compared with Sure Losers, ran campaigns that were better able to afford television advertising. For incumbents, the use of television advertising in markets with reasonable potential depended upon whether their opponents used television. Nearly three-quarters (73 percent) of the challengers in races with vulnerable incumbents used television advertising, and so did their incumbent opponents. Not only do incumbents who feel threatened by strong challengers react by raising and spending more money, but also they react to their challengers' specific campaign techniques.

For congressional races in districts with reasonable market potential, then, television is indeed an important vehicle for communicating with voters. Campaigns in these places are likely to purchase television advertisements, and their cost usually consumes a major portion of total campaign funds. For one-third of the contested races, however, a poor district-market overlap serves as a major structural constraint on the use of television in the race.

If television advertising is especially powerful as a means of reaching potential voters and if challengers tend to benefit disproportionately from television exposure, then it follows that certain locations provide greater opportunities than others for challengers in their uphill fight to unseat their incumbent opponents. Districts in highly urban settings have poor television markets. They also tend to be lopsidedly Democratic. To consider waging television campaigns, Republican challengers in urban districts have to raise great sums of money. Few are able to do so on their own, and the effectiveness of their challenge suffers as a consequence.

Television advertising is not the only source of voter information, but the same districts that have the poorest television markets also tend to have relatively poor markets for other media. Congressional districts imbedded in big cities present a multitude of structural difficulties to candidates in their efforts to reach potential voters. Metropolitan dailies circulate far beyond any single district's boundaries, and radio signals also reach far into the suburbs. Districts in the urban fringe, especially those across state lines from the major metropolitan centers, also present structural challenges to candidates. The television and radio markets are not only poor, but also their news coverage may be focused on a distant set of races. People in East St. Louis, Illinois, may become better informed about campaigns waged in Missouri than about those in their own state. Suburbs are likely to have their own daily newspapers, however, providing at least one useful vehicle for spreading campaign messages that is often absent in big-city districts.

Campaigns in places with poor mass media markets rely more on other vehicles such as campaign literature, direct mail, or advertisements in weeklies or ethnic newspapers. The reach of such campaign-generated information usually is more limited than the reach of television and major circulation daily newspapers. Even if handouts or mail are delivered to every household in the district, they can be ignored and easily discarded. Weekly or ethnic newspapers may be read, but it is a difficult campaign task to select the set of papers that, taken together, will reach most of the people in the district without lapping over into other districts as well. In contrast, advertisements appearing in the mass media are likely to be seen or heard in passing even by people who pay attention to the media primarily for other, nonpolitical reasons. Therefore, campaigns waged in districts with good media markets have an easier time reaching potential voters than those in poor markets. The quantity of information about congressional campaigns that potential voters see and hear depends substantially on where they live.

Campaign Themes

Operating within these constraints of media markets, campaign strategists decide which themes to emphasize in their materials. The data in Table 8-4 show which types of themes were important in which kinds of campaigns.[13] Virtually all incumbents stressed their personal and political characteristics, especially incumbency or other prior political experience, and ignored their opponents altogether. Vulnerability encouraged incumbents to present a richer set of campaign themes, including issues and constituent services; few Sure Winners emphasized issues in their materials, and fewer than half of them stressed constituency services. On the other hand, most challengers tended to focus on issues. In addition, Sure Losers attacked their opponents, while Hopefuls highlighted their own characteristics in a positive way. Negative campaigning, to the extent that it appeared, was a tactic of decided underdogs who had few options to capture either the media's or the voters' attention. Sure Winners could stay on the high road, confident in their chances of reelection.

Personal characteristics and issues were important themes for many candidates in open races. Partisan affiliation was seldom an important emphasis for anyone except in lopsidedly Democratic districts where Sure Winners were confident of victory, in districts where Democratic candidates in open races tried to capture partisan loyalists, and in places where Democratic challengers had no reasonable alternatives. One-half of the Republican incumbents and one-third of the Democrats never mentioned their partisan affiliation at all, even in a peripheral way.

Except for Sure Winners, many candidates stressed issues as important campaign themes. Therefore, one should not assume that most House candidates avoid discussing issues. Moreover, many candidates appeared

Table 8-4 Important Themes in Candidates' Campaign Materials, by Party, Status, and Assessments of Electoral Chances, 1978*

	Candidate Characteristics	Issues	Constituency Service	Partisan Affiliation	Criticism of Opponent	(N)
All Candidates	65	47	30	24	24	(159)
Candidate Status and Party						
Incumbents						
Democrats	71	39	48	30	2	(44)
Republicans	96	36	44	12	4	(25)
Challengers						
Democrats	57	57	18	36	50	(28)
Republicans	40	55	15	20	48	(40)
Candidates in Open Races						
Democrats	73	46	27	36	9	(11)
Republicans	73	55	18	0	18	(11)
Assessments of Chances						
Sure Winners						
Democrats	65	21	43	32	0	(34)
Republicans	93	29	36	21	0	(14)
Vulnerables						
Democrats	100	100	75	13	13	(8)
Republicans	100	67	67	0	17	(6)
Hopefuls						
Democrats	68	63	26	26	42	(19)
Republicans	44	48	22	22	39	(23)
Sure Losers						
Democrats	33	44	0	56	67	(9)
Republicans	33	60	7	13	67	(15)

* Cell entries are the percentage of campaigns with materials containing a particular type of theme judged to be "predominant" or "important." Because a set of materials could have several important themes, the percentages do not add up to 100 percent.

to address issues with clarity and in considerable detail. A count of the number of clear issue positions taken by House candidates in 1978 shows that, on average, candidates were relatively unambiguous in their positions on five separate issues covered in their campaign literature.[14]

As anticipated, greater competitiveness appears to encourage issue clarity. Vulnerable incumbents took well-defined positions more frequently and on more issues (nine on average) than did Sure Winners (three on average). Benjamin Page's finding—that very heavy news attention to the positions presidential candidates took forced the candidates to be clearer in their issue statements—also applies in the congressional case. However, as discussed in greater detail below, the amount of news attention devoted to issues in House campaigns seldom was very heavy. Only rarely was there enough news attention to make any difference to the clarity of the candidates' issue presentations. When newspaper coverage was unusually heavy, as measured by the number of articles about issues appearing in print, issue clarity increased.

The content of the mass media has a much better chance of reaching most district residents than campaign materials do, in large part because they attend to the media habitually for a variety of nonpolitical reasons. Much of the candidates' literature goes unread, except by a fairly small subset of politically active citizens. The content of campaign news, therefore, gives a better indication than does the candidates' literature of the amount and types of information that are realistically available to most people in the district.

Mass Media Content

Citizens become aware of candidates primarily by reading about them in the newspaper, hearing about them on the radio, or seeing them on television (Parker, 1980). But exactly how much chance is there for citizens to be exposed to House candidates through the mass media? Indeed, how much campaign information of any type is available in different kinds of districts?

Campaign Coverage and Media Markets

A detailed content analysis was completed for stories in 33 separate newpapers covering races in 43 of the 86 districts studied in 1978.[15] On average, there were 6 news stories and 12 articles of all types about a district's race per newspaper over the three weeks studied. This coverage amounts to an average of about one story every two days, hardly an overwhelming quantity of attention. Statements about average newspaper coverage, however, neglect substantial variation across newspapers and districts. The quantity of coverage of the 1978 races varied tremendously, from 1 to 51 items of any type, or from less than 1 item per week to nearly 2.5 items per day. The number of mentions of the Democratic candidate in a newspaper ranged from 0 to 359, and Republican mentions varied from 0 to 265. Some newspapers endorsed a candidate; others did not. Newspapers also varied in the amount of negative and positive tone in the coverage of each candidate.

As with television, the amount of coverage depended largely on how closely a newspaper's circulation area overlapped a district's boundaries. When the circulation area coincided more nearly with district boundaries, campaign coverage was heavier. A measure of newspaper efficiency in a district was developed that was equal to the number of households in the district taking a newspaper divided by the total circulation of that paper.[16] A newspaper's efficiency alone accounted for more than half of the variance (53 percent) in the number of news stories in different papers, and 58 percent of the variance in the total amount of campaign coverage, including advertisements and letters. On average, for each additional 10 percent increase in efficiency, campaign content increased by 2.8 stories and ads over the three-week period. Therefore, the wide range of newspaper efficiencies, from nearly 0 to 100 percent, was associated with large differences in the quantity of coverage. Moreover, as efficiency increased, the newspapers ran longer, more detailed stories. Readers of highly efficient newspapers could find out a great deal more about their House candidates than readers in other places. House contests became more newsworthy as the fit between the newspaper's circulation and district population improved.

Newspaper efficiency in congressional districts is inversely related to total newspaper circulation. Large circulation papers tend to reach multiple districts in a metropolitan area and therefore to be relatively inefficient for any one district. The reach of small circulation papers within the town and environs where they originate often falls completely within one district, although there are exceptions in places where district boundaries cut through their borders. Because of their higher district efficiency, smaller newspapers tend to cover a particular congressional race more heavily than larger papers. The reverse relationship is found in campaigns for other national offices; larger circulation newspapers cover presidential contests more completely than smaller papers (Danielson and Adams, 1961). With larger staffs, more space available for news stories, and a larger number of news services, newspapers with large circulations have more resources to devote to political coverage. In the case of congressional contests, however, these resources must be divided among several different districts, leaving any particular race with relatively little coverage. Therefore, typical urban residents, who read newspapers that are inefficient in their congressional districts, usually have available to them very little news about their House races.

This same relationship between efficiency and quantity of coverage pertains to other media as well. In dense urban areas, radio and television broadcasts reach millions of people in many separate House districts. Coverage of any particular race is irrelevant to most of the broadcast audience, and detailed attention to all of the races would consume large amounts of news time. In contrast, there are rural areas and small towns and cities with local broadcasting outlets that reach an audience roughly equivalent to one or two districts' populations. In those places, the structure of media markets is less a hindrance to campaign coverage. The 1978 study showed that substantially more respondents living in districts with good televison markets saw their House candidates on television during the campaign than those living in poor markets.

Not surprisingly, campaign coverage also increases with the vitality and competitiveness of the race. With the newspaper's efficiency in the district controlled, open races were covered more heavily than any other type of race except those with vulnerable incumbents, which in turn were covered more heavily than contests between Sure Winners and Hopefuls. The lowest levels of coverage went to races with obvious outcomes, those between Sure Winners and Sure Losers. Together, efficiency and competiveness accounted for 70 percent of the variance in the amounts of news coverage across newspapers and districts.

Peter Clarke and Susan Evans (1983) also noted that vital campaigns receive more news attention, but, in apparent contradiction, they found that candidates in open races received almost no news attention at all.[17] The findings presented here diverge from theirs on two points. First, candidates need not spend large sums of money before they receive coverage in the daily press. Some who are fortunate enough to run in districts with highly efficient newspapers are covered frequently in spite of running low-budget campaigns. Others spend large sums of money, yet receive no news attention from the inefficient daily newspapers in their districts. Second, reliance upon a clipping service led Clarke and Evans to underestimate seriously the amount of news coverage of open races.[18] The analysis of more complete data showed six times as much coverage, or 2.5 news stories about open races per week in an average newspaper district, which was roughly the same amount as in contests between incumbents and challengers.

Of course, newspaper efficiency and campaign vitality do not account for all the variation in news coverage. Some newspapers are more attentive, and others less attentive, than would be predicted based on these factors alone. Although systematic data are not available to verify this notion, the newspaper editor's interest in politics probably accounts for a substantial part of the remaining variation. Some editors see elections as the most critical process in our democracy, and they feel a strong sense of responsibility to provide information to voters. Editors who feel that way are likely to devote greater amounts of newspaper resources—both personnel and news space—to cover House races (Goldenberg, 1975).

Differences in Mass Media Coverage

Both candidates in a given race are not equal beneficiaries of news attention or editorial endorsements. As Steven Coombs (MacKuen and Coombs, 1981) observed, the usual Republican advantage in presidential endorsements does not necessarily carry over to endorsements for, or coverage of, lower levels of office. Incumbency and competiveness matter more than party. If endorsements were made in 1978, incumbents were almost always chosen.[19] Moreover, incumbents received greater news coverage as well. As the data in Table 8-5 show, incumbents were mentioned more frequently than challengers in the newspapers.[20] Sure Winners were mentioned an average of 52 times as compared with 37 mentions of their hopeful opponents and only 12 mentions of the Sure Losers. Vulnerables received the most news attention of all, with 161 name mentions as compared with 107 for their hopeful challengers.

Most of the incumbents' advantage came in references to candidate characteristics, such as background and experience, but incumbents also enjoyed substantial advantages in issue coverage. Newspaper attention to other campaign news, such as the candidates' party affiliations, was divided in nearly equal amounts between incumbents and challengers. There was more positive and negative coverage of incumbents than challengers.[21] On average, a substantial proportion of stories about incumbents was complimentary. Incumbents also received slightly more negative coverage than their challengers, although the amounts in each case were quite small. An analysis of coverage in a small subsample of weekly papers with predominant circulation among black readers revealed similar patterns (Campbell, 1983). Incumbents received greater quantities of coverage, more positive tone, and more endorsements than challengers, even controlling for the race of the two opponents.[22]

Some newspapers scrupulously mentioned each candidate equally, while others mentioned the incumbent many times more often than the challenger. One possible explanation for a lopsided coverage advantage of incumbents is that media personnel cover only those challengers who are viable. Clarke and Evans (1983) concluded that challengers fall behind in news coverage because they do not have the experience and background to make themselves newsworthy. The sample data from 1978, however, do not support such an interpretation. Challengers who were considered serious threats by their opponents were as likely to suffer disadvantages in media coverage as those whose prospects were minimal. Furthermore, in five of the six districts where more than one newspaper was analyzed, incumbents had a significant advantage over their challengers in one newspaper but not in the other. In other words, the same challenger captured roughly as much news attention as the incumbent in one newspaper, but captured much less than the incumbent in another newspa-

Table 8-5 Coverage of Candidates in Daily Newspapers, by Status and Assessments of Electoral Chances, 1978

	Incumbents		Challengers			Candidates in Open Races
	Sure Winners (N=33)	Vulnerables (N=8)	Hopefuls Opposing Sure Winners (N=18)	Hopefuls Opposing Vulnerables (N=8)	Sure Losers (N=15)	(N=22)
Name Mentions*	52	161	37	107	12	70
Content Themes**						
Personal/political characteristics	12	39	4	14	2	8
Partisan affiliations	5	13	5	13	3	8
Issues	5	14	2	7	1	4
Content Tone***						
Positive	41	21	10	6	11	28
Negative	6	7	3	6	3	6

* Cell entry is the mean number of name mentions for a candidate in a newspaper in the district.

** Cell entry is the mean number of articles with particular types of content themes.

*** Cell entry is the mean proportion of total articles with positive or negative tone.

per in the district. Obviously, the challenger's background and experience cannot account for these differences across newspapers in the same district.

Leon Sigal (1973) provided a perspective that may account for these differences. He observed that some editors and reporters follow standard operating procedures that unintentionally benefit organized, official sources of news. Incumbents generate news relatively easily by casting votes on bills, announcing government actions of interest in their districts, or appearing at public functions. Unless newspaper editors devote *greater* efforts to producing news material about challengers than incumbents and insist upon equal treatment of both candidates, incumbents easily will outdistance their opponents in the news columns. Some editors and reporters feel a special obligation to treat opposing candidates equally. They insist as a matter of policy that each candidate receive roughly equal amounts of space. Equal time provisions for radio and television coverage provide some legal protections for challengers against such an imbalance, but daily newspapers are under no similar legal obligation to be fair. Their fairness derives from the application of professional standards and editorial policy.

Issue Coverage in the Press

The minimal attention to issues in the daily newspaper coverage of House campaigns, apparent in the data provided in Table 8-5, is somewhat startling given the emphasis that many candidates placed on issues in their own materials. Only in the competitive races between vulnerable incumbents and hopeful challengers did issue coverage exceed a total of 10 stories over the three weeks studied. There were many more stories about candidate characteristics, which is not surprising given the emphasis that candidates themselves placed on their backgrounds and credentials for public office. However, even the candidates' partisan affiliations received more play than issues in the press. This kind of reporting reflects the journalists' tendencies to simplify and codify important attributes of newsworthy individuals, with candidates' party affiliations certainly among the most important. Whether or not candidates are specific about issues in their public speeches, reporters can read campaign literature and use the considerable issue content there to generate news stories. The fact that they seldom do lends support to the view of the media as more interested in candidate images, controversy, and predictions of who is likely to win the election than they are in policy differences.

Once again, however, newspapers varied in this regard. Some contained fairly large amounts of issue content, while others had none at all. How much they contained was largely a function of the efficiency of the newspaper in the district and the competitiveness of the race. The importance candidates' placed on issues also could be traced through their literature to newspaper coverage. The content of the literature served as an indicator of major campaign themes that were stressed in speeches and interviews, providing cues to reporters covering the race.

The linkages between campaign strategy and campaign-generated material, such as literature, are direct. Those between campaign strategy and media content are more indirect. Nonetheless the linkages are there. For challengers, those who emphasized issues in their literature received six times as much issue coverage in the news (2.4 articles) as those who had no prominent issue themes in their campaign materials (0.4 articles). Challengers must emphasize issues to gain media attention. They have no record, and their opponents tend to ignore them. Other than the information they generate themselves, there are few sources of information available to the public about their issue stands.

For incumbents, the situation was different. Their challengers' emphasis on issues was what mattered. If their opponents emphasized issues in their literature, then the incumbents received more than three times as much issue attention in the newspaper (8.6 articles) as did incumbents opposed by challengers who ignored issue themes (2.3 articles). If the challengers intended to use issues to attack the incumbents' records or policy positions, it is not clear that they were successful because there was no corresponding increase in the negative tone of the incumbents' coverage. Although the challengers' strategy may sensitize reporters to important issues in the campaign, journalistic norms dictate that the articles they write be balanced in their presentation. As a consequence, charges by the challenger may be addressed by the incumbent in the same article in a fashion that blunts the critical thrust of the challenger's strategy.

What people learn from newspapers about candidates for the House in their district depends largely on where the people live and which newspapers they read. If their local editor is interested in politics, if their district race is hotly contested, and if their hometown newspaper circulates largely within one congressional district, readers may learn a great deal about the campaign. If the newspaper editor is committed to equal news treatment of opposing candidates, readers may learn as much about the challenger as about the incumbent. Otherwise, news information about congressional contests is likely to be scant and to favor the incumbents, adding to the problems challengers already face. The incumbent's advantage is as likely to occur in competitive as in noncompetitive races. Being seen as a serious contender by the opposition is insufficient as a spur for equal news treatment of the challenger.

Similarly, what people learn from radio and television about House races also is dependent on the quality of media markets in their district. In places with a good overlap of market and district boundaries, broadcasting is an important campaign tool. Political advertising is relatively plentiful, and news coverage is apt to be more extensive. On the other hand, in dense metropolitan areas voters cannot expect to learn much from radio or television about their House candidates. Political advertising costs too much, and news coverage of any particular district race is limited.

Even in places where media coverage is considerable, the amount of attention to candidate backgrounds and personal characteristics far exceeds that paid to issues. This kind of coverage parallels the heavier emphasis given to candidate factors in the materials produced by the campaigns themselves, but the absolute amount of media attention to issues generally fails to reflect a rather substantial and detailed level of discussion of issues in the literature of many campaigns. Nevertheless, what campaigns choose to emphasize does affect what gets covered, and the issue content, to the degree it exists, reflects an emphasis on issues in the race.

The quality of a district's mass media market has important consequences for the amount of information available to district residents. Obviously there are sources of information other than the mass media. Many campaigns are energetic in providing materials of various sorts, but in most cases the mass media remain the public's major sources of campaign information. Where media markets are poor and media content is scant, challengers need vast sums of money to produce and deliver enough campaign materials on their own to make themselves visible. Without visibility, their challenges are doomed to failure.

Notes

1. For a summary of this literature, see Barbara Hinckley, *Congressional Elections* (Washington, D.C.: CQ Press, 1981), chap. 2.
2. See Mark Westlye (1983) for a description of how this name recognition varies in Senate races.
3. For discussions on this point, see Bernard Berelson, Paul F. Lazarsfeld, and William N. McPhee, *Voting* (Chicago: University of Chicago Press, 1954), 321; Samuel Popkin, John W. Gorman, Charles Phillips and Jeffrey A. Smith, "Comment: What Have You Done for Me Lately? Toward an Investment Theory of Voting," *American Political Science Review* 70, 787-788; Hinckley (1981), 10.
4. Richard Stout, review of *Covering Campaigns: Journalism in Congressional Elections*, by Peter Clarke and Susan H. Evans, *Washington Journalism Review*, June 1983, 56.
5. Mann and Wolfinger, 629.
6. Benjamin Page, *Choices and Echoes in Presidential Elections* (Chicago: University of Chicago Press, 1978), 153. Patterson arrived at similar conclusions based on his study of the presidential election of 1976. See Thomas Patterson, *The Mass Media Election* (New York: Praeger Publishers, 1980).
7. Page, 171.
8. Patterson and McClure, *The Unseeing Eye* (New York: G. B. Putnam's Sons, 1976). Also see Page on this point.

9. Cover and Brumberg's imaginative study of the effects of sending "baby books" to new parents demonstrates the usefulness of this technique. See Albert D. Cover and Bruce S. Brumberg, "Baby Books and Ballots: The Impact of Congressional Mail on Constituent Opinion," *American Political Science Review* (June 1982): 347-359.

10. Occasionally free time was available on television and radio for use in the campaign. Under equal time provisions, if a station gives or sells time to one candidate, it also must provide equal time to other candidates for the same office. An additional 10 percent of all managers in the 1978 races said that they used free television time, and an additional 9 percent used free radio time. Although the differences by status and uncertainty hold regardless of whether the broadcast time was paid or free, Sure Losers were the biggest beneficiaries of free broadcast time.

11. Detailed data on television reach are available from the *Broadcasting Yearbook* (1977); data on advertising costs came from "SQAD Offers Spot TV Cost Projections," *Advertising Age,* July 30, 1979, 30. Rate data were for an average prime time 30-second spot for each DMA (the Nielsen equivalent of Arbitron's Area of Dominant Influence). The precise cost listed in *Advertising Age* is only an approximation (and a high one) of what television advertisements actually cost congressional campaigns in 1978, both because costs increased between 1978 and 1979 and because political campaigns are eligible by law for the lowest rate (not the average rate) available.

   An Area of Dominant Influence (ADI) is Arbitron's designation for a unique television market based upon viewing patterns within counties. Each ADI consists of all counties in which the home market stations are the most heavily viewed; each county is assigned exclusively to only one ADI.

   Television reach in a district was calculated for each ADI by determining the overlap between ADI and district maps. ADI households in counties wholly within a district were summed. Then the number of households in counties only partially within the district was either added in entirely or halved depending on whether nearly all or only some of the county's population lived in the district. In large cities, where districts are imbedded within the ADI, the district reach was set at a maximum of 180,000, which was the approximate average number of households per congressional district in 1978, according to the U. S. Census. For districts covered by more than one ADI, the ADI with the best efficiency was chosen. ADI efficiency was calculated as the ADI's district reach divided by the estimated total audience of the ADI.

12. Although the West is not an area of high population density compared with other parts of the country, a large number of the districts in the West that fell into the American National Election Study and, therefore, into our sample as well were districts in densely populated urban areas.

13. As part of the 1978 American National Election Study, interviewers visited the candidates' campaign headquarters and gathered whatever campaign materials were available from the office: posters, buttons, bumper stickers, literature, position papers, texts of advertisements, and direct mail. Trained coders assessed each set of campaign materials in terms of its important themes. Summary codes were assigned to the entire set of materials collected from each candidate's campaign. A number of campaigns had run out of posters, position papers, advertisements, and newsletters by the time the interviewers arrived, but nearly every campaign made its literature available. The summary codes can be used to describe the thematic content of this campaign literature.

   Interviewers ascertained whether each type of campaign material had been used, and noted whether each was obtained, used by the campaign but not obtained by the interviewer, or not used at all. Materials both produced and distributed by the campaign tended to be available. Materials produced by the campaign but distributed by someone else, such as advertisements prepared for inclusion in the mass media, often were unavailable. Therefore, although coders noted that a campaign's themes generally were the same across whatever different types of materials had been collected, summary codes based upon available campaign materials are not adequate descriptions of the content of advertisements in newspapers, radio, or television. Each set of campaign materials was examined for its predominant, important, secondary, and peripheral themes.

14. The American National Election Study coders assessed the clarity of the positions taken by candidates on each of the issues covered in their campaign materials. Each issue was rated in terms of the degree of clarity in the position taken from "clear position taken" to "general, nonspecific statement or solution voiced" to "mention of the issue without further discussion or elaboration." For this analysis, only those issues with the highest clarity ranking were counted as clear.

15. Thirty-three newspapers covering 43 separate congressional districts in the 1978 sample were included in the content analysis. More than one newspaper was analyzed in 7 of the districts, resulting in 55 different newspaper-district combinations. Districts included both close and lopsided races as well as those involving Republican incumbents, Democratic incumbents, and contests for open seats. Because of limited resources, only three of the six weeks prior to the election were examined. Because the amount of news attention devoted to electoral campaigns increases as election day nears, selecting three weeks that include the week preceding, the third week and the fifth week before the election somewhat overestimates one-half of the total six-week coverage.

The newspapers selected for content analysis were a subset of those included in the 1978 American National Election Study. ANES employed a service to clip all campaign news and advertising in daily newspapers in 108 congressional districts over a six-week period from September 27, 1978, through election day. To obtain newspapers that were likely to have readers among the ANES respondents, newspapers with the largest circulation in each district were selected, as well as the newspaper with the largest circulation in places where the ANES interviewed potential voters. A check of the accuracy of the clipping service revealed that roughly two-thirds of the campaign articles and advertisements were missed, and the amount overlooked varied across the sampled newspaper-districts from none to all. Therefore, the amount of campaign coverage in local dailies could not be estimated using the ANES data, and an independent effort was made to secure additional clippings on microfilm and to code them for as many newspaper-district combinations as practicable.

All of the news content about the campaign (news stories, opinion columns, editorials, letters to the editor, advertisements) in selected daily newspapers was clipped for every other week during the last six weeks of the campaign: from October 3 through October 9, October 17 through October 23, and October 31 through election day, November 6, 1978.

16. The efficiency measure required a check on the overlap of district and circulation areas by county, using Circulation. If a county was completely imbedded within a congressional district, then all of the newspaper penetration in that county was attributed to the district. If there was more than one congressional district in a county, then only part of a newspaper's penetration in that county was attributed. Either all or half of the penetration was attributed in these cases, depending on whether nearly all or only some of the county's population lived in the district. In large cities, the proportion of penetration in the city was multiplied times 180,000, the U. S. Census estimate of the average number of households in a congressional district in 1978, to estimate the number of households in the district that read the newspaper.

17. See Clarke and Evans (1983), especially 32 and 47.

18. Ibid., 88 and 95. They reported finding 30 news articles about 22 open race candidates, or 0.4 articles per week in an average newspaper district. This was substantially less coverage than they found for incumbents or their challengers.

19. Clarke and Evans reported that when incumbents ran against challengers, 30 percent of the large circulation dailies did not endorse either candidate. If an endorsement was made, 9 out of 10 went to incumbents (74).

20. The number of mentions of each candidate, including personal pronouns, was counted in

each newspaper story The total number of a candidate's mentions in a particular newspaper is simply the sum of mentions across all stories about the campaign. The content measures were based on coding every paragraph regarding its major emphasis, whether on issues, candidate characteristics, partisan affiliation, or some other theme. In each case, the theme was linked to one or both of the candidates. Summary thematic measures count the number of articles that contain a specific type of thematic content in even one paragraph.

21. Trained coders also assessed each campaign story's tone as positive, negative, or neutral toward each candidate. Positive stories included articles announcing candidate endorsements, articles about a candidate's legislative successes, letters-to-the-editor or editorials with obvious laudatory comments, or stories about a candidate's lead in the polls. Negative stories included editorials and letters-to-the-editor with critical comment, as well as articles about negative candidate ratings by groups, news stories about candidate speeches containing content correcting the candidate's mistakes or quoting nonsupportive observers, and articles about a candidate trailing in the polls. Summary tone measures for each candidate are the number of stories with positive (or negative) tone about that candidate. A story with both positive and negative references was counted twice.

22. Campbell's analysis (1983) was based on campaign coverage in black weeklies in nine districts; eight of the races involved an incumbent and a challenger, and one was for an open seat. All of the incumbents in the nine urban districts were Democrats, so partisan differences in coverage were not in question. There were four pairs of white opponents, three pairs of black opponents (including an open race), and two contests involving one black and one white candidate.

Chapter 9

Voters' Responses to the Campaign

Candidates and their staffs develop campaign strategies and select tactics to appeal for votes. But how can their success be measured? Are campaigns effective in informing potential voters and winning their support? Answers to these questions require data from surveys of voters containing information about their awareness of the candidates, their assessments of them, and their vote choice.

Two types of campaign effects are explored here. First, campaigns, and the information they generate, may inform voters about the candidates and influence individuals as they decide to cast a ballot for one candidate rather than the other. Campaigns may also stimulate voters' interest in the election, increase their political involvement, and propel them to the polls. The most important campaigns for stimulating voter interest and participation, however, are those at the top of the ticket—senatorial or gubernatorial races in a nonpresidential year. House contests only rarely have independent significance for levels of voter turnout.

Recognizing the Candidates

Designing winning strategies is what campaigns are all about. Getting information to the voters about who the candidates are and what they stand for is an important part of campaign strategy for both incumbents and challengers, but their circumstances differ markedly. In addition to campaigning just before the election, House incumbents provide service to their districts and communicate frequently with constituents during their entire two-year term. In effect, the incumbents are campaigning all the time. As a result, voters are more likely to recognize them than their challengers even before the official campaign period begins. During the campaign, this initial recognition advantage can either grow or shrink. Which course it takes depends in part on how vital a campaign the challenger is able to wage and in part on how receptive voters are to the challenger's appeals.

Whether an individual voter recognizes only the incumbent, only the challenger, both candidates, or neither affects who that voter is likely to support. A voter's evaluation of the two candidates has a substantial effect on vote choice as well. Because voters generally have to recognize candidates before they can evaluate them, recognition is a pivotal factor in voting decisions. A voter's partisan identification serves as an initial screen for candidate appeals: messages from the candidate of the same party are received more clearly and positively than appeals from the candidate of the other party.

The general model pursued here and elsewhere (Goldenberg and Traugott, 1981), and that others have pursued in closely related form (Abramowitz, 1975; Mann and Wolfinger, 1980; Ragsdale, 1981) suggests that the voters' choices are a composite of their being able to recognize the candidates and to evaluate them, filtered through the screen of the voters' partisan identifications.

Voters are more likely to recognize incumbents than challengers at the outset. As a result, the election campaigns that incumbents wage are assumed to have less impact on their levels of recognition. This hypothesis has not been rigorously tested, however. Such a test would require the measurement of *changes* in the voters' recognition of a candidate during the campaign period as levels of campaign effort and activity also change. The necessary longitudinal data to test this relationship in nonpresidential contests generally are not available.[1]

Data from the 1978 American National Election Study of voters are presented in Table 9-1 showing the levels of recall and recognition for incumbents and challengers. Recall is defined as the ability of potential voters to remember the names of the candidates on their own. This test of the respondent's knowledge generally is considered more stringent than a test ascertaining their ability to recognize the names on a list. The latter is all that is required of voters after they enter the polling booth.

The levels of both recognition and recall are much greater for incumbents than for challengers.[2] Regardless of party affiliation, one-third of those interviewed after the 1978 election could recognize and recall the incumbents, and another one-half could recognize incumbents without being able to recall their names. Incumbents were about three times as likely as challengers to be both recognized and recalled (34 percent to 10 percent). A majority of those interviewed could not recognize the challengers at all. The candidates in open races had recognition levels that fell in between the incumbents' and challengers'.

Table 9-1   The Relationship Among Candidate Status, Party, and Voters' Recognition and Recall, 1978

| | Respondent Can | | |
	Recognize and Recall	Recognize but Not Recall	Not Recognize
Incumbents			
Democrats	33%	47	19	(892)
Republicans	35%	48	17	(631)
Challengers			
Democrats	12%	35	53	(633)
Republicans	8%	27	64	(884)
Candidates in Open Races			
Democrats	28%	40	32	(227)
Republicans	24%	38	38	(224)

These differences in candidates' recognition and recall are affected by the kinds of campaigns they run. Most incumbents are relatively well known when their campaigns begin. Nevertheless, their levels of recognition by election day are somewhat higher if they spend a great deal of money on their campaign than if they spend little. Controlling on length of service, the incumbents with well-financed campaigns (over $100,000) were more likely to be recognized than incumbents who spent less. However, as the data in Table 9-2 show, spending is even more important for the challengers' level of recognition. They begin as relative unknowns; the more money they can raise and spend, the more familiar they become in their districts.

It is the challenger's spending that determines whether both candidates can be recognized or only the incumbent. At the highest level of challenger spending, two-thirds of those interviewed could recognize both candidates. Only 26 percent could recognize both candidates when the challenger spent less than $25,000, and more than one-half of those interviewed (54 percent) could recognize only the incumbent when spending by the challenger was this low. In contrast, only one in six (17 percent) failed to recognize both candidates when spending by the challenger was at its highest.[3] In open races, spending also is important to recognition of the candidates. The more the candidates spend, the higher the proportion of voters who recognize them.

The translation of money into recognition is, of course, indirect. Money buys organized campaign events at which potential voters can meet the candidate in person, and it buys a variety of contact through the media. Some of this takes the form of campaign-produced materials like direct mail and advertising on television and radio. Straight news coverage is important

Table 9-2 The Effects of Candidate Spending on Levels of Recognition in Congressional Races, 1978

Candidates' Expenditures*	Respondent Can Recognize			
	Incumbent	Challenger	Open Race Democrat	Open Race Republican
Less than $25,000	78% (437)	27% (867)	— (0)	44% (9)
$25,000-$49,999	80% (375)	44% (254)	30% (20)	48% (21)
$50,000-$99,999	77% (355)	59% (192)	68% (124)	53% (71)
$100,000 or more	87% (367)	70% (221)	77% (83)	71% (123)

Challengers' Expenditures	Respondent Can Recognize			
	Incumbent & Challenger	Incumbent Only	Challenger Only	Neither
Less than $25,000	26%	54	1	19 (867)
$25,000-$49,999	41%	40	2	16 (241)
$50,000-$99,999	56%	25	3	16 (192)
$100,000 or more	66%	17	4	14 (221)

* These expenditures correspond to the appropriate recognition variable. To assess recognition of the Democrat, for example, they represent the Democrat's expenditures; likewise for the Republican candidate, the incumbent, and the challenger.

as well, and sometimes it can be generated by staging newsworthy events.

Data are presented in Table 9-3 that demonstrate the importance of personal and media contact with the electorate for levels of candidate recognition.[4] There is no substitute for direct contact between the candidates and their potential constituents. Any personal contact usually leads to recognition among the voters. In fact, levels of recognition for challengers quickly approach those of incumbents when equivalent levels of contact are made. However, incumbents are twice as likely as their challengers to be recognized when there is no contact (75 percent to 38 percent), and the proportion of respondents who have had direct contact with the incumbent is far greater than the proportion who have had a similar opportunity with the challenger. Their permanent supporting staff, especially in district offices, and the opportunities to assist constituents are among the incumbents' clearest advantages.

In lieu of personal contact, some form of media contact is the next most important link to voters. Establishing these links is a primary tactical concern of campaigns. Direct mail advertising and coverage in the news media are important resources for the development of candidate recognition. Because challengers start with lower levels of recognition, the proportionate increase in their recognition levels is greater when contact with potential voters takes place.

Table 9-3   The Relationship Between Direct and Media Contact and the Recognition of Congressional Candidates, 1978

	Respondent Can Recognize	
	Incumbent	Challenger
Personal Contact*		
None	75% (1174)	38% (1467)
Little	98% (209)	81% (43)
Some	99% (103)	87% (15)
A lot	100% (48)	100% (9)
Received Mail		
No	64% (674)	35% (1333)
Yes	94% (860)	74% (201)
Read about the campaign in any paper?		
No	67% (409)	28% (409)
Yes	86% (1098)	44% (1098)
How many articles did you read about the campaign for the U.S. House of Representatives in your district?		
Didn't read any	67% (409)	28% (409)
Just one or two	73% (74)	28% (74)
Several	83% (518)	42% (518)
A good many	92% (486)	49% (486)
Overall Media Exposure		
No media	63% (167)	23% (167)
One medium	75% (291)	32% (291)
Two media	82% (441)	40% (441)
Three media	85% (458)	43% (458)
Four media	92% (177)	58% (177)

* This index is composed of the number of positive responses to questions related to meeting the candidates personally, attending a meeting or gathering where they spoke, or talking to a member of their staff or someone in their office.

Frequent newspaper reading as well as heavy coverage of the campaign in local newspapers also lead to increased levels of candidate recognition. In the sample of districts for which daily newspapers were content analyzed, the more a candidate's name was mentioned, the more widespread was voter recognition of that candidate. Heavier news coverage led to a greater tendency to recognize the candidates even for nonreaders of the newspapers.[5] Recognition among nonreaders probably was increased because heavy newspaper coverage indicates an active campaign that also is covered on radio and television.

Moreover, the difference in levels of recognition for pairs of candidates was related directly to differences in the amount of newspaper coverage they received.[6] That is, when the coverage for two opposing candidates was close to equal, both the challengers and incumbents were recognized by an almost equal proportion of respondents. If coverage of the incumbents was substantially greater than the challengers', then recognition of the challenger faded in relation to the incumbent. There were no instances of substantial coverage advantages for the challengers.

Evaluating the Candidates

Another measure of the electorate's familiarity with candidates is an ability to associate specific issue positions with them. As the data in Table 9-4 make clear, knowing the candidates' position on an issue is unlikely without first recognizing their names. These data show that voters were three to six times more likely to indicate that they could place a candidate along a variety of issue dimensions when they could recognize the candidate.

Some people could place candidates whose names were unfamiliar, and this may have reflected assumptions that people made about probable positions based upon the candidates' party affiliations. Some of these placements probably were inaccurate. Being able to place a candidate on an issue scale is only a minimal test of knowledge because there was no way to verify the accuracy of the respondents' answers. Under this measurement rule, they could place a candidate on an issue, do it incorrectly, and still have it count as "an ability to place." Under a more stringent condition of requiring "correct" placements, the ratio of correct placements for recognized to unrecognized candidates is likely to be even greater.

The relationship between recognizing and being able to place candidates on issues implies that, for most potential voters, knowing the candidate's name is a necessary first step before more demanding judgments are possible. Without basic information on the candidates' identity, explicit comparisons of one candidate to the other cannot be made. In the absence of other information, potential voters are left to cast a ballot for (or against) a party or for (or against) the one candidate who is recognizable—the incumbent.

What is usually considered a candidate's "positive image" is really a composite of two different factors: a voter knowing something about the candidate and then evaluating the information favorably. Positive or negative feelings toward a candidate can be measured by the use of a "thermometer." Each person interviewed by the American National Election Study was asked to assign a warm (positive), neutral, or cold (negative) thermometer rating to each candidate. Relative evaluations of the candidates could be measured by the difference in the thermometer ratings. These differences have been found to be one of the most important predictors of vote choice (Kelly and Mirer, 1974; Miller et al., 1976).

Table 9-4   The Relationship Between Recognition of Congressional Candidates and Ability to Place Them on Issues, 1978

	Proportion of Respondents	
	Who Can Recognize the Candidate	Who Cannot Recognize the Candidate
Who place the Incumbent on		
Liberal/conservative political views[a]	74% (965)	20% (195)
Government guaranteed jobs[b]	71% (1025)	20% (220)
Rights of the accused[c]	59% (1100)	18% (245)
Government aid to minorities[d]	64% (1148)	17% (258)
Government/private medical insurance[e]	52% (1056)	17% (232)
Equal rights for women[f]	56% (1184)	24% (176)
Who place the Challenger on		
Liberal/conservative political views[a]	47% (496)	13% (660)
Government guaranteed jobs[b]	38% (592)	11% (719)
Rights of the accused[c]	38% (541)	12% (799)
Government aid to minorities[d]	40% (574)	12% (834)
Government/private medical insurance[e]	35% (524)	11% (763)
Equal rights for women[f]	41% (582)	11% (873)

[a] We hear a lot of talk these days about liberals and conservatives. Here is a seven-point scale on which the political views that people hold are arranged from extremely liberal to extremely conservative. Where would you place (the Democratic/Republican candidate) on this scale?

[b] Some people feel that the government should see to it that every person has a job and a good standard of living. Others think that the government should just let each person get ahead on his own. Where would you place (the Democratic/Republican candidate) on this (seven-point) scale?

[c] Some people are primarily concerned with doing everything possible to protect the legal rights of those accused of committing crimes. Others feel that it is more important to stop criminal activity even at the risk of reducing the rights of the accused. Where would you place (the Democratic/Republican candidate) on this (seven-point) scale?

[d] Some people feel that the government in Washington should make every possible effort to improve the social and economic position of blacks and other minority groups. Others feel that the government should not make any special effort to help minorities because they should help themselves. Where would you place (the Democratic/Republican candidate) on this (seven-point) scale?

[e] There is much concern about the rapid rise in medical and hospital costs. Some feel there should be a government insurance plan which would cover all medical and hospital expenses. Others feel that medical expenses should be paid by individuals and through private insurance like Blue Cross. Where would you place (the Democratic/Republican candidate) on this (seven-point) scale?

[f] Recently there has been a lot of talk about women's rights. Some people feel that women should have an equal role with men in running business, industry, and government. Others feel that women's place is in the home. Where would you place (the Democratic/Republican candidate) on this (seven-point) scale?

Table 9-5 The Relationship Between Recognition of Congressional Candidates and Relative Evaluations of Them, 1978

	Relative Evaluation			
Relative Recognition	Favors Challenger	Neutral	Favors Incumbent	
Both Incumbent and Challenger	17%	25	58	(583)
Incumbent Only	8%	17	75	(656)
Challenger Only	52%	30	18	(27)

Data are presented in Table 9-5 that compare the relative recognition of pairs of candidates and relative evaluations of them.[7] When only one of the candidates could be recognized, the evaluation advantage fell to that candidate. Three-quarters of those who could recognize only the incumbents evaluated them more favorably; likewise, one-half (52 percent) of those who could recognize only the challengers evaluated them more favorably. A positive evaluation was more likely to follow recogition of the incumbent than the challenger. And there were many more people who could recognize only the incumbent than could recognize only the challenger. When both of the candidates could be recognized, the evaluation advantage went to the incumbent by a margin of about three to one (58 percent to 17 percent). This result probably can be attributed to the higher levels of information the electorate has about incumbents, including voting records, service, and previous contact with constituents. Overall, incumbents have the edge; their advantages clearly extend beyond recognition to evaluation. Both concepts are important to victory at the polls.

Recognition, Evaluation, and the Vote

At the individual voter's level, candidate recognition and evaluation are significant in explaining whether and how people vote. Several studies have illustrated how candidate preference can be explained using these two concepts in conjunction with the voter's party identification.[8] The essence of these more complex analyses is presented in the data in Table 9-6. The relationship between evaluations of the candidates and vote choice is neatly captured there. When respondents evaluated one candidate more positively than the other, the favored candidate received the lion's share of the vote. This was as true when the challengers were favored as when the incumbents were, but few respondents evaluated the challengers more positively. When the relative evaluations were neutral, incumbents always held an advantage in votes over their challengers.

Table 9-6   The Relationship Among Recognition, Evaluation, and Vote Choice, by Candidate Status, 1978

	Respondent Voted for		
	Incumbent	Challenger	
Respondent Could Recognize			
Both Candidates and Evaluation			
Favored Incumbent	94%	6	(125)
Was Neutral	53%	47	(51)
Favored Challenger	3%	97	(58)
Incumbent Only and Evaluation			
Favored Incumbent	93%	7	(302)
Was Neutral	79%	21	(42)
Favored Challenger	35%	65	(26)
Challenger Only and Evaluation			
Favored Incumbent	—	—	(1)
Was Neutral	—	—	(0)
Favored Challenger	0%	100	(8)
Neither and Evaluation Was Neutral	67%	33	(45)

These relationships endure despite the party identification of the voters. Democrats were more than twice as likely to assign positive evaluations to Democratic candidates than to Republicans, but Democrats who felt more positively toward Republican candidates voted for them by a three-to-one margin (74 percent to 26 percent). By the same token, most Republicans favored Republican candidates, but they supported Democratic candidates by a five-to-one margin (83 percent to 17 percent) when they assigned more positive evaluations to the Democrats. In virtually all of the cases where voters' relative evaluations favored candidates of the other party, those candidates were incumbents. The respondents voted for them because the incumbents' positive images outweighed the pull of partisan affiliations.

Defections in contests for other offices also are affected by these same considerations, but without such strong advantages to incumbents. In statewide races, which involve higher levels of expenditures by all candidates and substantial visibility for the challengers, the potential for being able to evaluate both candidates is greater. As a result, defection rates in statewide races are different from those in House races. As the data in Table 9-7 show, defections of voters from their own party's candidate to an incumbent of the other party were more frequent in the House races than in higher level contests. Defections to challengers were less frequent in House than in statewide races. As a consequence, House incumbents pick up much more support from voters of the other party than they lose from voters

Table 9-7 Defection Rates of Partisans in Elections for Governor, U.S. Senator, and U.S. Representative, in Races Involving Incumbents, 1978

Races Involving	Governors' Races		U.S. Senate Races		U.S. House Races	
	Democrats' Defection Rates	Republicans' Defection Rates	Democrats' Defection Rates	Republicans' Defection Rates	Democrats' Defection Rates	Republicans' Defection Rates
Other Party's Incumbents	40% (100)	31% (126)	30% (141)	29% (31)	56% (137)	52% (132)
Other Party's Challengers	14% (159)	10% (82)	15% (74)	9% (102)	5% (253)	3% (146)
Ratio of Defection Rates (Incumbents/ Challengers)	2.86:1	3.10:1	2.00:1	3.22:1	11.20:1	14.00:1

of their own party. The ratio of the two defection rates—incumbent to challenger—was four to five times greater in House races than in the senatorial or gubernatorial races.

The model presented here has general utility for understanding the voters' response to candidates' campaign activity. A campaign's net effect on individual voters' choices is a consequence of whether the voters recognize one or both opponents and how evaluations of them compare. The vitality of their campaigns has significance for recognition and evaluation, although campaign messages are filtered through the voter's partisan identification.

Campaigns and Voter Turnout

Campaigns are designed to stimulate, inform, and mobilize potential voters. One of the important purposes of a campaign is to communicate the idea that electing one candidate rather than the other will make a significant difference to government performance. By convincing potential voters that their participation is important, campaign strategists hope to encourage high turnout among their own supporters.

The level of interest in political campaigns has been recognized as a significant predictor of voter participation since the initiation of survey-based electoral research (Campbell et al., 1960). Variations in levels of interest, which have been observed between presidential elections in the "on year" and congressional elections held at the same time or separately in the "off year," have been used to explain characteristic differences in voter turnout. A pattern of "surge and decline" (Campbell, 1966) is the most visible manifestation of this phenomenon, resulting in a saw-toothed pattern of overall turnout in national elections that rises in presidential years and declines in the off years. Even in the on year, the turnout rate for election of the president exceeds turnout for congressional races on the same ballot.

The usual explanation for this pattern is the variation in the stimulus of the campaigns. This, in turn, is a result of a number of factors, including the differences in the visibility of presidential candidates and those running for lower office, the relative amounts of money they spend on their campaigns, and the relative amount of media coverage they receive. These factors taken together form the essence of the vitality of the campaign. Politics is not ordinarily a very important part of the daily lives of most citizens. Campaigns and the media coverage and political discussion they engender signal an approaching election, and this combined hoopla arouses the interest of many citizens on a cyclical basis.

Demonstrating a linkage between the vitality of House campaigns and voter interest even in an off year is a difficult research proposition for a number of reasons. First, most states run concurrent senatorial or gubernatorial elections that generate much more campaign activity than the House race. These higher level campaigns, not the House campaigns, stimulate people to participate. Without appropriate attention to the entire electoral context, the impact of House races on turnout cannot be isolated.

Second, high levels of political interest are associated with high levels of education and past political activity, as well as the voters' recognition of the importance of participation in the political process. All of these factors are associated with information seeking and knowledge about politics. Vital campaigns might affect peoples' interest in politics in different ways, depending on their levels of education. Consequently, the simultaneous effects of these factors also need to be considered.

Third, money can be spent in many ways to further a candidate's interests, including conveying messages to people who are already quite interested in politics. These include political activists, loyal party workers, and potential contributors. Because of their substantial involvement in politics at the outset of the campaign, their levels of interest, as measured by a standard survey question, might not be expected to increase. Sometimes money is spent lavishly on techniques and activities without commensurate payoff. For example, some campaigns choose to pay high prices for the production and placement of advertisements on television in places where the market potential is poor. Therefore, research attention also must extend to the products that result from campaign spending and the constituents who are contacted by or through them.

Last, and most important, the relationship between campaigning and interest is a dynamic one. Before the campaign, one normally would expect to observe low levels of interest in politics; then, as the campaign gets under way, the candidates' activities provide the stimulus for levels of interest to increase. The general election campaign is a period filled with extraordinary political content and greater opportunities for the discussion of politics. An appropriate demonstration of this dynamic process requires longitudinal data with repeated measures of voter interest and campaign activity across the campaign period. However, most of the data that are available come from only one time point, frequently from a postelection survey. Given this methodological problem and others, most researchers either have chosen to accept or been forced to treat political interest as a relatively fixed characteristic of members of the electorate rather than as a consequence of the campaign itself.

Thomas Patterson's study of the 1976 presidential campaign is a notable exception (Patterson, 1980). His project involved a panel study of potential voters in two cities, combined with content analysis and exposure measures related to the media the voters saw or heard. Over time and locale, Patterson found that interest increased early in the candidate selection process—through the primaries—but did not increase further during the general election period. Moreover, he found that interest was a function of exposure to the media. There is clearly a dynamic process depicted here: over time, attention to the news resulted in increased levels of interest in the campaign, even when controlling on the individuals' prior levels of political interest. Patterson also found stronger recognition effects from exposure to reporting in newspapers than to television news, although both effects were significant and consistent throughout the campaign.

As has been noted, television's reporting of congressional races is less thorough than its coverage of presidential elections because of the generally poor fit between the stations' signal areas and congressional districts. Some newspaper circulation areas may present the same problem, but others are more closely aligned with district boundaries. They usually provide more coverage, in greater detail, than television. Even in districts with good markets, however, the overall level of coverage devoted to House races is much lower than that given to presidential contests and much more concentrated in the period just prior to election day. As a consequence, the effects that Patterson identified should be stronger for newspaper exposure than television exposure in House races, and growth in the level of interest stimulated by media coverage should begin much later in the campaign and continue through most of the election period.

Does exposure to the media actually heighten interest in the campaign, or do people already interested in politics seek out media coverage? The answer is probably both. In the 1978 study, people who said they were interested in the campaign reported that they had read more stories about it. The stories were available to all the readers, but only the interested group chose to read them. On the other hand, in a subset of districts in which detailed content analysis of selected papers was performed, there was a positive relationship between the quantity of coverage and the level of campaign interest of readers within the coverage area. That is, people who read quite a few articles about the campaign in newspapers with heavy campaign coverage were more likely to be interested (58 percent) than were readers of newspapers with relatively light campaign coverage (46 percent). The very highest levels of interest in the campaign were found among heavy readers in places where newspapers covered the local contest generously.

People can choose whether to read their local newspaper and whether to pay attention to the articles in it. Those who are already interested in politics probably pay closer attention than others to whatever campaign articles are available. People who want to read a local newspaper, however, usually have little opportunity to select one that appeals to them. Today many cities and towns have only one newspaper. As a consequence, heavy readers could not choose a newspaper to reflect their prior campaign interest. Rather, the content of the newspaper that happened to circulate where they lived enhanced their interest in the House campaign.

Turnout, too, was related to media exposure and media content. As the data in Table 9-8 show, turnout was the highest for those who indicated

Table 9-8   The Relationship Between Media Exposure and Turnout, 1978

	Voter Turnout	
Do you read a daily newspaper?		
No	31%	(844)
Yes	60%	(907)
Read about the campaign in any paper?		
No	26%	(470)
Yes	62%	(1243)
How many articles did you read about the campaign for the U.S. House of Representatives in your district?		
Didn't read any	26%	(470)
Just one or two	45%	(82)
Several	56%	(566)
A good many	71%	(572)
Overall Media Exposure		
No media	22%	(190)
One medium	36%	(324)
Two media	52%	(522)
Three media	64%	(510)
Four media	72%	(205)

most exposure to campaign coverage for each of the media-related predictors, even when levels of education were controlled. Moreover, turnout among the heaviest readers was higher in districts with more newspaper coverage of the race than in districts with less coverage, indicating an independent effect of the media content on political participation.

Although it is difficult to trace a direct and consistent link between the vitality of House campaigns and levels of voter interest or participation, there are strong indications that the media affect political interest and voter turnout. A definitive demonstration of these relationships will have to await research that is designed specifically to test for their existence.

In this chapter, the foundation for the study of the effects of congressional campaigns on individual voters and the role of the media in them has been established. The concepts of candidate recognition and evaluation are central for explaining vote choice, and the concept of interest is central for explaining turnout.

Contact with the candidates—both direct and indirect—affects whether voters recognize individual candidates. Recognition usually is a precondition for evaluation of the candidates, which, in turn, is the essential determinant of vote choice. While party identification plays an important role in this process, information about the candidates and their issue positions is very important, too. Furthermore, exposure to the media appears to heighten voter interest and turnout, although a full investigation of the role that House campaigns play in inducing participation awaits a design more appropriate to the research task.

Notes

1. In a panel study Traugott conducted for the *Detroit News* during the 1982 Michigan senatorial campaign, Sen. Donald Riegle's recall level in the electorate increased from 18 percent to 40 percent from August through late October. At the same time his Republican opponent Philip Ruppe, less well financed and organized, had levels of recall that rose from 11 percent to 25 percent in the same period. This case suggests that incumbents are not always well known, or even substantially better known than their challengers, at the start of their campaigns. It also suggests that any candidate's familiarity to the voters can benefit from campaign effort and activity and the associated news coverage.
2. Eubank and Gow (1983) have suggested that the placement of the recognition items in the 1978 survey questionnaire inflates levels of recognition for incumbents. The consequence for the analysis reported here is that the relationships between media exposure/content and candidate recognition probably are understated when compared with those that would appear with alternative measurement.
3. The effects of spending on recognition persist when the spending patterns of pairs of contestants are combined. It is only when expenditures by both the incumbent and the challenger were higher that the challenger's recognition level increased. There were a few races in which the challengers outspent the incumbents, but none in which a challenger's expenditures were high and those of the incumbent were low.
4. In comparisons of Democrats and Republicans, the patterns of effects are similar.
5. Because of the limited amount of data with information from both sources (911 respondents in 43 congressional districts where content analysis was also available), the coverage measure was categorized as low (fewer than 10 articles), medium (10 to 25 articles), and high (26 or more articles). One simple measure of readership was obtained from the question "Did you read about the campaign in any newspaper?" But the more discriminating measure for readers was "How many newspaper articles did you read abut the campaign for the U. S. House of Representatives in your district—would you say you read a good many, several, or just one or two?"
6. The concept of "relative coverage advantage" was measured as the ratio of the difference in the number of name mentions of the Democratic candidate to the number of mentions of the Republican candidate divided by the total number of mentions for both. Some Republican challengers received more coverage than their Democratic incumbent opponents, but it was never substantial. There was no coverage advantage at all for Democratic challengers.
7. The thermometer ratings are treated here differently from the way they are treated in the measurement of recognition. For evaluative purposes, the inability to recognize a candidate was treated as a neutral (exactly 50 degrees) thermometer rating. If the other candidate was evaluated positively (above 50 degrees), the relative evaluation was positive; similarly for a negative evaluation (less than 50 degrees). Hence, an evaluation difference could be based entirely on the assessment of only one candidate. A neutral relative evaluation of zero, therefore, reflected an inability to evaluate either candidate or the assignment of equal ratings to them.

Looking at the assessment of pairs of candidates based on their partisan affiliation, one can see that the effects of relative recognition are clear. When both of the candidates are recognizable, the evaluation is as likely to favor the Democrat as the Republican, and the proportion of neutral relative evaluations is high. When only one candidate in the pair can be recognized, the candidate is overwhelmingly evaluated in a positive way.

8. Three different methodologies have been used to confirm the utility of this model. Goldenberg and Traugott (1981) demonstrated its utility in predicting the vote using regression, with appropriate controls on newspaper readership and levels of education in the electorate. Ragsdale (1981) employed simultaneous equations to demonstrate the differential effects recognition and evaluation in races for the U. S. House and U. S. Senate. Abramowitz (1980) used path analysis to identify the genesis of evaluation differentials in these races as well.

	Understanding
Chapter 10	Electoral Success

Understanding how a campaign affects individual voting decisions is important, but it represents only one perspective on campaign effects. The voters are subject to two simultaneous campaigns, the net consequences of which are the candidates' vote shares on election day. Allowing for the baseline partisan support in the district, some candidates do better than expected while others do worse. Winning obviously is important in the short run, and predicting the outcome usually is straightforward: in nearly all cases, incumbents win and challengers lose. In recent years, only about 1 incumbent representative in 20 who sought reelection failed to recapture the seat—better odds than for most sporting events. When district-level votes are analyzed, it is possible to assess the consequences of the campaign process on the direction and size of the victory margin.

Winning is not everything in electoral politics. Election results have long-term significance as well because successive campaigns are part of a dynamic process of candidate selection and retention. For almost every candidate, the most difficult general election campaign is the first, even for the winner. Early in their careers, incumbents are more vulnerable to defeat (Cover, 1977). With reasonable attention to their work and constituents, incumbents find retention of their seats becomes easier with seniority. As tenure increases, they commonly face successively weaker challenges or no challenge at all. As a consequence, long-term incumbents frequently achieve larger margins of victory.

Despite the fact that they usually win, not all incumbents perform equally well in defense of their seats. Discounting important differences in the basic political properties of their districts, there is still remarkably wide variation in the vote-getting ability of different incumbents. The following analysis shows that these variations can be attributed largely to the vitality and sophistication of their campaigns, as well as to the quality of their challengers and the campaigns they wage.

Measuring Electoral Success

One of the most commonly used measures of electoral performance or success is the candidate's proportion of the total vote cast. For incumbents, a derivative measure is their share of the vote in the current election compared with their last race; the challengers' performances sometimes are assessed in terms of their share of the vote relative to the previous efforts by their party. These measures present a number of conceptual and methodological problems.

The division of the vote cast on election day is a measure that encapsulates all of the characteristics of the district—both political and demographic—as well as the status of the candidates and their activity and behavior during the campaign. As such, the size of a candidate's vote share reflects not only the campaign activities and the candidates in the current contest but also long-term characteristics of the district that are largely beyond the campaign's control. Therefore, it is not a satisfactory measure of how campaign techniques affected electoral success.

Similarly, the difference between a candidate's vote share in the last election and the current one captures more than the campaign effects of the latest contest. It also reflects campaign effects of the earlier race. It is quite possible to win a greater vote share in the current election, even though the candidate's campaign is less vital and effective than the last time, because the opposition is also much weaker than last time. To relate campaigning to outcomes, a different measure is needed.

An alternative, the deviation from the normal vote, avoids many of the problems cited above. The long-term political characteristics of a constituency, represented in its underlying distribution of partisanship, are captured in the normal vote estimate. As a measure of underlying partisanship, it represents the *expected* outcome of an election in lieu of a specific pair of candidates and their campaigns. The actual results of the election deviate from the normal vote, and this difference reflects short-term factors such as the contestants' specific personal characteristics, resources, strategies, and issue agendas.[1] The relative success of candidates can be assessed in terms of how well they ran against an expected performance based on partisanship in the district. Given the underlying support that reasonably could be translated into votes on election day, how much better or worse did the candidates do? Deviations from the expected outcome indicate that one candidate had a net advantage over the other in short-term factors associated with the campaign.

In two-person races, one candidate's gain is the other's loss. The direction of the deviation from the district's basic partisanship indicates which candidate did better and which worse than expected. The size of the deviation reflects the magnitude of short-term effects. Factors that are important in explaining the size and direction of the deviation are campaign advantages (or disadvantages) of one candidate over the other. For example, one can look at what each candidate spent and assess the consequences of a spending advantage for the difference between the actual voter response and the expected outcome.

A Model of Electoral Success

The model developed for individual voters in Chapter 9 also applies at the congressional district level with only slight modification. The dependent variable that captures electoral success shifts from the vote preference or defection of an individual to the deviation from the normal vote of a district. The significant predictors remain candidate recognition and evaluation, although for analysis at the district level these concepts are measured as the relative recognition and evaluation advantages in the district of one candidate over the other.[2]

The general model that combines these factors is depicted in Figure 10-1. There are two sets of concepts associated with deviations from the normal or expected vote. One consists of factors related to candidate recognition, such as incumbency status, the media attention given to the two opposing campaigns, and the other types of campaign activity that result in contacts with members of the electorate. The second set of concepts is associated with voters' evaluations of the two candidates. They include the quantity and quality of campaign coverage, which are, in turn, a function of the workways of the press in the district, the vitality of the two opposing campaigns, and their resource allocations, especially their media efforts.[3]

Candidate recognition is central because it has a direct effect on electoral success as well as an indirect influence through candidate evaluation. Being better recognized than the opponent is an important advantage. In fact, unlike candidates for the Senate and other statewide offices, both candidates for the House usually are not evaluated one against the other (Ragsdale, 1981). House incumbents often are opposed by "invisible" challengers who cannot be recognized, let alone evaluated, by the electorate. Therefore, a recognition advantage in House races often is enough to ensure reelection. Only in cases where the challengers have sufficient resources to improve their familiarity in the district or where they are unusually well-known are the challengers likely to be evaluated. When that happens, differences in how the two candidates are evaluated become an important influence on vote choice.

The effects of media strategies on electoral outcomes are of particular

Figure 10-1   A Model of the Relationship Among Media Factors, Relative Candidate Recognition and Evaluation, and Electoral Success

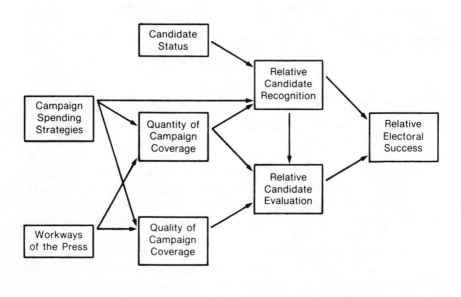

interest. A growing body of literature from the 1970s suggests that media coverage is important to the outcome of elections, although the evidence offered is rather indirect. Most commonly, broadcast expenditures have been linked to the partisan vote division (Dawson and Zinser, 1971; Jacobson, 1975; Palda, 1973). Typical of these efforts, Jacobson reported that a candidate's radio and television expenditures, taken as a proportion of total expenditures, are a positive predictor of the candidate's proportion of the total vote. This relationship held even when incumbency status and the partisan division of past district votes were controlled.

Although media expenditures capture the advertising effort of a campaign, they do not represent the effects of editorial endorsements or the consequences of more or less extensive news coverage. Newspaper endorsements have been shown to make a difference in contests for national and statewide offices (Coombs, 1980; Robinson, 1974). They are likely to be important in congressional contests as well, where serious name recognition problems and low levels of voter interest and information are present. Regular news coverage contributes to candidate name recognition, and one candidate's advantage over the other in news attention is important to electoral outcomes.

Testing the Model

The analysis was conducted in two parts, each employing a multivariate analysis technique, which permitted an assessment of the effects of multiple factors on electoral outcomes. First, the relative recognition of two opposing candidates was examined as a function of how much coverage they received in the media. Four measures of coverage were used, including advantages in endorsements, television advertising, other media advertising, and newspaper coverage. Second, the electoral success of the two candidates was examined as a function of their recognition and the quantity and quality of their coverage in the media.[4]

The first phase of the analysis employed five independent variables to predict recognition advantage for the Democrat. One measure was developed from the American National Election Study survey responses, two were developed from information obtained from the surveys of the campaign managers, and two from a combination of the expenditure reports to the Federal Election Commission and television market penetration data from *Broadcasting Yearbook.* Each was constructed along a dimension ranging from relative advantage for the Republican candidate to relative advantage for the Democratic candidate.

Ideally, each candidate's name recognition would be measured through a preelection survey of potential voters in the district just before election day. Because such a measure was unavailable, recognition was measured with an agreement index that was based on the campaign managers' judgments about which candidate was better known by election day.[5] At either extreme, the index showed that both managers agreed that one candidate held the recognition advantage, while its midpoint indicated agreement that neither candidate was advantaged.[6]

Measures of various kinds of media content ideally would draw on detailed analysis of the relevant media in the districts. Because the content of newspaper coverage of the races was available only for a subset of districts and the content of television coverage was unavailable altogether, alternative measures had to be developed. The first two of these—coverage advantage and editorial endorsement advantage—were drawn from the managers' survey. To check against the bias of self-interested reports, the measure of quantity of coverage was formed as an index of agreement between the Democratic and Republican managers in each district. The two managers were asked whether either candidate was advantaged with respect to the quantity of media coverage and, if so, which candidate. The two managers' responses were then combined to form scales that ranged from agreement on Republican advantage to agreement on Democratic advantage. The midpoint is agreement that neither candidate was advantaged.

The measure of editorial support was somewhat different. Although

managers were asked about the endorsements of both their own candidate
and their opponent, they were well informed only about their own candidates; many said that they had no idea whether or not their opponents had
any newspaper backing. As a consequence, only knowledge about their
own candidates was used. The index assumed a high value if only the
Democratic candidate was endorsed, a low value if only the Republican was
endorsed, and an intermediate value if both or neither received editorial
support.

The best approximations of relative amounts of media advertising were
separate measures of the amounts the candidates spent for television and
for other media. The two measures of expenditure advantage were calculated from the detailed reports of general election expenditures filed with the
FEC from July 1, 1978, onward. They provided information on total
expenditures in this period, as well as allocations to advertising in general
and to broadcasting in particular. One measure included all advertising
expenditures except television. It was constructed as the difference between
the Democrat's and Republican's expenditures divided by their sum. This
resulted in a number that varied between -1 and +1. The other used a
similar ratio of television expenditures. Because both opponents ran in the
same district and paid the same rates for advertising in the same media, the
difference in their total television advertising dollars provides a reasonable
estimate of their relative media efforts. A large effort by a candidate in a district with poor television market potential, however, will yield less payoff than
a large effort in a district with a good television market. Therefore, the ratio
of television expenditures was multiplied by the indicator of TV market
potential.[7]

Data are presented in Table 10-1 that show the results of the first phase
of the multivariate test in which recognition advantage was predicted from
advantages in general advertising expenditures, news coverage, endorsements, and television, taking market potential into account.[8] All of the signs
are positive as expected. Together, the independent variables explain one-
half of the variation in recognition advantage. The most important factors
are endorsements, virtually all of which went to the incumbents, and the
quantity of coverage in newspapers. The measure of television expenditures
for each candidate also is important. However, the measure of relative
advantage in other forms of media spending is not statistically significant.

If a variable that indicates incumbency is added to this equation, the
proportion of explained variance increases to 81 percent, virtually all of it
due to the incumbency measure.[9] The conceptual significance of the results
presented in Table 10-1 is that three media variables can explain a large
portion of the variance that normally is attributed to an incumbency
advantage in recognition. Being an incumbent means, in addition to other
things, receiving more news coverage, more endorsements, and having
more money to spend on television advertisements.

Table 10-1   The Regression of Candidate Recognition on Media Effects in Congressional Races, 1978

Variable	Partial Correlation Coefficient	Regression Coefficient	T-Statistic
Proportion of TV Expenditures x Potential Market	.23	.04	2.13**
Proportion of Other Media Expenditures	.10	.18	.92
Endorsements	.45	.55	4.55*
Quantity of Coverage	.30	.33	2.85*

Multiple R   =   .71 (F = 20.8)
Standard Error   =   1.16
Constant Term   =   .57
N   = 85

* Significant at the .01 level.
** Significant at the .05 level.

The results from the second part of the model, in which deviations from the normal vote were predicted, are presented in Table 10-2. The dependent variable required the generation of estimates of the normal vote for congressional districts that could be subtracted from the actual election returns to yield a deviation in favor of one party or the other. The procedure used is described in the Appendix. Five predictor variables account for 81 percent of the variation in candidate successes. A candidate's recognition advantage clearly is the most powerful factor: greater recognition of one candidate over the other produces a deviation from the normal vote in the first candidate's favor.

Both the quantity of coverage and the proportion of television expenditures are strongly related to electoral success, suggesting their importance in the support of recognition and in the process of evaluation as well. In particular, television expenditures play a more important role in increasing vote margin than might be expected based solely on their impact on candidate recognition. This suggests that television advertising plays an additional campaign role because its thematic content is designed to influence voters' evaluations of the candidates.

Exploring this possibility further requires information gathered over time on the evaluations potential voters make of each candidate in each district

Table 10-2   The Regression of Democratic Deviations from the Normal Vote on Media Effects and Candidate Recognition in Congressional Races, 1978

Variable	Partial Correlation Coefficient	Regression Coefficient	T-Statistic
Recognition	.74	6.84	9.74*
Quantity of Coverage	.36	2.63	3.46*
Proportion of TV Expenditures x Potential Market	.25	.31	2.25**
Proportion of Other Media Expenditures	−.09	−.99	−.81
Endorsements	.12	.94	1.10

Multiple R   =   .90 (F = 66.1)
Standard Error   =   7.30
Constant Term   =   −32.70
N   =   85

* Significant at the .01 level.
** Significant at the .05 level.

and detailed content data from television ads. Neither endorsements nor other media expenditures contributed independently to extraordinary electoral success.

The importance of television advertising in stimulating positive evaluations of candidates is supported by a replication of these same equations with the data transposed to represent the incumbents' advantages relative to their challengers. In general, all of the predictor variables operate in the same fashion although with less explanatory power.[10] The effects of television advertising in these replications were the strongest for Republican nonincumbents. This finding may result from partisan differences identified in previous chapters, in particular that the National Republican Congressional Committee, more often than its Democratic counterpart, targets money and highly skilled in-kind assistance to challengers and candidates in open races who have the best chances of success.

As a consequence, Republican nonincumbents are in an excellent position to gain maximum advantage from their generally higher television expenditures. If the NRCC makes advertisements available at lower than commercial rates, then Republican advantages in television advertising are even greater than their dollar advantages suggest. These are all areas for further research.

A preoccupation with the turnover of seats from one party to another in congressional elections overlooks substantial variation in campaign performance in races for the U. S. House of Representatives. In each election virtually every district outcome deviates from the expected partisan division of the vote, and the range of these deviations is quite wide.

It is important to understand variations in electoral performance because, across elections, they contribute to the security or insecurity of the incumbents who occupy office. Candidates who can win by larger margins than suggested by the underlying partisanship in their district can add to their attractiveness as candidates for higher office and advance their careers in the party. Relatively poor performances and the feelings of insecurity they produce may prompt more aggressive behavior by incumbents in providing constituent service and raising additional campaign funds for their next reelection bids. Important political consequences of the current campaigns may be seen in the level of competition and the vitality of subsequent electoral contests. Key party activists judge candidate performance by various criteria, some of which are quite different from deviations from the normal vote. What these criteria are and how they are used are additional questions for future research.

Media content is demonstrably important to electoral outcomes. Advantages in the quantity of attention by the news media as well as endorsements and greater resources to purchase campaign-controlled advertisements are of obvious benefit to the favored contestant. Media advantages translate directly into recognition and evaluation advantages that in turn lead to favorable margins at the polls. Examples of all of these factors at work are given in the case studies of congressional campaigns presented in the next chapter.

Notes

1. Deviations from the normal vote also reflect more than the general election campaign. An incumbent who wins support because of constituent service throughout the term, or in earlier terms, benefits from that behavior in terms of a positive deviation from the normal vote in the district. Of course, some voters may ask, "What have you done for me lately?" In the absence of recent incumbent effort on their behalf, voters may be expected to revert to support of their own party's candidate.
2. There is no need to include a measure of district-level partisanship advantage in this model because it is already incorporated into the measurement of the dependent variable.
3. As demonstrated in Chapter 8, the potential of the media market is an important determinant of both the campaign's media effort and the amount of news attention devoted to the campaigns. But the market potential is the same for each candidate in the same district and therefore has no effect on one candidate's advantage over the other unless their financial resources are taken into account as well.
4. Ideally, data on candidate evaluations from representative samples of constituents would be used to construct a measure of relative evaluation to test this model. Neither these data

nor an appropriate substitute from the managers' survey was available. Therefore, the media coverage variables were included because of their expected significance for voters' evaluations of the candidates.

5. The 1978 American National Election Study postelection survey did include a question about recognition, but there were problems with using it. See Eubank and Gow (1983). In addition, the samples of potential voters in each district were too small and too clustered to produce accurate estimates of recognition levels per district.

6. For these agreement scores, a value of "1" indicates that both managers agreed that the Republican candidate was advantaged; "2" that one manager felt the Republican was advantaged, but the other didn't know who was; "3" that both agreed that neither candidate was advantaged; "4" that one manager felt the Democrat was advantaged, but the other didn't know who was; and "5" that both agreed that the Democrat was advantaged. In virtually no races did the managers disagree by indicating that different candidates were advantaged. When that was the case, the district was eliminated from the analysis.

7. The measure used here is the same as the one called "market potential" in Chapter 8, divided by 1,000. Therefore, it represents the number of households (in thousands) that could be reached by television in the best Area of Dominant Influence (ADI) in the district. The market potential measure ranged from 0.7 to more than 33, and the other variables in the equation ranged from -1 to +1 or 1 to 5. Dividing market potential by 1,000 is a scale transformation that does not affect the results of this equation.

8. Ordinary least squares regression was used in this analysis. The model presented in Figure 10-1 functions equally well for predicting deviations from the incumbent's (or challenger's) normal vote as for deviations from the Democrat's (or Republican's) normal vote in each district. In the first case, only the contested races involving incumbents can be analyzed; in the second case, open races can be added to the analysis.

9. For the purposes of the regression in Table 10-1, the incumbency variable was measured with the values of 1 = Democratic challenger, 2 = Democratic candidate in an open race, and 3 = Democratic incumbent.

10. This model would be improved with additional specification to account for incumbents' contact with constituents and the various services they provide to them. These activities are part of their "continuous campaigning," which can elevate their recognition levels far above their challengers. Without taking these factors into account, the proportion of variance explained in their relative recognition advantage is almost certainly attenuated.

Four Campaigns
Chapter 11 and Their Consequences

Case descriptions of several typical congressional contests can illuminate the development and effects of campaign strategies because they bring together the various parts of the campaign process. They complement statistical analysis by providing a more complete and detailed sense of the reality of each campaign. Where individual cases fail to fit the general patterns identified through statistical analysis, they challenge our general understanding and frequently point toward directions for future inquiry.

The following case studies are composites of races from the 1978 sample. The information for each case is based on the interviews with managers, reports from the Federal Election Commission, materials collected by the American National Election Study, newspaper coverage, and various other public sources. The names of the candidates in the cases are fictitious to protect the confidentiality promised to those who were interviewed.

Because of the central role played by the managers' assessments of likely electoral outcomes, the cases were selected to represent the circumstances of four typical campaigns. The first illustrates a race in which a confident incumbent is opposed by a challenger whose manager expects to lose. In the second case, a challenger whose manager is hopeful of victory is pitted against a confident incumbent. The third is the campaign of an incumbent whose manager feels vulnerable because of a vigorous challenge by a serious opponent. And finally, an example is presented of an open race in which both sides work hard in the face of uncertainty about the result.

Previous chapters have presented a model of campaign behavior that suggests managers develop particular strategies and employ tactics that take into account the unalterable realities in the district, their theories of election, and their overall assessments of their candidates' chances of winning. Therefore, each case begins with a description of the district setting, the beliefs of both managers about who and what matters in waging successful campaigns in their district, and the managers' assessments of who will win. The resulting campaign strategies and tactics of the two opponents are then described. Included in this description are the breadth of each campaign's targeting in the district, the primary campaign themes, the techniques selected to carry those themes to potential voters, and the allocation of campaign funds.

These cases illustrate the connections between strategic behavior and election outcomes. How much the potential voter learns about House candidates depends in part on the campaigns that are waged and in part on characteristics of mass media content beyond the campaign's control. Many citizens never become aware of their district's candidates, especially the challengers. Recognizing the candidates may be unimportant for voters who habitually support one party or the other. For them, campaigns hardly matter anyway. Candidate recognition also may be unimportant for those citizens who use their votes for House candidates to express approval or disapproval of the performance of national party leaders. In the main, however, House races are local affairs, and before a voter will support a candidate of the opposite party, that candidate must become visible and known. To the extent that House campaigns make a difference, they do so by generating information and raising the level of candidate recognition. Each case, therefore, also includes a description of the information environment of the contest, the level of each candidate's recognition in the district, and the outcome of the race. Obviously no single case can capture all the variety found in each of the four general types of campaign circumstances. The conclusion of each case describes interesting variations on the predominant themes it typifies.

Case 1: Congressman Confident vs. Mr. Choice

The Setting

In this big-city district in an industrial state, the manager for the long-term incumbent felt like a sure winner. Representative Confident was a Democrat in a district that everyone agreed was heavily Democratic. He was well known. He had run unopposed in the primary and appeared unassailable, given his large pluralities in the past several elections.

The challenger, Mr. Choice, acknowledged that "the incumbent will win and it won't be close at all." He acted as his own manager and ran his campaign out of his home with a skeletal staff and a minimal budget. Mr Choice had decided to run the day before the filing deadline. His decision rested on the strong belief that "Nobody should run for public office unopposed. Voters should have a choice." He faced no opposition in the primary because few were interested in waging what was widely regarded as a losing battle. At the time he was interviewed, Mr. Choice said he had no real campaign organization in place yet and that it would be difficult to do much in the short time remaining before the election.

The incumbent's campaign manager had been one of his administrative assistants, previously on his congressional staff payroll with responsibility for running a local office. He had logged considerable experience in earlier campaigns. His role in this campaign was to see that the proper filing took place, to take advantage of any free media opportunities, to evaluate the opponent, and generally to monitor campaign developments and alert the incumbent if he needed to raise more money or become active in the campaign. There were no plans to raise any substantial amount of money unless it was needed. The campaign staff was composed of a few volunteers, with professionals available should their services become necessary.

Theories of Election

Both managers believed traditional party loyalties would be a very important, indeed the most important, factor in the race. Both said the experience of the incumbent also would be important. Neither manager expected issues to sway many votes, although both candidates were outspoken on the issues anyway.

Both managers described the district population in much the same terms: blacks, including white collar and blue collar workers, and the poor. Other groups in the district included unions, churches, and various community organizations. Most voters were expected by both managers to support the incumbent.

Campaign Strategy and Tactics

For different reasons, both managers planned to target very broadly in their campaigns. Mr. Choice, a Republican, had no alternative but to appeal to Democrats and independents because there were so few Republicans among the district's voters. He needed to reach out beyond his own partisans to attempt to forge a winning coalition. He said he wanted to reach "independent thinkers, willing to hear the Republican point of view." Congressman Confident could take the high road, appealing to all eligible voters in the district to go to the polls on election day, regardless of their preference. His manager admitted that "we had enough of a buffer (in a registration advantage) to do that."

Despite the certainty of his loss, Mr. Choice exerted himself in the campaign. His positions on major issues were substantially more conservative than the incumbent's. By his own admission, Mr. Choice's positions were more distant than the incumbent's from the preferences of most people in the district. Nevertheless, Mr. Choice persisted in presenting his viewpoints in campaign literature and newspaper interviews and through free radio and television time.

Overall, Mr. Choice spent less than $1,000 on his campaign, nearly all of which went for campaign literature. His opponent spent less than $5,000, but could have raised and spent considerably more had it been necessary. Most of Congressman Confident's campaign spending went toward paying rent for a campaign office. He produced only one piece of campaign literature—on economic issues—and otherwise relied on free media time and space. Given the poor television market in this urban district and the low-cost nature of both campaigns, television advertising never was considered. Some radio time was provided by candidates for other offices who asked Representative Confident to speak on their behalf. The direct mailing to potential voters was sent early by Congressman Confident's staff so that it could be mailed for free using his franking privilege as a member of Congress.

The Information Environment

Both managers identified the same three newspapers as the most influential in the district and the best sources of campaign news. Two of these newspapers were content analyzed as part of the study. Neither was very efficient in the district, and together they contained only 5 news stories and 12 articles or advertisements of any kind referring to this campaign during the three-week period studied. Confident was mentioned 16 times, and Choice only 4 times. Both newspapers endorsed the incumbent.

In spite of this sparse coverage, both managers said newspapers provided better coverage of the candidates and the campaign than radio or television. Broadcasting alternatives were very inefficient in this big-city district. That tended not only to discourage campaigns from purchasing advertising on radio or television but also to diminish the amount of news attention devoted to any one campaign—especially to this lopsided campaign—by local radio and television stations.

The Outcome

With such low levels of campaign activity and information, the challenger remained invisible to potential voters. Not a single American National Election Study respondent in this district recalled the challenger's name or even recognized it when his name was offered. Congressman Confident was recognized widely, but only 10 percent of the ANES survey respondents recalled his name on their own.

Neither manager was surprised by the outcome of the election—a landslide victory for Congressman Confident, who garnered more than 90 percent of the vote. He performed much better than would be expected based solely on the district's 70 percent Democratic edge.

Conclusions

The outcome of nearly half the congressional races in 1978 was never in doubt: one in five was uncontested and another one in four was a certain victory for the incumbent. Of the Sure Winner-Sure Loser races, more than half involved low-level campaigns, such as this one, occurring in urban districts with normal votes better than 55 percent in favor of the Democrat. Clearly, even though these races were contested in a technical sense, the campaign had little impact on citizen knowledge, preference, or action on election day. Only in the event of some unusual circumstance, such as an incumbent's death, would the presence of a challenger on the ballot in this kind of race make any appreciable difference.

But not every Sure Winner-Sure Loser race is as inactive as the one described above. As we saw in Chapter 7, sometimes incumbents spend a great deal of money even in races against weak challengers to win decisively and to further other political goals. Moreover, some incumbents spend money by giving it to other candidates for office. That, too, contributes to their political influence, although it has little consequence for their own campaigns.

For example, one incumbent soundly defeated his opponent but outspent him 25 to 1 in doing so. Congressman Record ran an active media campaign, placing advertisements on 8 television stations, on 16 radio stations, and in 9 daily and 41 weekly newspapers, stressing his record as an incumbent representative. His challenger was unknown, poorly funded, and inactive. The challenger, according to his own assessment, offered not the slightest threat to Congressman Record's reelection. Record's manager agreed. The incumbent's 1978 campaign was primarily an investment for the future, not a response to any current threat.

Case 2: Congressman Aplomb vs. Mr. Wealthy

The Setting

Congressman Aplomb ran as a Republican incumbent in this conservative, well-to-do, suburban district. In spite of a constituency closely divided between Democrats and Republicans, both managers considered this district traditionally safe for Republicans candidates. Although facing an unusually aggressive challenger, Representative Aplomb's manager was certain of victory. "He won two to one last time and has a better campaign organization this time with the same opponent," he said. There had been no opposition in the primary, and Aplomb's staff had raised much more money by primary time than was required. He was well known and thought to be in tune with the views of his constituents. He had paid careful attention to constituent service for the past two years.

Mr. Wealthy was making his second try to unseat the incumbent. Money was plentiful because of Mr. Wealthy's independent means. His professional, hard-driving campaign staff, provided with generous amounts of cash, was hoping to stage an upset. Wealthy's manager was a young salaried consultant from outside the state who worked along with eight other paid employees. The campaign used a paid telephone bank. The manager thought the opposition was poorly organized and believed Wealthy could win by running a highly professional campaign. "We are going to put together a much better campaign than the incumbent will," he claimed.

Congressman Aplomb's manager was a volunteer with little previous campaign experience. The campaign relied heavily on volunteer coordinators in each of the many separate communities in this district. However, others on the staff were paid professionals, including an accountant, a press aide, and an advertising specialist.

Theories of Election

Both managers described the district population in similar terms: diverse and middle class. In addition, Mr. Wealthy's manager expected the growing Hispanic population to prove an important element in the district's electorate. Both managers acknowledged the slight Republican majority in the district. They also mentioned that there was a substantial number of registered Democrats, who nevertheless tended in past elections to vote for the Republican incumbent.

Before the election, the opposing managers had different views of which factors would be most critical to voters' decisions. Congressman Aplomb's manager thought his candidate's background and experience as an incumbent would be the most important consideration for voters, with partisan identification only moderately important and issues relatively unimportant. "In this district, people don't tend to discuss issues much," he said. Mr. Wealthy's manager acknowledged that incumbency and party were two big advantages for the opponent, but he felt that his candidate's energy and attractiveness, when combined with several hot local issues, could produce a winning campaign. He did not expect partisan affiliations to be very important to voters' choices. By the time of the postelection interview, both managers' views had shifted in similar directions. Both believed partisan affiliation was the most important factor in the campaign, followed by incumbency and the name recognition and experience that it implied. Both agreed that neither national or local issues had been important.

Campaign Strategy and Tactics

The targeting strategy of Congressman Aplomb's campaign concentrated on traditional conservative Republicans to ensure their turnout and on Democrats in areas that had supported a previous referendum calling for tax limitations. There were three campaign messages: "support the incumbent," "we want the votes of Democrats, too," and "please be sure to vote." Mr Wealthy's campaign had a more diverse set of targets—people living in an area near a proposed sewage disposal site, Democrats, senior citizens, women, and people with Spanish surnames. The messages stressed by Wealthy's campaign concentrated on safety from environmental pollution, safety from domestic abuse, concern for the Hispanic community, and personal attacks on the character of the incumbent. Each campaign engaged in fairly specific targeting and tried to communicate appropriate messages to different sets of residents.

The district presented difficult communications challenges to both campaigns. Television, radio, and major daily newspapers were highly inefficient vehicles for reaching district residents. Although there were a number of small efficient daily and weekly newspapers, neither manager was convinced that they were especially effective in the district. Both campaigns ended up trying a wide variety of techniques to convey their messages. Congressman Aplomb relied on direct mail and literature, especially to appeal to conservative Democrats, as well as advertisements in daily and weekly newspapers and radio spots. He also was the beneficiary of advertising done on his behalf by powerful political action committees in various national media. In contrast, Mr. Wealthy spent nearly half his campaign funds on television advertisements, in spite of the highly inefficient market. He also used billboards, yard signs, literature, direct mail, and radio spots—in short, every vehicle available—but his was primarily a television campaign.

Wealthy bought substantial television time to run advertisements about two weeks before the election. He spent more than Congressman Aplomb or his manager had expected. The incumbent, as a consequence, did some last minute fund raising and poured additional money into radio advertising; it was too late to buy television time. More money was raised than could be spent, and his campaign ended up with a surplus of about $25,000. Even with the last minute media blitz, nearly half of Aplomb's funds went to staff and office expenses, and less than a quarter went to advertising. In contrast, Mr. Wealthy's office expenses consumed a much smaller proportion of the total amount spent; the largest category of spending by far was advertising. In total, Mr. Wealthy outspent Congressman Aplomb more than three to one in advertising dollars.

For these two candidates, national issues were unimportant—their positions on most issues were indistinguishable. Each manager judged constituent views on national issues the same way and felt both candidates properly reflected district preferences. Only on local issues was there disagreement, and Mr. Wealthy was unable to make these differences work for him.

The Information Environment

Both managers identified the same newspaper as most influential in the district, and it was content analyzed. This newspaper circulated far beyond the district boundaries. It contained only three news stories and five articles of any type concerning the election during the three weeks studied. Both managers anticipated that the incumbent would have the advantage in news coverage, and indeed he did. Congressman Aplomb was mentioned 14 times, and Mr. Wealthy was not mentioned by name even once. The newspaper endorsed the incumbent. The challenger, Mr. Wealthy, ran one advertising insert in this paper, but it did not appear during the three weeks of coverage that were analyzed.

In spite of the inefficiency of the most important daily newspaper and the sparse amount of news attention devoted to this race, both managers agreed that campaign coverage was better in the daily newspapers than on radio or television. The broadcast markets were even more inefficient, and news coverage on radio and television was relatively rare. Nonetheless, one particular television news story was judged by both managers to be critical to the decisions of some voters. During the campaign, a natural disaster occurred in the district, and lives were lost. Congressmen Aplomb was interviewed on television; he was presented as a concerned and effective representative. Mr. Wealthy called a press conference, but local television did not use any of the material from the conference, nor was he identified by name anywhere in the story.

In the absence of an unusual media event, neither candidate could have expected news attention from television or radio stations in such an inefficient market. When such events occur, however, they are defined by media personnel as disaster stories, not campaign stories. As such, they provide an important advantage to incumbents who can capture news attention in their official capacity as they react to the event. Because this kind of story rarely is covered by the political reporter assigned to the campaign, the press is unlikely to provide partisan balance to the incumbent's remarks. Ignoring the challenger is perfectly acceptable according to the professional norms of news reporters and editors. In this particular instance, with so little other news coverage of the race in any of the major media, one news story was judged by both managers to be quite important.

The Outcome

In spite of running an aggressive and costly campaign, Mr. Wealthy lost by a large margin. He captured only 35 percent of the vote, nearly the same margin as two years earlier. On the other hand, by the time of the postelection ANES interviews, more than half (58 percent) of those interviewed in this district recognized Mr. Wealthy's name. Although his active campaigning undoubtedly improved Wealthy's name familiarity in the district, the fact that 42 percent of the respondents still did not recognize him is an indication of how poor the television market was that he relied on.

Conclusions

This case demonstrates that money does not always make a difference to an election's outcome, especially in a poor media market where television strategies cost a great deal. The marginal vote advantage of each additional dollar of campaign funds depends on how, where, and when the money is spent, not simply on the total amount. Some would judge that Mr. Wealthy's campaign simply wasted great sums of money by concentrating on such an inefficient means of communication.

Before the election, it is difficult for challengers or their managers to admit that they have no hope of winning. Of the contested races in 1978, those pitting a Sure Winner against a Hopeful were the most common type. Some of the Hopefuls were either fooling themselves or trying to maintain a confident public image. But some of them were seriously hopeful and acted in ways that can be understood better once this feeling is recognized. Three-quarters of the races where managers for challengers hoped to defeat the incumbent were in districts with almost equal partisan divisions. More than half the Hopefuls were able to raise and spend substantial amounts of money either in absolute terms or relative to their opponents.

If victory on election day is the sole criterion of success, then Hopefuls who ran campaigns against Sure Winners were dismal failures. Even those challengers with credible reasons for hopefulness were unsuccessful in capturing House seats from confident incumbents in the 1978 sample. Nevertheless, the campaigns that Hopefuls ran and the campaigns of their incumbent opponents were active in terms of the amounts of money spent. Sure Winners spent much more money when they ran against Hopefuls than when they ran against Sure Losers.

Moreover, campaign activity yielded real dividends in terms of better informed voters. In Hopeful versus Sure Winner contests, not only were the challengers recognized by more than twice as many potential voters on average as were challengers in Sure Winner-Sure Loser races, but even the incumbents were more widely recognized than were their counterparts in less hotly contested races. To the extent that information on the issue positions and capacities of candidates accompanies familiarity with their names, voters in districts with active campaigns can make better informed choices. In addition, challengers who succeed in making themselves known in the district, even if they lose the race, may become formidable opponents in the future.

Case 3: Congressman Quaking N. Boots vs. Mrs. Conservative

The Setting

Congressman Boots, a member of the Watergate class of Democrats first elected in 1974, ran a tough race for reelection in this district, which is composed of several medium-sized cities surrounded by rich agricultural land. The district showed obvious Republican leanings in votes cast for president and the Senate, but the partisan division of voters in the district was extremely close, and Congressman Boots had won two previous elections with small but respectable margins of 2 to 3 percent. Both managers acknowledged the closeness of the district, but Boots's manager said it tilted toward the Republicans, and Conservative's manager said it was becoming more independent.

Congressman Boots's manager was a paid staff member, and he had several paid employees working with him. Nevertheless, he was essentially an amateur who had little campaign experience before 1978. There had been no opposition in the Democratic primary that year, so his skills and campaign organization had not yet been tested. He acknowledged that both Boots and Conservative had a good chance of winning and that the result would be close.

The challenger, Mrs. Conservative, employed a professional manager with a great deal of prior campaign experience, including managing four congressional races and coordinating the state campaign for Ronald Reagan's presidential bid in 1976. He supervised five other paid employees. Mrs. Conservative had prevailed over strong competition in the Republican primary, raising and spending more than $100,000 to do so. She had won despite her total lack of experience in elective, appointive, or party office, overcoming unanimous newspaper support for her primary opponent. Mrs. Conservative's manager acknowledged that Congressman Boots was ahead in October but thought Conservative might win on election day because of her campaign's strong organizational skills.

Theories of Election

Both managers believed the incumbent's record would be a very important factor in the race. They agreed that Boots would benefit from the excellent service he had provided in his district over the past two terms. They also agreed that inflation, property taxes, and government spending were the major issues facing the country and the people in their district and that the challenger would benefit from her strong conservative stands on those issues. The incumbent's manager saw the district as quite attentive to issues, crediting almost half the people with following national issues closely.

Neither manager expected party affiliations to be very important. Both thought high turnout would help the Democratic incumbent, but Conservative's manager predicted that turnout would be low, with the exception of conservative Republican voters stimulated by the challenger's campaign.

Their theories of election did not shift noticeably from the preelection to postelection interviews. Mrs. Conservative's manager still believed the incumbent's record and associated issues, personal characteristics of the candidate, and turnout levels were very important, while party was relatively unimportant. Congressman Boots's manager also cited issues, personal characteristics, and turnout as key factors in the race.

The two managers described the district's population in roughly the same terms: identifiable swing groups included farmers and former farm residents who had moved recently to the cities. Organized labor was mentioned prominently as an electoral force behind Congressman Boots, along with students at a local college, while Catholic opponents of abortion were seen as likely supporters of Mrs. Conservative.

Campaign Strategy and Tactics

These two candidates naturally used very different targeting strategies. Congressman Boots, a Democrat, concentrated on independents to build a winning coalition in a slightly Republican district. Mrs. Conservative focused on her own supporters—conservative rural residents and "right-to-lifers."

According to their managers, the candidates' issue stands also were quite different. Mrs. Conservative was placed at the extreme conservative end of each issue scale by her own manager as well as by her opponent's manager. Conservative's manager felt her views accurately reflected those of the people in her district, while he described Boots as extremely liberal and out of touch with district views. In contrast, Congressman Boots's manager placed his candidate toward the center, only slightly to the left of people in the district who were described as leaning toward the conservative end. In other words, both managers agreed that the challenger was quite conservative in her views and that most people in the district were more conservative than the incumbent. The managers disagreed sharply, however, in their assessments of how distant the views of each candidate were from the preferences of most district residents. Therefore, they also disagreed in their overall judgments about how much Conservative would benefit.

In his campaign messages, Congressman Boots emphasized his service to constituents and his experience as an incumbent. He raised considerably more than $100,000, with the help of 30 PACs, and spent it primarily on airing four separate television advertisements. Television was a very efficient medium in this district. For relatively modest amounts of money, candidates could place advertisements on stations that reached virtually every person within the district and few people beyond it. Daily newspapers also were highly efficient advertising media, although most of them had such small circulations that few people could be reached with any particular advertisement. Congressmen Boots also placed ads in 12 daily newspapers, in 25 weeklies, and on 20 radio stations. His staff conducted two surveys during the campaign and received free polling assistance from the Democratic Study Group. His campaign produced three pieces of issue-oriented direct mail, specifically targeted at the elderly, veterans, and small business owners, and two general handouts that focused on the incumbent's image as a good representative.

Mrs. Conservative spent nearly twice as much as her opponent in the general election campaign, having already spent a great deal to win the nomination. She benefited from help provided by various sources outside of the district—the National Conservative Political Action Committee (NCPAC) provided free publicity, Ronald Reagan's Citizens for the Republic helped with polling, and the party and various PACs provided free targeting and research assistance. Reagan appeared with her in the district. Conservative relied heavily on television appeals, with substantial amounts spent as well on direct mail, get-out-the-vote drives, and radio and newspaper advertisements. Her campaign themes emphasized her honesty and reliability and her commitment to solve important public problems by using conservative approaches. Mrs. Conservative employed sophisticated direct mail techniques to raise even more money than expected through issue appeals and attacks on her opponent's record. In all, more than 50 separate mailings were sent, each carefully targeted to a specific occupational or other interest group. More than three dozen PACs responded by contributing to Mrs. Conservative's effort. With money in hand, she ran essentially a television campaign that emphasized her personal qualities. She also produced multiple handouts and placed advertisements in 6 daily newspapers, in 44 weeklies, and on 17 radio stations. Hers was an aggressive and well-funded challenge.

Midway through the campaign Congressman Boots was surprised by his unknown opponent's ability to raise such large amounts of money for television advertisements and to command national support and visibility. In reaction, Boots's campaign raised an additional $40,000, hired a professional advertising agency, and ran more television spots. Boots felt threatened, and he reacted by increasing his active campaign effort. Vice President Walter Mondale and Lillian Carter, the president's mother, stumped for Congressman Boots in the district. At that later point in the campaign, Boots was still leading in the polls and did not attempt to raise any more money.

The Information Environment

Conservative's manager mentioned four daily newspapers as influential in the district; Boot's manager mentioned two. Both said that newspapers provided better campaign coverage in their district than television or radio. Each picked the same daily newspaper as the most influential, and the content of that paper was analyzed.

During the three weeks covered in the analysis, this newspaper published 30 articles of all types about the House campaign, including 17 news stories. Although Mrs. Conservative's manager anticipated that the incumbent would have an advantage in the amount and tone of news coverage, he thought some aspects of the coverage favored the incumbent and others favored the challenger. The incumbent was mentioned 127 times to Mrs. Conservative's 94 mentions. Boots was mentioned more often in stories about the two candidates' political background and experience. Because Conservative never had held a previous political or governmental post, it is hardly surprising to find that her experience was mentioned fewer times. Coverage of other topics was much more equal. Boots was endorsed by every one of the four newspapers considered most influential in the district, and both managers felt the media's coverage of the candidates' debate favored the incumbent. On the other hand, Mrs. Conservative outdistanced Congressman Boots slightly in the number of complimentary references that appeared in the newspaper, and she suffered only one-quarter as many negative comments.

Efficient newspaper, radio, and television markets, together with two aggressive and well-funded advertising campaigns, produced a rich information environment. Virtually every ANES respondent in this district recalled reading about the campaign in the newspaper and seeing something about the campaign on television.

The Outcome

Mrs. Conservative won a surprising upset by a margin of less than 2 percent. By election day, both candidates were recognized by almost every ANES respondent, and well over half of the respondents could recall on their own the names of both candidates. Mrs. Conservative's growth in recognition represented a dramatic improvement over her nearly total invisibility at the outset of the campaign.

Conclusions

It is rare for House incumbents to lose elections, even when they are challenged by aggressive, well-financed opponents. Nonetheless, it can and does happen occasionally, and that reality contributes to the nervousness other incumbents feel. By all traditional measures other than money, Mrs. Conservative did not appear a formidable challenger. Although her opponent was a short-term incumbent who was disadvantaged somewhat by the partisan division of voters in his district, she was inexperienced and unknown. Modern fund-raising techniques and outside help provided generous financial support for Mrs. Conservative, and her campaign staff used that money efficiently and effectively in a district with a good television market. This case is an example of what can be accomplished by a well-financed and well-managed challenger under highly favorable circumstances.

In a similar contest between a Democratic incumbent and a conservative Republican challenger in a slightly Republican district with a poor television market, the outcome was different. The challenger spent nearly three times as much as his opponent, an amount in excess of $150,000. The challenger concentrated on issue themes through a television campaign in spite of the poor market. The incumbent reacted by trying to raise additional funds, but he was only marginally successful. His campaign budget was never adequate to buy much television time in such an expensive area.

The challenger's television effort had only a moderate pay off. Half the ANES respondents recalled seeing television coverage of the campaign, and slightly fewer recognized the challenger's name when asked. Virtually no respondents were able to recall the challenger's name on their own. On the other hand, very few of those interviewed were able to recall the incumbent's name either, and fewer than half of them recognized the incumbent's name when it was provided. The challenger's campaign strategy raised his visibility in the district to the level of his opponent, but it was not very high for either.

The newspaper market in this district also was poor, lacking a single efficient daily newspaper. Although district residents were educated, relatively affluent suburbanites who tend to be well informed on national issues, they relied on metropolitan news sources that carried virtually no stories about the House race. For local news, they read small weekly newspapers. The modest levels of candidate recognition in a district with an active campaign and with potential voters who were interested in politics can be attributed to the poor overlap of media markets and district boundaries.

In addition to money, this challenger enjoyed other advantages. He hired an experienced, professional manager, he benefited from strong local and national party support, and he ran in a district with Republican leanings. Despite all this, he lost by a narrow margin in 1978. However, his aggressive campaign set the stage for a successful challenge in the next congressional election.

Case 4: Mr. Primary vs. Ms. Experience

The Setting

The long-term Democratic incumbent of this urban/suburban district decided to retire before the 1978 election. For years, he had enjoyed easy reelections and considerable popularity in the district. His retirement prompted a serious effort by Ms. Experience, a Republican, to capture the seat and a highly competitive contest among the Democrats for the nomination, in which Mr. Primary surprisingly defeated two well-known area politicians.

Ms. Experience had held local elective office for some time. She was seen by her opponent's manager as hard working, service oriented, good at raising money, and well recognized in the district. She had little competition in her primary, but she nevertheless raised and spent nearly $100,000, much of it on advertising. Her staff had five paid members, including her manager, who expected to win a close contest.

Mr. Primary's manager was an experienced advertising professional and political consultant. Five additional paid employees worked for him. Although he expected to win based on polls that showed his candidate in the lead, he acknowledged that "it could change." Mr. Primary raised and spent more than $200,000 dollars staging his upset in the primary. More than half of that paid for advertisements on local television stations in a saturation effort lasting seven weeks in the spring. That effort was credited widely with transforming a certain loss into a respectable primary victory. Television exposure improved Mr. Primary's name recognition in the district considerably over its initial low level. However, according to Ms. Experience's polls, by early October she was still more widely recognized than her opponent.

Theories of Election

Both managers recognized that the Democrats enjoyed a small registration edge in the district but saw the district population as becoming more conservative over time. Before the election, Ms. Experience's manager attributed little importance to the partisan inclinations of potential voters. "People will not vote down party lines because of my candidate's experience, energy, and responsiveness," he said. He cited survey evidence to support his view. To impress potential voters with his candidate's qualifications and to counter expected claims by the opponent, he knew that large sums of money would be essential. Ms. Experience's manager expected national issues to be quite important in the race, not because the candidates differed sharply on the issues, but because he expected voters to support Republican candidates in reaction to President Jimmy Carter's poor performance. By the postelection interview, Experience's manager had changed his mind. Based on his campaign experience, he saw partisan affiliation as very important and issues as relatively unimportant. However, he persisted in his belief that adequate funding was essential and speculated that more money would have enabled Ms. Experience's campaign to overcome the partisan disadvantage in the district.

Mr. Primary's manager held a different view. He expected the election to hinge on the voters' perceptions of the personal characteristics of the two candidates—their decisiveness, energy, and wisdom. To wage a successful campaign based on building a positive image for his candidate relative to the opponent, large sums of money were needed. Primary's manager did not expect candidate positions on national issues to be at all important. Rather, he anticipated a considerable advantage for his candidate based on the partisan affiliations of voters in the district. His election theory did not change over the course of the campaign.

Campaign Strategy and Tactics

According to their managers, both candidates targeted their campaign appeals to white, middle-class Democrats and some Republicans. In addition, Ms. Experience targeted women. Mr. Primary used issue themes in television advertising to praise his decisiveness and to condemn Ms. Experience's ineffectiveness. According to his manager's account, these advertisements relied upon the stereotyping of women as unable to make decisions. Ms. Experience's campaign messages emphasized that she was experienced, hard working, and female.

Television advertising was a moderately good buy in this district. Primary's manager was convinced that their district was "uniquely suited to television." During the primary he had reacted to their opponents' heavy use of television by doubling Mr. Primary's television advertising. This tactic had proved so successful that he decided to repeat it during the general election. He concentrated more than $100,000 of campaign funds on television in the general election and spent virtually nothing at all on radio or newspapers. In his judgment, the kind of message he wanted to emphasize was well suited to television. He developed 15 separate advertisements for use on four television stations.

Ms. Experience used a variety of communications vehicles, but throughout the campaign she reacted in kind to her opponent's use of television. Her campaign produced five advertisements for use on three television stations. They also ran several advertisements on two radio stations and in two daily and two weekly newspapers.

Raising money was a major preoccupation of both campaigns. Each raised a great deal and spent all of it. Mr. Primary's manager described fund raising as "astronomically difficult," and his opponent agreed. Because both campaigns felt a need for such large amounts of money, their difficulty in raising enough is not surprising. In the contest for PAC support, Primary came out ahead in total dollars, thanks to extensive union support. But Experience received support from more than 20 PACs and benefited from substantial targeting and research assistance from the National Republican Congressional Committee. She also had survey help from the Citizens for the Republic.

The Information Environment

The same newspaper was identified by both managers as the most influential in the district, and its content was analyzed. A second newspaper also was mentioned as important because, as a traditionally Republican newspaper, its endorsement of the Democrat was "devastating" to Ms. Experience.

The most influential paper, fairly efficient in the district, published 7 news articles and 17 stories of all types about the campaign. Primary was mentioned considerably more often than Experience, and he received four times as much complimentary coverage and roughly the same amount of critical coverage as his opponent. Primary's advantage was evident across all types of content, including references to the candidates' backgrounds and experience, personal characteristics, campaign organization, issues, and group support. Given Ms. Experience's background and the vigor of her campaign, her disadvantage in coverage cannot be attributed to a lack of newsworthiness. In fact, a vital Republican campaign in this district might have been considered unusual and very newsworthy.

The press's treatment of Ms. Experience probably resulted from the standard operating procedures of news collection that tend to benefit candidates like Mr. Primary who create stories for reporters to cover. Primary's manager, a skilled media and advertising specialist, handled press relations for his campaign. He was much more aggressive than Ms. Experience's staff in planning events intended to capture free media attention. President Carter, Vice President Mondale, House Speaker Tip O'Neill, and other prominent political figures came to the district to stump for Mr. Primary. In each case, coverage on television, on radio, and in local newspapers followed.

Although the television market in this district was moderately good, the daily newspaper market was even better. Both managers agreed that the newspaper provided more campaign coverage than either radio or television news. Therefore, the information environment was judged moderately rich, with good news coverage in the newspapers and advertisements on television and radio. Three-quarters of those interviewed by the ANES in this district said they saw something about the House race on television, three-quarters read something about it in the newspaper, and more than half heard something on radio.

The Outcome

The heavy media advertising and moderate amounts of coverage led to widespread recognition of both candidates. Mr. Primary won in a close election, but his margin of victory was much smaller than his predecessor's. His disappointed manager attributed the small margin partly to a conservative trend in the district and partly to an unusually low Democratic turnout. In addition, Primary's manager cited friction among the campaign staff and blamed himself for failing to react to the opponent's aggressive radio advertising. Ms. Experience was not elected, but she came very close indeed, even with fewer dollars and with less professional management of her resources.

Conclusions

Despite a history of Democratic representation in his district, Mr. Primary was far from secure. The partisan division of voters was close, he was a relative unknown, and his opponent's campaign was well funded. By raising enormous sums of money for the primary and general election and by advertising heavily on television in this moderately good market, Mr. Primary was able to improve his level of recognition dramatically.

The amount of money available and the way it is spent appear to be especially important in open races, so long as the district is about evenly divided between Democrats and Republicans. Candidates typically begin the campaign with low levels of name recognition and need active advertising strategies to overcome this deficiency. Because many open races are viewed as targets of opportunity by both parties, it is not unusual for both candidates to raise large sums of money. The general election budgets of most of the open races studied in 1978 exceeded $100,000, with several approaching a quarter of a million dollars; only one candidate spent less than $50,000. Because primary expenses also were substantial for candidates in open races, their total campaign spending was quite high. Spending in open races has grown even higher in the 1980s.

The amount spent by a candidate in an open race is not a reaction to what the opponent spends but simply a response to the perceived opportunity a race without an incumbent presents. Candidates raise and spend as much as they can. However, the specific allocations of campaign dollars may result from a reaction to the opponent's strategy. Television advertising begets television advertising.

Even when open races occur in congressional districts that appear to be safe for one party's candidate, a certain measure of nervousness still prevails. In another race, Mr. Officeholder ran against Mr. Persistent in a suburban district recognized as safely Republican by both managers. Persistent, the Democratic candidate, was running for the second time. His manager was hopeful of winning but knew victory was a long shot. Although Mr. Officeholder's manager said his candidate would win easily, telltale signs of concern were revealed in his interview. For example, he worried about whether enough money could be raised for their campaign, and he fretted over a magazine article intimating that Mr. Officeholder might be guilty of a conflict of interest in his current elected position. After the election, Mr. Officeholder's manager said the results had been better than expected and that in late September he had been worried that it might be close.

Mr. Officeholder put together a highly professional campaign staff that conducted a sophisticated direct mail campaign. They raised and spent $45,000 in an uncontested primary to "capture people's attention early." They conducted six surveys during the campaign and distributed eight separate mailings, three during the primary and five during the general election. Four of the five mailed during the general election were targeted carefully, one to a neighborhood in the district where support was thought to be high, one to contributors, one to Democrats thought to be receptive to Republican appeals, and one to newly registered voters. Mr. Officeholder's campaign placed advertisements in five daily and two weekly newspapers. All in all, they spent more than $100,000, several times as much as their Democratic opponent.

But Mr. Persistent's campaign was not regarded as hopeless. He was able to raise a respectable amount of money, despite a well-known opponent and the disadvantage of running in a Republican district. He received contributions from more than a dozen political action committees.

Incumbency is regarded widely as an important advantage. When neither candidate has it, even the obvious front-runner feels less confident, and the underdog attains additional credibility. In open races, therefore, virtually every candidate and manager feel more uncertain about the outcome than the objective indicators of competitiveness would suggest.

The four cases presented here demonstrate the considerable variety that exists in congressional campaigns. Occasionally incumbents spend a great deal of money, even though they are certain of winning, to further their ambitions for higher office or political influence. However, on the whole, the amount of energy and resources devoted to a campaign depends on whether the principals are confident or uncertain in advance about the outcome. These feelings hinge on judgments about who and what will matter to the outcome of the election and whether those important factors realistically are manipulable by a campaign run in that district.

Because campaigns vary substantially in terms of their vitality, no one should expect to find that all campaigns have similar effects on election outcomes. Some campaigns are so inactive that they are barely visible; as a result their effects are minimal. Others are very hard fought; they can and do generate information that reaches potential voters and leads to vote totals that can represent substantial deviations from the outcome expected in the absence of the campaign.

Campaigns do not exert total control over the information available to voters, however. Reporters are more or less active in covering House races. Their activity depends substantially on how well or poorly media markets fit with the district boundaries. As a consequence, even very active campaigns in some places face a difficult task reaching voters through the news and an expensive task reaching them through media advertising.

Although most challengers lose, they can set the stage for future success if they can achieve a high level of visibility in the district and capture more votes than expected. They might do better themselves next time or their efforts might encourage an even stronger challenger to step forward. Understanding campaign effects requires an appreciation of the dynamic properties of electoral politics and attention to how candidates perform relative to expectations as well as to who wins and who loses particular contests.

Campaigning and
Chapter 12   the Democratic Process

Campaigns for Congress are part of a continuous and dynamic process of national political activity. Because of their number, frequency, and diversity, they provide an important perspective on campaigning in general. House campaigns evolve, they have effects, and they play an important role in a democratic society. Understanding how they work and their consequences provides important insights into the relationship between political elites and voters in contemporary America.

The Nature of the Contests

Not all congressional candidates are created equal, and the discrepancies within individual pairings make for very substantial variations in the campaigns. Some differences are the product of party affiliation and incumbency; others of how confident or uncertain the candidates and their staffs feel about their chances of winning. Not all challenges to incumbents are alike. Even open races do not imply that each candidate stands the same chance of winning or is equally confident of victory.

For incumbents, the perception of vulnerability is the driving force behind their behavior. Most of them are quite sure they are going to win, but a considerable minority realizes that victory can be assured only with concerted effort. There is some chance, even if slight, that they could lose. How confident they are of victory distinguishes incumbents in terms of how much money they raise and spend, as well as their patterns of resource allocation during the campaign.

It can take a great deal of money, often $200,000 or more, to run for Congress, and the financial demands increase with each cycle of races. A major advantage of incumbency is the ability to raise about as much money as needed. Just as important, incumbents can raise money when they want it. Incumbents appear to be raising and spending larger amounts of money earlier in the period between elections. By spending preemptively, they hope to enhance their own reelection bids and to dissuade serious challenges.

For those who seek to make politics their career, congressional campaigns provide a stepping-stone for advancement. These incumbents try to maximize the size of their victories to secure leadership positions in Congress or to increase their visibility and eligibility as potential candidates for higher office. One indicator of such aspirations is that these incumbents raise and spend much more money than their vulnerability or district characteristics indicate is necessary to win. Ambitious candidates have to demonstrate to their political peers, as well as to other influential elites, an ability to raise large sums of money and to campaign arduously and effectively. In addition to contributing to electoral security, such behavior demonstrates a suitability for representing the party in a political role with increased responsibility.

The challengers also embark on their campaigns with a variety of motives. Many believe, against the odds, that they have a good chance to win. They raise a lot of money and campaign hard. But a substantial number begin resigned to eventual defeat. They are loyalists preserving the party's line on the ballot or gaining campaign experience for the future. These candidates usually raise little money and run minimal campaigns.

To defeat incumbents, most challengers have to spend a considerable amount. Typically, challengers begin with a severe recognition disadvantage. Increasing their visibility in the electorate can be expensive, and outspending their opponents is difficult because most challengers find it harder to raise money. Incumbents have an inherent strategic edge in this regard: they need to raise and spend money only in response to the resources and allocation patterns of the challengers. Financing is another area where the deck is stacked against the challengers.

It is also the case that not all congressional districts are created equal. One of the stark realities the candidates face is the underlying distribution of partisanship in the constituency. Through accidents of history and gerrymandering by state legislatures, many congressional districts no longer are competitive in any real sense. Even before the race begins, one candidate has the advantage of running on behalf of the majority party, and the other carries the burden of representing the minority party. Most incumbents secured their office initially because they had this kind of head start in their first race, and this represents one of the most significant advantages they bring to each reelection effort.

Differences in partisanship are related closely to variations in the demographic and ideological composition of a congressional district. These factors must be regarded as given when the campaign begins. They serve to structure the nature of the candidates' appeals, including the issue agenda around which the policy debate between the candidates will center.

Campaign Strategies and Tactics

The division of the district's partisan loyalties determines in large part the basic form of the opponents' strategies. Candidates try to form a coalition of sufficient size to capture a majority of the expected vote on election day. To do so, majority party candidates can concentrate on mobilizing their core supporters and getting them to the polls. The minority party candidates, on the other hand, have to run campaigns based on converting at least some of the partisans from the other side.

Managers for different kinds of candidates necessarily pursue different campaign strategies and employ different tactics based on what they have to work with. Incumbents enjoy advantages here as well because their managers are more experienced and their campaign staffs more professional. Their managers know what works, and, with the backing of sufficient money, they go about applying these techniques. Challengers' managers are likely to be learning on the job, and even those who hope to win generally lose. In light of their experiences during the campaign, they often change their views about what actually matters to voters. Typically, these managers develop more respect for partisan forces and become more modest in their assessments of the importance of issues and the candidates' personal characteristics.

As a result of these fundamental considerations—candidate status, party, and assessments of chances—the form and content of congressional campaigns take on predictable colorations. Sure Winners tend to run relatively limited campaigns that emphasize the candidate's personal characteristics and party to the relative exclusion of issue content. Appeals are narrow and focused, targeted at mobilizing loyal supporters to vote. Sure Winners use advertising techniques that allow them to control the distribution of information as well as its content. Hopeful challengers and vulnerable incumbents make broader appeals to the electorate as they try to forge winning coalitions. Their campaigns are based more frequently on issues because they must supply voters with reasons for defecting from their party. To the extent that resources are available, Hopefuls and Vulnerables are likely to use radio and television ads to reach as many potential voters as possible. Sure Losers have little money available to wage vigorous campaigns. They take advantage of equal time provisions in seeking free television and radio attention but otherwise rely heavily on handouts and whatever personal contacts they can make with voters. Sure Losers may try to make broad appeals to a wide range of potential voters, often criticizing the incumbents' records and offering policy alternatives, but their appeals largely go unnoticed by the press and the public.

In implementing their strategies, congressional candidates will be more or less successful depending on how well the media market fits with the congressional district boundaries. Relatively invisible challengers have a difficult time overcoming their initial disadvantages in name recognition where the purchase of television time is not cost effective and the newspaper circulation area covers many other congressional districts. Advertising costs will be higher, and the media will be less inclined to cover the race. This relationship is most striking in urban America where all of these factors come together to favor the firmly entrenched Democratic incumbents who represent geographically compact constituencies. Both the television broadcast signals and newspaper circulation areas cover many districts, and the coverage of individual races suffers. Furthermore, the costs of access to media audiences usually are prohibitively high.

Public Information and Voter Response

Information flow varies within and across districts. Because of factors beyond their control, voters in different congressional districts receive qualitatively different information about their House candidates. These differences are caused by variations in candidate resources, strategic intent, and the quality of the media markets.

If the candidates have enough money, they can use increasingly sophisticated campaign technology to send highly specific messages to very distinct subgroups in the electorate. To a degree not feasible in the past, candidates can exert control over political communication, and different voters in the same constituency can receive different amounts and types of information.

The quantity and quality of information available to voters have consequences for constituent interest in the campaign, turnout, familiarity with the candidates' names and reputations, assessments of the candidates, and eventual vote choice. News attention to the campaign and other products of campaign activity act as stimuli to citizen interest. The messages the candidates formulate for public consumption are a critical element in the evaluation process, once the public knows who is running.

Candidate control over the content and targeting of their political messages would not be so serious a problem if the news media provided independent and ample information. But research shows increasingly that many media outlets do not. Those in large urban areas may cover congressional races in general more heavily than those in more efficient markets, but media attention in large metropolitan areas to any one House race within their audience area is limited. As a consequence, people get more or less news about the campaign and the candidates in their districts simply because of where they live.

What campaign coverage appears is likely to favor the incumbent, even when a serious challenge is under way. Because of the workways of the press, particularly reporters' reliance on news produced by familiar figures and on the daily routines of news gathering, incumbents who prepare and distribute press releases usually can generate more coverage than their opponents. Some of this "news" relates to official duties. Furthermore, incumbents raise and spend more money, giving the impression of running more vital and effective campaigns. If they arrange for more dinners and speeches to which the press can be given advance notice, these scheduled "media events" also can boost their coverage.

When all of these incumbent advantages are considered, the voter's response to the candidates is quite understandable. The substantial success rate of incumbents in seeking reelection is a function of their inherent advantage in partisanship in the district, their greater visibility in the electorate, and the more positive evaluations they generally receive because they are running against invisible, underfinanced challengers. It is no wonder, then, that as the number of voters who defect from their parties has increased over the last 20 years, House incumbents have been the overwhelming beneficiaries. Few House challengers have sufficient resources to induce voters of the other party to defect and support their challenge. In fact, their resources typically are so limited and their media coverage so infrequent that challengers often cannot hold on to the support of their own partisans.

A better understanding of how these incumbent advantages operate improves the chances for restoring some competitiveness to congressional races and thereby encouraging more attentive and responsive representation for constituents. Defeating incumbents is not an appropriate goal in and of itself. High rates of turnover could lead to a diminished quality of government as legislative positions become occupied by inexperienced politicians. Shortened careers also could lead to a smaller talent pool for filling leadership positions and to fewer experienced candidates running for higher office. However, a virtual absence of competition for House seats in many districts does not serve the democratic process.

Some sense of vulnerability among incumbents leads them to wage broader, more active campaigns oriented toward issues and toward more voter contact. Their activity stimulates media attention. As a result, constituents become better informed, and candidates become more attentive.

In the absence of active campaigning and ample media attention, voters are likely to respond to different kinds of cues in making their decisions. They may simply pull their party's lever. They also may be more inclined than voters in districts with competitive House contests to use their votes to express their judgments of the president's performance in office.

Regardless of voter intent, the shifting of seats from one party to another has important consequences for the operation of our national government. The press widely interprets victories and defeats in particular races as referenda on the president's popularity and performance. Even if they were not meant as such, electoral outcomes in House races have unquestionable importance for the president's ability to operate effectively during the next two years. The party holding the majority of seats in the House assumes the position of leadership in that body and enjoys the substantial advantages that accompany it in committee leadership and increased staff support. Legislative outcomes and the presidential resources required to influence them obviously are affected by the partisan makeup of both chambers of Congress.

Political analysts and columnists also interpret individual district outcomes. They are impressed by unusual successes, and their commentary can bolster popular perceptions of an emerging political career. Of course ambitious incumbents also have to demonstrate effective legislative and administrative skills to their colleagues during their service in Congress. As long as those skills are adequate, the rewards for their extraordinary campaign efforts can include increased responsibility through selection for leadership positions in the House or a party nomination for statewide office.

Implications for Other Campaign Settings

The results of this investigation of House campaigns have some relevance for other partisan races. Although national presidential election campaigns represent a special case, the basic ideas and models employed here are applicable to contests for statewide and lower level offices and even for presidential primaries.

For example, candidate visibility is critical to any successful campaign. Recognition usually precedes evaluation. During the past 20 years, while House incumbents have maintained a substantial electoral edge over their opponents, Senate challengers have become increasingly successful in unseating incumbents. In 1980 they won about as often as they lost. In 1982 senatorial incumbents were more successful in winning reelection than they had been for years, but whether this represents a sustainable shift in the earlier trend remains to be seen. In a virtual reversal of constitutional intent, the members of the upper chamber now lead a less secure life than members of the lower chamber.

One possible explanation for increased electoral risk is that interstate shifts in population have altered the fundamental distribution of partisanship in many states, leaving them more competitive than in the past. Another is that six-year and four-year terms are sufficiently attractive to draw much stronger senatorial and gubernatorial challengers who usually have high visibility either from previous elective office or from some other public occupation.

The communication environments of statewide campaigns offer a third plausible explanation of challenger success. It is much easier and more straightforward to organize a media campaign within state boundaries than within congressional district boundaries. Resources are more plentiful in senatorial and gubernatorial races, and campaigns of broader scope are possible. Even if they are not well known to begin with, senatorial challengers can use the mass media effectively—television in particular—to develop name recognition and pave the way for voters to compare them with the incumbents. By timing their campaigns carefully through the primary period, challengers can begin the general election contest with about the same levels of recognition as the incumbents.

News coverage of senatorial and gubernatorial races is more ample than coverage of House campaigns, and this contributes to the familiarity of challengers in the state. With only two major party candidates running for senator or governor, there is little competition for news attention. Even in bistate metropolitan areas where the local media must cover all of the races, the number of senatorial or gubernatorial candidates is modest. The mass media do not have to divide their attention among so many contests. Moreover, the senator's or governor's constituency encompasses the entire circulation or signal areas in most cases. News editors need not worry about devoting space to candidates who are irrelevant to most of their readers. Consequently, the constraints imposed by media market structure typically are less severe for senatorial or gubernatorial than for House campaigns.

Unfettered by any real limitations on spending, the costs of senatorial races is skyrocketing. One candidate in 1982, Mark Dayton of Minnesota, spent $9 million on his campaign and lost. Incumbents are raising more money sooner and flaunting it in attempts to diminish the seriousness of the challenge they might face. Running against an incumbent senator is becoming more and more a game for the wealthy. The high return rate for incumbent senators in 1982 may be only a temporary interruption in the pattern of increasing vulnerability or it may reflect a sustained improvement in security for incumbents, particularly Republicans supported by their national party, who have finally developed effective strategies to counter their challengers.

With so much energy and money flowing into campaigns for public office, one might expect that significant scholarly attention would follow. In fact, presidential campaigns have been the favorite subject of numerous books and articles, many by journalists and a few by scholars, but generalizations drawn from presidential case studies cannot be applied casually to lower level contests. Understanding the campaign process requires attention to the considerable diversity among races.

That attention means renewed interest in the context of campaigns, especially in the information generated by and about opposing candidates. The political environment varies from race to race, but there are patterns of variability that can be described and understood. They vary in terms of the incumbency status of opposing candidates, their assessments of their chances, and the structural constraints of media markets. The current preoccupation with presidential contests needs to be complemented by greater interest in congressional, state, and local campaigns. Systematic inquiries at various levels of office seeking will enhance our understanding of the role of campaigns in our political system.

The significant effects of a campaign may not be seen until long after the election is past—when a new challenger emerges, additional money is raised by the opposing candidates, and the political aspirations of the incumbent become clear. By performing better or worse in one election than their political peers or the media expected, candidates create opportunities or risks for their future careers. Instead of focusing solely on who wins or loses any particular contest, researchers need to think about campaigns as part of a dynamic process—a series of events with both short- and long-term consequences for the character of governance in our system.

Appendix

The procedures used to estimate the normal vote for each congressional district in the sample are described in detail here. This estimate was based on the distribution of party identification in the district, adjusted for differences in turnout and defection rates that have been observed historically for Democrats and Republicans.

The normal vote is based primarily on the long-term consideration of the partisanship of the constituency. The deviation from the normal vote is the simple subtraction of the normal vote estimate from the actual electoral outcome. This deviation reflects the net short-term effect of the campaign, the candidates' personal characteristics, the issue agenda in the campaign, and even the incumbent's service to constituents while in office.

The fundamental requirement for estimating the normal vote of a constituency is the distribution of the party identification of the constituents who reside there. This distribution, measured through surveys, is adjusted by weighting for the greater propensity of Republicans to turn out and of Democrats to defect or vote for the candidates of the other party (Converse, 1966). These weights have changed slightly over time and within major regions of the United States (Miller, 1979). But the method, and the estimates it generates, has proved very useful as an analytical framework for understanding voting behavior in presidential elections.

Generating normal vote estimates for congressional districts requires knowing or estimating the distribution of party identification in each district. Because the 1978 American National Election Study (ANES) was based on a congressional district sample, initially the survey results were examined as a potential source of such data. Within each of the 108 districts that formed the full sample, and therefore also within the subset of 86 districts that had

contested races, small samples of approximately 22 adults were interviewed. While there was some concern about using a seven-point distribution of party identification based on such a small number of respondents, a
more substantial problem was the clustering effect of conducting the
interviews in only a few geographic locales within each district rather than
distributing them randomly across the whole district. This presented a
serious problem in heterogeneous districts with different ethnic or racial
groups located in separate areas. The partisan identifications of respondents from only one area were not representative of partisan identifications
in the district as a whole.

As a result, a decision was made to secure data from larger,
districtwide samples of voters. Contacts were made with private pollsters
and with other political scientists who had worked in the area of congressional elections.[1] The marginal distributions for party identification in 37
congressional districts were obtained from these sources. The information
came from 1 survey conducted in 1974, 6 in 1976, 21 in 1978, and 9 in
1980. The sample sizes generally were between 300 and 400 respondents,
except for two districts with samples of more than 500 respondents and two
districts with samples of only 154 and 54 respondents. All of the data were
obtained from telephone interviews, and some studies involved prescreening
for registration or other forms of likelihood of voting.

To apply the Converse methodology with the revised Miller weights, a
seven-point distribution of party identification would have been necessary
for each of the 86 districts in the sample.[2] With data available on only 37
districts, an alternative estimation technique had to be developed for the
other 49. In addition, only 12 of the districts with available data had the full
seven-point range of strong and weak Democrats, strong and weak
Republicans, independents, and independents who felt closer to the Democrats or Republicans. As a result, an adjusted set of weights was applied to
some three-point distributions of party identification to generate the normal
vote estimates.

The first step in this process was to apply the parameters and
methodology described in Miller to the full seven-point distributions available
for 12 districts. The estimation parameters for turnout and partisanship
effects in the 1960s were taken from Table 1 of Miller, with appropriate
allowance for the South/non-South location of the district. The vector
multiplication method was used to compute the expected vote for each of
the five groups of identifiers, and then the composite estimate of the normal
vote was made.

As a second step in the process, the known seven-point party
identification distributions in these 12 districts were then combined into
three-point scales. The broad categories of partisans were then subdivided
into strong and weak identifiers using the national proportions of identifiers
who are strong and weak Democrats or strong and weak Republicans, as in-

Table A   A Comparison of Normal Vote Estimates Derived from Alternative Distributions of Partisan Identification in 1978 Congressional Districts.

State & Congressional District	5-Point Distribution of Partisan Identification	3-Point Distribution of Partisan Identification	Difference
Delaware At Large	51.3	51.3	0.0
Indiana 3	52.4	51.1	1.3
Indiana 9	53.8	53.4	0.4
Kansas 2	46.2	45.7	0.5
Maine 1	48.4	48.3	0.1
Michigan 7	56.6	55.7	0.9
Missouri 6	55.8	55.6	0.2
Ohio 3	53.4	52.6	0.8
Pennsylvania 2	63.0	61.9	1.1
Wisconsin 4	58.1	57.6	0.5
Wisconsin 6	47.4	47.9	−0.5
Wyoming At Large	45.8	46.4	−0.6

dicated in the 1978 ANES national sample. With the data now divided into five categories, the Miller parameters were applied again. A comparison of the estimates derived from aggregating the five-point distributions and disaggregating the three-point distributions showed no difference of more than 1.3 percentage points in the estimates of the normal vote for the Democratic party. A summary of the results obtained by this process is presented in Table A. Because of the small differences that were observed, and hence the confidence placed in the method based on the disaggregation of the three-point distribution of partisan identification, normal vote estimates were generated for all 37 congressional districts for which data were available, 12 on the basis of seven-point distributions and 25 on the basis of three-point distributions.

In the third step, a regression procedure was used to develop an estimation equation in the 37 districts that could then be applied to the remaining 49. Several variables were selected from the *Congressional District Data Book for the 95th Congress* and the *Political Almanac for 1978*, three of which produced a parsimonious ordinary least squares (OLS) regression estimate of the survey-derived normal vote measures calculated from the 37 district-level samples of party identification. The most significant of these variables was the proportion of the vote Jimmy Carter received in the district in 1976, one of the most "normal" presidential elections since 1960. The percentage of non-whites in the district was used because of this group's strong positive relationship with Democratic partisanship. Finally, the number of incumbents' terms, adjusted by sign to reflect a Democratic (+) or Republican (−) incumbent, was used as an indicator of the safety of the seat and hence the relative imbalance of the distribution of partisanship in the district.

The complete three-variable equation for 37 districts resulted in an R of .71 (R^2 = .51), and this equation was used to generate estimates of the normal vote for the other 49 districts. All calculations were performed in terms of support for the Democratic party, and the deviations were calculated by subtracting the normal vote estimates from the actual election outcome. This deviation was used as the measure of the net effect of the campaign in each district.

Notes

1. Our thanks to Thomas Mann, Robert Teeter, and Mary Lukens is acknowledged in Chapter 2.
2. The historical defection and turnout rates for a congressional district probably vary from the equivalent parameter values for a national sample interviewed in conjunction with a presidential election. Because there was no equivalent set of parameters available, it was necessary to assume that the national weights could be applied to each of the congressional district-level distributions of party identification.

Bibliography

Abramowitz, Alan I. "A Comparison of Voting for U. S. Senator and Representative in 1978." *American Political Science Review* (September 1980): 633-640.

___. "Candidates, Coattails, and Strategic Politicians in the 1980 Congressional Elections: Explaining the Republican Victory." Paper presented at the annual meeting of the American Political Science Association, Chicago, Ill., September 1983.

___. "Name Familiarity, Reputation, and the Incumbency Effect in a Congressional Election." *Western Political Quarterly* (December 1975): 668-684.

___. "Party and Individual Accountability in the 1978 Congressional Election." In *Congressional Elections,* edited by Louis Maisel and Joseph Cooper. *Sage Electoral Studies Yearbook,* vol. 6, 171-194. Beverly Hills, Calif.: Sage Publications, 1981.

Abramson, Paul, John Aldrich, and David Rohde. *Change and Continuity in the 1980 Elections.* rev. ed. Washington, D.C.: CQ Press, 1983.

Adamany, David. *Campaign Finance in America.* North Scituate, Mass.: Duxbury Press, 1972.

Adamany, David, and George E. Agree. *Political Money: A Strategy for Campaign Financing in America.* Baltimore: Johns Hopkins University Press, 1975.

Agranoff, Robert. *The Management of Election Campaigns.* Boston: Holbrook Press, 1976.

Alexander, Herbert E. *Financing Politics: Money, Elections, and Political Reform.* 3d ed. Washington, D.C.: CQ Press, 1984.

___. *Political Finance.* In *Sage Electoral Studies Yearbook,* vol. 5. Beverly Hills, Calif.: Sage Publications, 1979.

___. *The Case for PACs*. Washington, D.C.: Public Affairs Council, 1983.

Alexander, Herbert E., and Brian A. Haggerty. *The Federal Election Campaign Act: After a Decade of Political Reform*. Los Angeles: Citizens' Research Foundation, 1981.

American Newspaper Markets. *Circulation '78/79*. Northfield, Ill.: American Newspaper Markets, 1978.

Becker, Lee B., Maxwell McCombs, and Jack M. McLeod. "The Development of Political Cognitions." In *Political Communication: Issues and Strategies for Research*, edited by Steven Chaffee. Beverly Hills, Calif.: Sage Publications, 1975.

Berelson, Bernard, Paul Lazarsfeld, and William McPhee. *Voting*. Chicago: University of Chicago Press, 1954.

Bogue, Allan G., Jerome M. Clubb, Carroll R. McKibbin, and Santa A. Traugott. "Members of the House of Representatives and the Processes of Modernization, 1789-1960." *Journal of American History* (September 1976): 275-302.

Bonafede, Dom. "Democratic Party Takes Some Strides Down the Long Comeback Trail." *National Journal*, October 8, 1983, 2053-2055.

Broadcasting Publications. *Broadcasting Yearbook 1977*. Washington: Broadcasting Publications, 1977.

Buchanan, Christopher. "House: Modest Gains for the Minority." *Congressional Quarterly Weekly Report*, November 11, 1978, 3250-3253.

Bullock, Charles S. III. "House Careerists: Changing Patterns of Longevity and Attrition." *American Political Science Review* (December 1972): 1295-1305.

Caldeira, Gregory A., and Samuel C. Patterson. "Contextual Influences on Participation in U. S. State Legislative Elections." *Legislative Studies Quarterly* (August 1982): 359-381.

Campbell, Angus. "Surge and Decline: A Study of Electoral Change." In *Elections and the Political Order*, edited by Campbell et al., 40-62. New York: John Wiley & Sons, 1966.

Campbell, Angus, Philip E. Converse, Warren E. Miller, and Donald E. Stokes. *The American Voter*. New York: John Wiley & Sons, 1960.

___. *Elections and the Political Order*. New York: John Wiley & Sons, 1966.

Clarke, Peter, and Susan H. Evans. *Covering Campaigns: Journalism in Congressional Elections*. Stanford, Calif.: Stanford University Press, 1983.

Clem, Alan L. *The Making of Congressmen: Seven Campaigns of 1974*. North Scituate, Mass.: Duxbury Press, 1976.

Converse, Philip E. "The Concept of the Normal Vote." In *Elections and the Political Order*, edited by Campbell et al., 9-39. New York: John Wiley & Sons, 1966.

Conway, M. Margaret. "Republican Political Party Nationalization, Campaign Activities, and Their Implications for the Party System." *Publius*

(Winter 1983): 1-17.

Copeland, Gary W. "The Effects of Campaign Expenditures on Turnout for Congressional Elections." Paper presented at the annual meeting of the Midwest Political Science Association, Milwaukee, Wis., April 1982.

Cover, Albert D. "One Good Term Deserves Another: The Advantage of Incumbency in Congressional Elections." *American Journal of Political Science* (August 1977): 523-542.

___. "Contacting Congressional Constituents: Some Patterns of Perquisite Use." *American Journal of Political Science* (February 1980): 125-135.

Cover, Albert D., and Bruce S. Brumberg. "Baby Books and Ballots: The Impact of Congressional Mail on Constituent Opinion." *American Political Science Review* (June 1982): 347-359.

Cover, Albert D., and David Mayhew. "Congressional Dynamics and the Decline of Competitive Congressional Elections." In *Congress Reconsidered*, 2d ed., edited by Lawrence C. Dodd and Bruce I. Oppenheimer, 62-82. Washington, D.C.: CQ Press, 1981.

Danielson, Wayne A., and John B. Adams. "Completeness of Press Coverage of the 1960 Campaign." *Journalism Quarterly* (Autumn 1961): 441-452.

Dawson, Paul A., and James E. Zinser. "Broadcast Expenditures and Electoral Outcomes in the 1970 Congressional Elections." *Public Opinion Quarterly* (Fall 1970): 398-402.

___. "Characteristics of Campaign Resource Allocation in the 1972 Congressional Elections." In *Changing Campaign Techniques*, edited by L. Maisel, *Sage Electoral Studies Yearbook*, vol. 2, 93-138. Beverly Hills, Calif.: Sage Publications, 1976.

___. "Political Finance and Participation in Congressional Elections." In *Annals of the American Academy of Political and Social Science* (May 1976): 59-73.

Dodd, Lawrence C., and Bruce I. Oppenheimer. "The House in Transition: Change and Consolidation." In *Congress Reconsidered*, 2d ed., edited by Lawrence C. Dodd and Bruce I. Oppenheimer. Washington, D.C.: CQ Press, 1981.

Downs, Anthony. *An Economic Theory of Democracy.* New York: Harper & Row, 1957.

Epstein, Edwin M. "The Emergence of Political Action Committees." In *Political Finance,* edited by Herbert E. Alexander, *Sage Electoral Studies Yearbook,* vol. 5, 159-198. Beverly Hills, Calif.: Sage Publications, 1979.

Erbring, Lutz, Edie N. Goldenberg, and Arthur Miller. "Front-Page News and Real-World Cues: A New Look at Agenda-Setting by the Media." *American Journal of Political Science* (February 1980): 16-49.

Erikson, Robert. "The Advantages of Incumbency in Congressional Elections." *Polity* (Spring 1971): 395-405.

——. "Is There Such a Thing as a Safe Seat?" *Polity* (Summer 1976): 623-632.

Eubank, Robert B., and David John Gow. "The Pro-Incumbent Bias in the 1978 and 1980 National Election Studies." *American Journal of Political Science* (February 1983): 122-139.

Fenno, Richard. *Home Style.* Boston: Little, Brown & Co., 1978.

Ferejohn, John A. "On the Decline of Competition in Congressional Elections." *American Political Science Review* (March 1977): 166-176.

Fiorina, Morris P. "The Case of the Vanishing Marginals: The Bureaucracy Did It." *American Political Science Review* (March 1977): 177-181.

——. *Congress: Keystone of the Washington Establishment.* New Haven: Yale University Press, 1977.

——. *Representatives, Roll Calls and Constituencies.* Lexington, Mass.: D.C. Heath & Co., 1974.

——. "Some Problems in Studying the Effects of Resource Allocation in Congressional Elections." *American Journal of Political Science* (August 1981): 543-567.

Fishel, Jeff. *Party & Opposition.* New York: David McKay Co. 1973.

Fleishman, Joel L. "Private Money and Public Elections: Another American Dilemma." In *Changing Campaign Techniques,* edited by L. Maisel, *Sage Electoral Studies Yearbook,* vol. 2, 93-138. Beverly Hills, Calif.: Sage Publications, 1976.

Gibson, James L., Cornelius P. Cotter, John F. Bibby, and Robert J. Huckshorn. "Whither the Local Parties? A Cross-Sectional and Longitudinal Analysis of the Strength of Party Organizations." Paper presented at the annual meeting of the Western Political Science Association, San Diego, Calif., March 1982.

Glantz, Stanton A., Alan I. Abramowitz, and Michael P. Burkart. "Election Outcomes: Whose Money Matters?" *Journal of Politics* (November 1976): 1033-1041.

Goldenberg, Edie N. *Making the Papers.* Lexington, Mass.: Lexington Books, 1975.

Goldenberg, Edie N., and Michael W. Traugott. "Campaign Managers' Perceptions and Strategic Decisions in Congressional Elections." Paper presented at the annual meeting of the Western Political Science Association, San Diego, Calif., March 1982.

——. "Congressional Campaign Effects on Candidate Recognition and Evaluation." *Political Behavior* (Summer 1980): 61-90.

——. "Normal Vote Analysis of U. S. Congressional Elections." *Legislative Studies Quarterly* (May 1981): 247-258.

——. "Resource Allocations and Broadcast Expenditures in Congressional Campaigns." Paper presented at the annual meeting of the American Political Science Association, Washington, D.C., September 1979.

Goldenberg, Edie N., Michael W. Traugott, and Frank R. Baumgartner.

"Preemptive and Reactive Spending in U. S. House Races." Paper presented at the annual meeting of the Midwest Political Science Association, Chicago, Ill., April 1983.

Gore, William J., and Robert L. Peabody. "The Functions of the Political Campaign: A Case Study." *Western Political Quarterly* (March 1958): 55-70.

Graber, Doris A. *Mass Media and American Politics.* Washington, D.C.: CQ Press, 1980.

Heard, Alexander. *The Costs of Democracy.* Chapel Hill: University of North Carolina Press, 1960.

Hershey, Marjorie R. *The Making of Campaign Strategy.* Lexington, Mass.: Lexington Books, 1974.

Hibbing, John R. "Voluntary Retirement from the U. S. House of Representatives: Who Quits?" *American Journal of Political Science* (August 1982): 467-484.

Hinckley, Barbara. *Congressional Elections.* Washington, D.C.: CQ Press, 1981.

____. "House Reelections and Senate Defeats: The Role of the Challenger." *British Journal of Political Science* (October 1980): 441-460.

Huckshorn, Robert J., and Robert C. Spencer. *The Politics of Defeat.* Amherst, Mass.: University of Massachusetts Press, 1971.

Huntington, Samuel P. "A Revised Theory of American Party Politics." *American Political Science Review* (September 1950): 669-677.

Jackson, John E. "Intensities, Preferences, and Electoral Politics." *Social Science Research* (September 1973): 231-246.

Jacobson, Gary C. "Congressional Elections, 1978: The Case of the Vanishing Challengers." In *Congressional Elections,* edited by Louis Maisel and Joseph Cooper. *Sage Electoral Studies Yearbook,* vol. 6, 219-248. Beverly Hills, Calif.: Sage Publications, 1981.

____. "The Effects of Campaign Spending on Congressional Elections." *American Political Science Review* (June 1978): 469-491.

____. "The Impact of Broadcast Campaigning on Electoral Outcomes." *Journal of Politics* (August 1975): 769-793.

____. *Money in Congressional Elections.* New Haven: Yale University Press, 1980.

____. "Public Funds for Congressional Campaigns: Who Would Benefit?" In *Political Finance,* edited by Herbert E. Alexander. *Sage Electoral Studies Yearbook,* vol. 5, 99-128. Beverly Hills, Calif.: Sage Publications, 1979.

Jacobson, Gary C., and Samuel Kernell. *Strategy and Choice in Congressional Elections.* New Haven: Yale University Press, 1981.

Johannes, John R., and John C. McAdams. "The Congressional Incumbency Effect: Is It Casework, Policy Compatibility, or Something Else?" *American Journal of Political Science* (August 1981): 512-542.

Jones, Charles O. "The Role of the Campaign in Congressional Politics." In *The Electoral Process,* edited by M. Kent Jennings and L. Harmon Zeigler, 21-41. Englewood Cliffs, N.J.: Prentice-Hall, 1968.

Jones, Ruth, and Warren Miller. "Financing Campaigns: The Individual Contributor." Paper presented at the annual meeting of the Midwest Political Science Association, Chicago, Ill., April 1983.

Kayden, Xandra. "The Nationalization of the Party System." In *Parties, Interest Groups, and Campaign Finance Laws,* edited by Michael J. Malbin. Washington, D.C.: American Enterprise Institute for Public Policy Research, 1980.

Kazee, Thomas A. "The Decision to Run For the U. S. Congress: Challenger Attitudes in the 1970s." *Legislative Studies Quarterly* (February 1980): 79-100.

Kelley, Stanley, Jr., and Thad W. Mirer. "The Simple Act of Voting." *American Political Science Review* (June 1974): 572-591.

Key, V.O. *The Responsible Electorate.* Cambridge: Harvard University Press, 1966.

Kim, Dhang Lim, and Donald P. Racheter. "Candidates' Perceptions of Voter Competence: A Comparison of Winning and Losing Candidates." *American Political Science Review* (September 1973): 906-913.

Kinder, Donald R., and D. Rodney Kiewiet. "Economic Discontent and Political Behavior: The Role of Personal Grievances and Collective Economic Judgments in Congressional Voting." *American Journal of Political Science* (August 1979): 495-527.

Kinder, Donald R., and David O. Sears. "Public Opinion and Political Action." In *The Handbook of Social Psychology,* edited by G. Lindzey and E. Aronson. Reading, Mass.: Addison-Wesley Publishing Co. Forthcoming.

Kingdon, John W. *Candidates for Office: Beliefs and Strategies.* New York: Random House, 1968.

Klapper, Joseph. *The Effects of Mass Communication.* New York: Free Press, 1960.

Lazarsfeld, Paul, Bernard Berelson, and Helen Gaudet. *The People's Choice.* New York: Columbia University Press, 1948.

Leuthold, David A. *Electioneering in a Democracy: Campaigns for Congress.* New York: John Wiley & Sons, 1968.

MacKuen, Michael, and Steven Coombs. *More Than News: Media Power in Public Affairs.* Beverly Hills, Calif.: Sage Publications, 1981.

Maisel, Louis. *Changing Campaign Techniques.* In *Sage Electoral Studies Yearbook,* vol. 2. Beverly Hills, Calif.: Sage Publications, 1976.

Maisel, Louis Sandy, and Joseph Cooper. *Congressional Elections.* In *Sage Electoral Studies Yearbook,* vol. 6. Beverly Hills, Calif.: Sage Publications, 1981.

Malbin, Michael, ed. *Parties, Interest Groups, and Campaign Finance Laws.*

Washington, D.C.: American Enterprise Institute for Public Policy Research, 1980.

Mann, Thomas E. *Unsafe at Any Margin.* Washington, D.C.: American Enterprise Institute for Public Policy Research, 1978.

Mann, Thomas E., and Raymond E. Wolfinger. "Candidates and Parties in Congressional Elections." *American Political Science Review* (September 1980): 617-632.

Mayhew, David. "Congressional Elections: The Case of the Vanishing Marginals." *Polity* (Spring 1974): 295-317.

McAdams, John C., and John R. Johannes, "Does Casework Matter? A Reply to Professor Fiorina." *American Journal of Political Science* (August 1981): 581-604.

McCombs, Maxwell, and Donald L. Shaw. "The Agenda-Setting Function of the Mass Media." *Public Opinion Quarterly* (Summer 1972): 176-187.

McDevitt, Roland D. "The Changing Dynamics of Fund Raising in House Campaigns." In *Political Finance,* edited by Herbert E. Alexander, *Sage Electoral Studies Yearbook,* vol. 5, 129-158. Beverly Hills, Calif.: Sage Publications, 1979.

Miller, Arthur H. "Normal Vote Analysis: Sensitivity to Change Over Time." *American Journal of Political Science* (May 1979): 406-425.

Miller, Arthur H., Edie N. Goldenberg, Lutz Erbring. "Type-Set Politics: Impact of Newspapers on Public Confidence." *American Political Science Review* (March 1979): 67-94.

Miller, Arthur H., Warren E. Miller, Alden S. Raine, and Thad A. Brown. "A Majority Party in Disarray: Policy Polarization in the 1972 Election." *American Political Science Review* (September 1976): 753-778.

Miller, Warren E. "The Majority Rule and the Representative System of Government." In *Cleavages, Ideologies and Party Systems,* edited by E. Allardt and Y. Littunen, 343-376. Helsinki, Finland: Transactions of the Westermarck Society, 1964.

Miller, Warren E., and Donald E. Stokes. "Constituency Influence in Congress." *American Political Science Review* (March 1963): 45-57.

Nelson, Candace. "The Effect of Incumbency on Voting in Congressional Elections." *Political Science Quarterly* (Winter 1978/1979): 665-678.

Page, Benjamin. *Choices and Echoes in Presidential Elections.* Chicago: University of Chicago Press, 1978.

Palda, Kristian S. "Does Advertising Influence Votes: An Analysis of the 1966 and 1970 Quebec Elections." *Canadian Journal of Political Science* (December 1973): 638-655.

___. "The Effect of Expenditures on Political Success." *Journal of Law and Economics* (December 1975): 745-771.

Parker, Glenn R. "Incumbent Popularity and Electoral Success." In *American Politics Quarterly* (October 1980): 449-464.

——. "Incumbent Popularity and Electoral Success." In *Congressional Elections,* edited by Louis Maisel and Joseph Cooper. *Sage Electoral Studies Yearbook,* vol. 6, 249-279. Beverly Hills, Calif.: Sage Publications, 1981.

——. "Interpreting Candidate Awareness in U. S. Congressional Elections." *Legislative Studies Quarterly* (May 1981): 219-233.

Patterson, Thomas E. *The Mass Media Election: How Americans Choose Their President.* New York: Praeger Publishers, 1980.

Patterson, Thomas E., and Robert D. McClure. *The Unseeing Eye.* New York: G. B. Putnam's Sons, 1976.

Peters, John G., and Susan Welch. "The Effects of Charges of Corruption on Voting Behavior in Congressional Elections." *American Political Science Review* (September 1980): 697-708.

Popkin, Samuel, John W. Gorman, Charles Phillips, and Jeffrey A. Smith. "Comment: What Have You Done for Me Lately? Toward an Investment Theory of Voting." *American Political Science Review* (September 1976): 779-805.

Ragsdale, Lynn. "Incumbent Popularity, Challenger Invisibility, and Congressional Voters." *Legislative Studies Quarterly* (May 1981): 201-218.

Riker, William H., and Peter C. Ordeshook. "A Theory of the Calculus of Voting." *American Political Science Review* (March 1968): 25-41.

Robinson, John P. "The Press as King-Maker: What Surveys from the Last Five Campaigns Show." *Journalism Quarterly* (Winter 1974): 587-594.

Robinson, Michael J. "Three Faces of Congressional Media." In *The New Congress,* edited by Thomas E. Mann and Norman J. Ornstein. Washington, D.C.: American Enterprise Institute for Public Policy Research, 1981, 55-96.

Sabato, Larry J. *The Rise of Political Consultants.* New York: Basic Books, 1981.

Sigal, Leon. *Reporters and Officials: The Organization and Politics of Newsmaking.* Lexington, Mass: D.C. Heath & Co., 1973.

Stokes, Donald E., and Warren E. Miller. "Party Government and the Salience of Congress." *Public Opinion Quarterly* (Winter 1962): 531-546.

Stout, Richard. Review of *Covering Campaigns* by Peter Clarke and Susan H. Evans. *Washington Journalism Review,* June 1983, 56.

Tedin, Kent L., and Richard W. Murray. "Public Awareness of Congressional Representatives: Recall Versus Recognition." *American Politics Quarterly* (October 1979): 509-517.

Tufte, Edward. "Determinants of the Outcome of Midterm Congressional Elections." *American Political Science Review* (September 1975): 812-826.

Welch, William P. "The Allocation of Political Monies: Economic Interest Groups." *Public Choice* (1980): 97-120.

——. "Patterns of Contributions: Economic Interests and Ideological Groups." In *Political Finance,* edited by Herbert E. Alexander. *Sage Electoral Studies Yearbook,* vol. 5, 199-220. Beverly Hills, Calif.: Sage Publications, 1979.

Westlye, Mark C. "Competitiveness of Senate Seats and Voting Behavior in Senate Elections." *American Journal of Political Science* (May 1983): 253-283.

Yiannakis, Diana Evans. "The Grateful Electorate: Casework and Congressional Elections." *American Journal of Political Science* (August 1981): 568-580.

Index